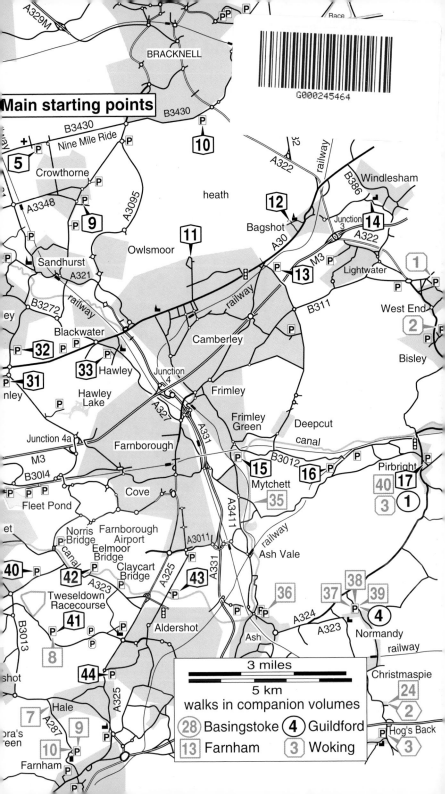

Main starting points

BRACKNELL

A329M

Race

G000245464

B3430

B3430

Nine Mile Ride

Crowthorne

5

10

A3348

A3095

9

heath

A322

railway

Windlesham

B386

12

Bagshot

Junction 3

14

A322

A30

M3

13

Lightwater

West End

1

Owlsmoor

11

B311

2

F

Sandhurst

A321

Bisley

B3272

railway

Camberley

Blackwater

32

33 Hawley

31

Hawley Lake

Junction 4

A327

Frimley

Deepcut

canal

Frimley Green

Junction 4a

M3

B30l4

Farnborough

A331

B3012

15

16

Pirbright

17

Cove

Mytchett

40

35

3

1

Fleet Pond

Norris Bridge

Farnborough Airport

A3011

A3411

railway

Ash Vale

canal

Eelmoor Bridge

40

42

A323

Claycart Bridge

A325

A331

43

36

38

37

39

Tweseldown Racecourse

41

A324

A323

4

Normandy

railway

Aldershot

Ash

8

B3013

44

A325

Christmaspie

24

Hale

7

A287

9

Hog's Back

2

3

ra's een

10

Farnham

3 miles
5 km

walks in companion volumes

28 Basingstoke **4** Guildford

13 Farnham **3** Woking

1 Swallowfield Park and Thatcher's Ford

About 7½km/4¾ miles with an extension of 1½km/1 mile; farmland and woods; undulating. OS maps 1:25000 159 Reading, 1:50000 175 Reading.

Start from Swallowfield Church, SU 732 647. There is parking in the village.

The Crown ☎ 0118 988 3260   **The George & Dragon** ☎ 0118 988 4432

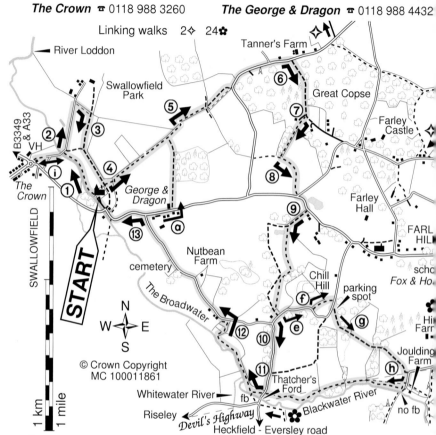

① From the inner corner of the car park at Swallowfield Church go through the trees to the field (20m) (no right-of-way) and on along the Blackwater to the bridge (400m).

ⓘ *If visiting the village pub, cross the bridge. When the drive bends L, stay ahead on the path past the lodge (200m). Go along the Street opposite to the* **Crown** *(150m). Return the same way to the bridge.*

② Follow the drive towards the big house, Swallowfield Park (350m).

③ Turn R along the garden hedge to the cart track (200m) and follow it back to the churchyard (500m).

④ Opposite the church R, turn L on the cross path from the churchyard to the field (60m). Enter the R field and follow the L edge past a side path R (from the road at the **George & Dragon**) (500m). Go on along the hedge to the gap (100m).

⑤ Continue on the other side of the hedge to the next field (200m) and keep on through that to the

2

oad (300m). Go on along the road ⌐ (350m). ✦ Soon after the timber-framed house L (80m) turn R at the forestry track.

⑥ Go up the track through Great Copse to the flat top (300m) and the first house drive R (70m).

⑦ Take the path L of the drive down through the trees to the field (100m) and continue outside the field to the bottom (200m).

⑧ Go L between hedges round to the road junction (300m) then L on the wider road curving R (120m).

⑨ At the next L bend turn R along the track between garden and field (200m). On the R curve take the side path into the 2nd field L. Make for the highest point (300m). At the summit spinney turn R down to the near corner of the field (100m). Don't cross the track into the field ahead but enter the side field L. Walk straight across the foot of the slope to the gate near the furthest corner and out to the road (400m).

ⓔ *Extension of 1½ km/1 mile: Walk L up the road, over the top and down to the R curve (200m).*

ⓕ *Turn off L up the stepped path. Follow the L hedge, until it bends and stay ahead to the road (150m).*

ⓖ *Turn R and diverge L down the track beside the wood. Keep on to the next road (550m) then turn R to Jouldings Farm (80m).* ✿

ⓗ *Just before the garden turn R into the field. Follow the path near the river from field to field (1000m) (on the line of the* Devil's Highway*) to Thatcher's Ford. Cross the road into the field opposite.* ➔⑪

⑩ Walk down the road R, and L at the junction, to Thatcher's Ford (550m). Enter the field R.

⑪ Walk through the field past the Blackwater footbridge L (100m) and the Whitewater confluence (150m) and as far as you can go (400m).

⑫ Take the path up R (150m). Go L along the road past the houses, round a bend at Nutbean Farm (400m) to the T-junction (500m).

⑬ Turn L for the church (400m) or

ⓐ Go R to the *George & Dragon* (150m) then follow the paths over the fields to the church (1100m).

Swallowfield is SELINGEFELLE in the Berkshire folios of the Domesday Book, a manor rated for 5 hides in the king's demesne. The estate became home to many noble families during the Norman period and in later times. The earliest surviving reference to the Park was in 1316 when it appears to have been used as a stud farm. The present house was built by William Talman around 1670 for Diamond Pitt. This was Thomas Pitt, the 2nd Earl of Clarendon and grandfather of Pitt the Elder. He bought the estate in 1719 out of the £125,000 he received from the sale of a diamond acquired when he was Governor of Madras, inspiring Wilkie Collins' *Moonstone*. (The Duke of Orleans bought the diamond and it is now part of the French crown jewels.) Sir Henry Russell bought the estate in 1820 and it remained in that family until 1965.

Swallowfield Church, All Saints, was re-built by Sir John le Despenser, Lord of the Manor, in 1256 but has fabric of the previous century when it was a chapel-of-ease to Shinfield. Points of interest: Backhouse family pew of 1690, the 14th century scissor bracing of the bell turret, a disused Norman doorway of around 1120; brasses of 1442 and 1554; the grave (near the kissing gate) of Mary Mitford, 1787-1855, author of *Our Village*, who lived in the parish. *Swallowfield and its owners* Lady Russell 1901 Longmans 362pp

2 Arborfield, Great Copse and the Loddon

About 9km/6 miles with an extension of 1200m/¾ mile and short cuts of
1½km/1mile or 4½km/2¾ mile through tranquil, gently undulating farmland
and woods. OS maps 1:25000 159 Reading, 1:50000 175 Reading.

Start at Arborfield Cross car park on Swallowfield Road, SU 760 669.

The Bull ☎ 0118 976 0204
The Swan ☎ 0118 976 0475

Linking 1◇ 3✦

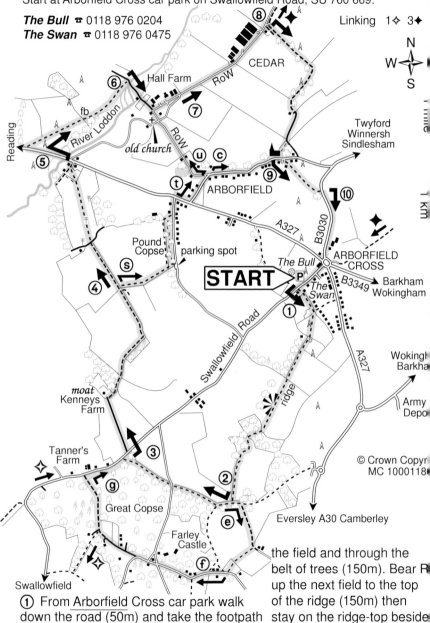

① From Arborfield Cross car park walk
down the road (50m) and take the footpath
L past the thatched house, up the edge of
the field and through the
belt of trees (150m). Bear R
up the next field to the top
of the ridge (150m) then
stay on the ridge-top beside
the trees and across a field

4

(700m). Go through the wood (100m) to the next field and on along the snaking R edge to the track in the belt of trees (500m).

(e) *Extension of 1200m/¾ mile: Go L on the track (70m) and take the side track R (300m). Just round the bend near the house, cross the fields R up to the road (200m).*

(f) *Walk along the road R (500m), over crossroads and on (150m). When the road curves down L stay ahead on the level track to houses. Disregard side drives ✧ and drop off the* plateau *down the forestry track to the road (700m).*

(g) *Follow the road R (350m). ➜(3)*

(2) Turn R along the track to the road (450m). Continue ahead to the next road (400m) then R (40m).

(3) Turn L along the long straight farm drive (400m). Go round the corner near Kenneys Farm and on up into the large field (200m). Stay at the R edge to the corner (350m) and round L to the end (350m).

(s) *Short cut of 1½km/1 mile: Just into the next field turn R into the side field. Follow the R edge to the corner at the wood (600m) then continue at the edge of the field or along the shady path in the wood to the end and out R (300m).*

(t) *Go L on the road to the main road (120m), R on the pavement (100m) and L along Church Lane, opposite, to the bend (300m).*

(c) *For the cut of 2½km/1½ miles stay on the lane past the church (500m) to the path R (50m). ➜(9))*

(u) *Turn L on the wide drive. Go round the bend and on past the Old Rectory to the cross drive near the ruins of Old Arborfield Church (400m). Take the next R. ➜(7)*

(4) Stay ahead along the edge of the field (400m), over the house drive and slightly R along the middle of the next field (400m). Cross the next, little field, corner to corner, and go out R to the main road (150m) almost opposite the drive to Hall Farm (University of Reading). (This drive is used by walkers without right-of-way.)

(5) Turn L over the River Loddon and go on along the main road (R verge) almost to the tree-lined end of the large field R (400m). Take the footpath back R across the fields, halfway between the pylons, from stile to stile (450m). After the footbridge keep to the R margin of the field to the hard track (400m).

(6) Follow the track R over the Loddon and up to the farm road and house R (250m). Turn L.

(7) Walk along the farm road (public footpath) through CEDAR. Arborfield church is visible far R. Carry on past numerous large barns L to the house R (1000m). ✦

(8) Turn R on the track: not next to the garden but in the trees after it (20m). Stay on the track up round R & L bends past Monk's Cottage (900m) to the next L bend (200m). then take the little path in the trees R up to the churchyard and cross to the road (120m). Turn L (50m).

(9) Take the footpath R which branches from the house drive (50m). Follow the path between gardens then fields to the main road, B3030 (400m).

(11) Walk along the road R; there is more verge on the L side (450m). At the roundabout, cross to the **Bull**, and go down the minor road beside it to the car park (150m).

3 Arborfield and the Coombes

About 7km/4¼ miles with an extension of 2km/1¼ miles to Barkham, mainly on wide tracks; farmland and woods; bluebells in season; no stiles; undulating. OS maps 1:25000 159 Reading, 1:50000 175 Reading.

Start at Arborfield Cross; park in Swallowfield Road at the layby opposite the *Bull*, SU 761 670, or the car park 100m lower down. There are parking spots at Arborfield Church and beside Coombes Lane off Bearwood Road, SU 781 678.

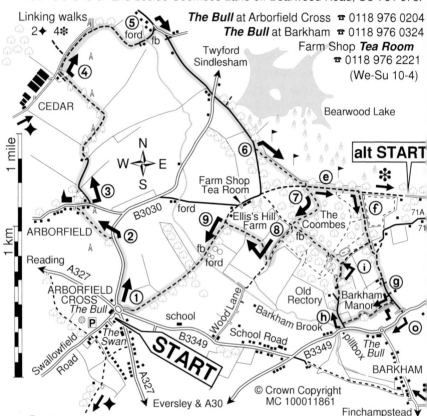

The Bull at Arborfield Cross ☎ 0118 976 0204
The Bull at Barkham ☎ 0118 976 0324
Farm Shop Tea Room
☎ 0118 976 2221
(We-Su 10-4)

Bearwood Lake

alt START

© Crown Copyright
MC 100011861

✦① From Arborfield Cross round-about follow the R verge of the Sindlesham road (450m). Watch out for a footpath L on the R curve.

② Go along the footpath between fields and gardens to the road near Arborfield Church (400m).

③ Along the road R (50m) turn L down the drive to Monks Cottage (500m). Stay ahead between fields almost to the concrete farm track of CEDAR (900m).

④ Bear R along the bridleway R of the concrete track. Stay on this bridleway round R, down to Barkham Brook (900m) and up the valley side to the lane (100m).

⑤ Turn R on the lane (60m) then bear R on the byway along the valleyside. Keep on to the next road (550m). Cross and go up the hard track opposite (450m). Watch out for the side path L, just over the brow and round a slight R bend.

(6) Take the side path L through the belt of trees to the golf course. (80m). Bearwood is visible beyond the lake and the pines. Keep on outside the boundary fence of the golf course (300m). In the trees bear L (30m) and go out R to the byway, Coombes Lane (20m). ✲

(e) *Extension of 2km/1¼ miles to Barkham: Go L on byway (400m).*

(f) *Turn R on the track beside the first field R. Keep on ahead and off the hill (450m). After a house L join the converging track and go on down between paddocks to the bridleway at the bottom of the R fields (350m). Either ➔(g) or ➔(o)*

(g) *(muddy when wet) Turn R along the bridleway past Barkham manor to the track at the end (500m).*

(o) *Stay ahead to the main road in Barham (120m) and go R on the pavement to the **Bull** (200m). Continue in the same direction out of the village to the track in the trees R opposite a pillbox (250m).*

(h) *Walk up the track to the Old Rectory (200m). Continue on the horse track, up, round R and along the top edge of a field to the side path L at the twist (250m).*

(i) *Follow the side path into the wood (70m). At the lumpy ground (old gravel workings) look for the onward path (on bridge) and follow it to the cross path at the corner of the next field (350m). Turn L. ➔(8)*

(7) Almost opposite, take the path into the wood soon curving down R to a cross path at the corner of the first field R (400m).

(8) Keep on down through the edge of the wood beside the field to the horse track (350m). Turn back R up between the fields to the ridge track (400m) near Ellis's Hill Farm (which has a farm shop and part time tea room).

(9) Go L off the ridge into the valley of Barkham Brook (350m). Stay ahead up to the roundabout and the **Bull** at Arborfield Cross (650m).

Bearwood is one of the grandest houses in Berkshire. It was built 1865-74 by John Walters III, to replace the house of his grandfather, John Walters I, founder of *The Times* in 1785. Now it is Bearwood College, a main-stream independent school. This was founded in 1827 as the Merchant Sailors Orphan Asylum in the City of London and became the Royal Merchant Navy School in 1921. A hunting lodge was here in ancient times and the name may derive from boar wood.

4 Barkham and the Coombes

About 7½km/4¾ miles or a shorter version of 5km/3¼ miles through the village; farmland and wood; undulating; bluebells in season. OS maps 1:25000 159 Reading, 1:50000 175 Reading.

Start at Barkham Church, SU 784 664, or at the kerbside in Coombes Lane, SU 781 678.

Linking walk 3✿   **The Bull** ☎ 0118 976 0324
Tea Room ☎ 0118 976 2221
(W-Su 10-4)

© Crown Copyright MC 100011861

ⓢ *Short version: From* Barkham Church go out to the road *(200m) and R along the pavement to the middle of the village (600m).*

ⓣ *At the* **Bull** *cross the main road and go R on the pavement (200m).*

ⓤ *At the end of the wall turn L. Cross the drive and follow the cart track (120m). After the garden take the bridleway L along the bottom of the fields past the manor house and stew pond, up round through the trees and on to the end (500m).*

ⓥ *Go up the track past the Old Rectory (200m). Continue on the horse track, up round a R bend and along the top edge of a field to the side path L at the twist (250m).*

ⓦ *Take the side path through the wood (70m). At the lumpy ground (old gravel workings) drop into the* hollow. Look for the path ahead (over bridge) and carry on up to the cross path at the corner of a field (350m). Stay ahead. ﹢④

① From Barkham Church walk out to the road (200m) and R on the pavement to the first house (100m). Take the footpath L beside the house and go on along the L edge of the fields (750m). At the next house follow the drive to the road (100m). Cross and go along School Road opposite (600m).

② After the dip and R bend, turn R on Wood Lane. Follow the concrete drive until it bends L (450m) then take the track (byway) R under trees between fields (250m).

8

3 When it bends up L join the footpath ahead. Keep on to the end of the L field (300m) and turn L on the cross path.

4 Go on at the edge of the wood, past the fields and up into the trees to the ridge track (300m). ✻ Stay ahead on the level track (300m) watching for a side path R, 40m before the slight L bend.

5 Take the side path through the belt of trees to the golf course (100m). Bearwood is visible far L beyond the lake and pines. Keep on outside the golf course fence (300m). In the trees bear L (30m) and go out R to the byway, Coombes Lane (20m).

6 Continue outside the golf course to the next field R (400m). Stay ahead on the track or walk along the edge of the field (250m). Go on past the Coombes Lane houses (300m), over Bearwood Road and along Sandy Lane (200m). After the houses descend the path ahead to the next tarmac and keep on to the bend (300m).

7 Follow the roads down R to the main road (250m). Continue on the narrow road opposite, almost to the power cables (500m).

8 Next to the stables drive R take the path under trees between the fields to the next road (550m).

9 Walk along the road R to the cross path at the R curve (300m) and turn L along the farm wall to the field (50m). Descend, slightly R (200m). Cross the farm track and belt of trees and go straight on from field to field towards the church spire (400m). Don't join the track, but cut through the churchyard (80m). Walk R of Church Cottages to see the moat.

The Domesday Book entry for Barkham

This is the original text, actual size. The book is now on display at the National Archives at Kew. The line through Barkham is red for highlighting, not deletion. The script is easy to read. The Latin words are abbreviated uniformly eg Tra = *terra*, land; m̊ = *modo*, now; TRE = in the Time of *Rex* Edward ie before the Conquest. The entries were written on loose parchment skins in 1086 probably at Winchester where the Exchequer resided until the 13th century. BERCHEHÃ was a manor, ie an estate, not a house or village. Forty pigsworth of woodland is larger than usual but a typical tax rating for a Windsor Forest manor.

BERKSHIRE.

LAND OF THE KING.
The king holds in demesne BERCHEHÃ. Elmer held it from king Edward Then & now for 3 hides. Land for 3 ploughs. In demesne is one; 6 villeins & 4 bordars with 3 ploughs. There are 5 acres of pasture. Woodland @ 40 pigs. Valued £4. T.R.E; later & now £3.

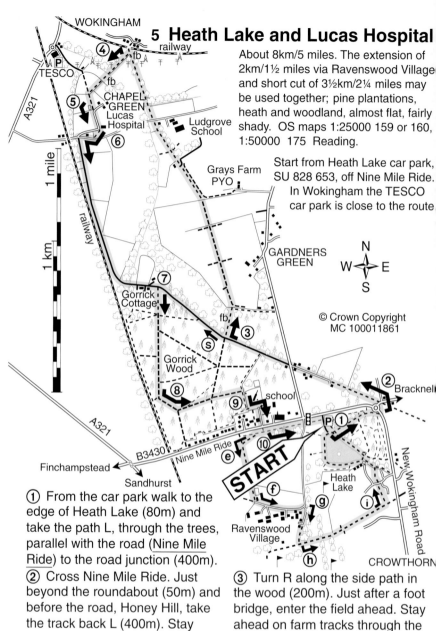

5 Heath Lake and Lucas Hospital

About 8km/5 miles. The extension of 2km/1½ miles via Ravenswood Village and short cut of 3½km/2¼ miles may be used together; pine plantations, heath and woodland, almost flat, fairly shady. OS maps 1:25000 159 or 160, 1:50000 175 Reading.

Start from Heath Lake car park, SU 828 653, off Nine Mile Ride. In Wokingham the TESCO car park is close to the route.

① From the car park walk to the edge of Heath Lake (80m) and take the path L, through the trees, parallel with the road (Nine Mile Ride) to the road junction (400m).

② Cross Nine Mile Ride. Just beyond the roundabout (50m) and before the road, Honey Hill, take the track back L (400m). Stay ahead on the tarmac lane (300m), over the road and along the track to the next track junction (450m).

Ⓢ *Short cut of 2¼km/1½ miles: Stay ahead on the track (600m) and turn L on the 2nd side path just before signs of habitation.* ➔⑦

③ Turn R along the side path in the wood (200m). Just after a foot bridge, enter the field ahead. Stay ahead on farm tracks through the fruit fields (800m). In the last fruit field the footpath is at the L edge (200m). Go on between the trees and small fields to the drive of Ludgrove School (300m). Cross and carry on between fields up to the railway line (500m).

④ Don't cross the footbridge but take the footpath back L. Continue in the same direction over the brook (200m) and up to the horse track between paddocks (150m).

⑤ Go L on the horse track (80m) and continue on the lane to Lucas Hospital L (150m).

⑥ At the bend pass into the field ahead and cross diagonally R (80m). Turn R on the drive to the junction (100m) then L on the track. Continue between fields and the railway (Reading-Guildford) (950m). Stay on the track round the L curve (250m) past Gorrick Cottage R and turn R at the next side path (70m).

⑦ Follow the path through the forest (150m) and continue ahead on the wide forest track. Disregard side tracks and paths (600m).

⑧ Carry on round the L bend (150m) but when the track bends R towards the road, fork L on the side track (250m). When the track bends ½L stay ahead on the lesser track to the cross path (250m).

⑨ Turn R along the path outside the cricket field (100m) then cross to the gate at the pavilion (80m). Walk out to the road (100m) and cross to the path in the wood (40m).

ⓔ *Extension of 2km/1½ mile: Turn R on the path parallel with the road (200m). At the end turn L on the path through the wood (100m). At the cross path bear R over the stream (20m) and carry on to the end (400m).*

ⓕ *Go L along the main drive of Ravenswood Village until it bends L beside the trees (350m).*

ⓖ *Go R on the side drive. When it bends to the buildings, keep on*

along the footpath to the golf course boundary path (250m).

ⓗ *Turn L along the public foot path straight across the fairways to the edge of the golf course (200m). Keep on under the trees between houses. Disregard the first side paths but watch out for the long straight side path L between back gardens (450m).*

ⓘ *Follow it to the road (120m). Slightly R carry on as before to the end of the housing estate (100m). Bear L along the edge of the wood to the footbridge R and Heath Lake (80m). Walk round the lake to the car park clockwise (500m) or over the bridge & anticlockwise (300m).*

⑩ Turn L and follow the path parallel with the road, under the trees (300m). Cross the Ravenswood drive and carry on to the car park (100m).

Lucas Hospital is Wokingham's only Grade I listed building. Built in 1666, it was endowed by Henry Lucas as an almshouse for 16 brethren & warden. It has recently been sold and replaced by modern almshouses elsewhere. This Henry Lucas also endowed the Lucasian professorship at Cambridge held by Newton, Charles Babbage, P A M Dirac and Stephen Hawking.

Ravenswood Village is a charitable home for the care and education of the mentally handicapped. It was set up in 1953 on the site of the house of the Ravenswood family and is now a division of the larger Norwood Trust. There are about 200 residents, 75% Jewish. Historically the Ravenswood estate corresponds to Bigshott Walk of the Easthampstead bailiwick of Windsor Great Forest and was called Bigshott Rayles after the Forest was enclosed and sold. It acquired the new name some time before 1860.

6 Around Finchampstead

About 8½km/5 miles with a short cut of 3km/2 miles; over fields, undulating. Avoid in wet winters. OS maps 1:25000 159 Reading, 1:50000 175 or 186.

Start near Finchampstead Church, parking beside the drive up to the church, SU 793 638, or from California Country Park, SU 785 649 (pay at weekends).

The Greyhound ☎ 0118 973 2269   **The Queen's Oak** ☎ 0118 973 4855

Linking wallks
7✳ 27✳ 29★ 30★

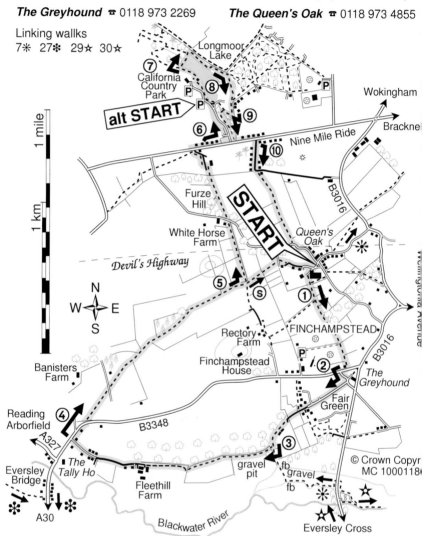

✳ **①** Walk up to Finchampstead Church. Identify the brickwork of the tower and the adjacent brick shed then go down the path behind the church, off the mound, into the trees. Keep on to the road (700m).

② At the road go down R (60m) and L into Longwater Lane to the first junction (80m). This is Fair Green. (The back entrance to the **Greyhound** is L 50m.) Turn R down the branch Longwater Lane

12

(350m). ✦ When the tarmac ends continue on a track (150m). When it bends L, stay ahead on the path outside the field (200m). ☆

③ Just round the L bend (50m) take the side path R into the field. Stay at the R edge of the fields beside the wood to Fleethill Farm (900m) then ahead on track and drive to the road (550m). ❊

④ Walk up the road R (100m). Just over the crest of the hill (50m) turn L along the path in the field (300m). Cross a tarmac drive and continue in the same line along a fenced footpath over several fields past the house on the hill (far R) to a 4-way path junction (1150m).

Ⓢ *Short cut of 3km/2 miles: Stay ahead on the path between hedges (250m) over a drive and up the hill past the church (300m).*

⑤ Enter the field L and follow the R edge to the road at White Horse Farm (400m). Cross and carry on between fields (400m) then follow the drive to the main road, Nine Mile Ride (150m).

⑥ Cross to the pavement and go R (250m) then L on the drive into California Country Park (300m).

⑦ From the first car park make your way to Longmoor Lake then follow the bank round the end to the far corner (400m) and back on the other side (200m).

⑧ Keep to the tarmac path which bends L away from the lake past the end of the field (100m), then R below the wooded slope. Continue to the boundary and R of the houses into the trees (200m).

⑨ Go round the U-bend in the path (50m) then cross the footbridge L (20m). Take the path L

parallel with the drive, out of the wood and bear L over the grass to the road (250m). Walk along the pavement L (150m).

⑩ Cross the road and walk along Warren Lane (200m). Just round the bend go R on the path between fields (500m). Walk up the road L to the **Queen's Oak** crossroads and the church drive (200m).

English bond, alternate courses of stretchers and headers, was the first fixed pattern used in all-brick walls. It was in the 16th century that bricks came into use; they were thinner then.

Flemish bond - alternating stretchers and headers in each course - appears first in 1631 in Dutch House, Kew, but took a century to become widely used - sometimes with burnt end headers. It soon went out of general use but is still applied in decorative brickwork.

It gave way to courses with two, three or more stretchers between headers - common throughout the 19th century.

Stretcher bond became the norm for cavity walls early in the 20th century for headers could not bridge the gap.

7 Finchampstead and the Blackwater River

About 9km/5½ miles; over fields, undulating. Avoid before summer because of muddy bridleways. OS maps 1:25000 159 Reading, 1:50000 175 Reading.

Start near Finchampstead Church, parking beside the drive up to the church, SU 793 638. Alternatively start from Colebrook Lake car park, SU 805 628. There is parking on the verge on Finchampstead Ridges, SU 809 634.

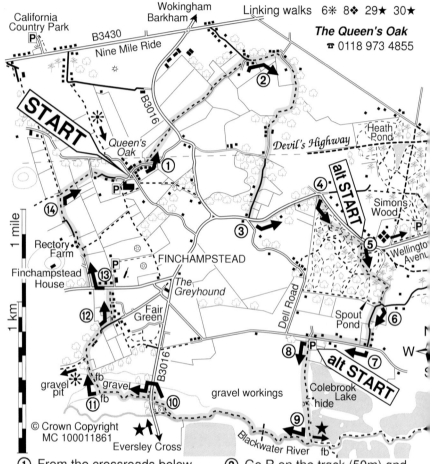

Linking walks 6✳ 8❖ 29★ 30★

The Queen's Oak
☎ 0118 973 4855

① From the crossroads below Finchampstead Church take the road past the front of the **Queen's Oak** (200m). Enter the corner of the 1st field L and make for the bottom L corner (250m). Cross the road slightly L and continue up the R edge of the field on the other side. Stay ahead between fields to the track with houses (700m).

② Go R on the track (50m) and continue on the path down to the tarmac drive (200m). Go R (120m). At the end of the tarmac continue on the bridleway under trees and up round the edge of a field to the drive and houses on top (450m). Stay ahead past a side drive (near the Devil's Highway) (250m) to the road (400m).

③ Cross the road and go L along the verge to the R bend (500m).

④ On the R bend turn R into the trees of <u>Finchampstead Ridges</u> and make your way along the hillside paths, keeping within 50m of the road, to the National Trust stone pillar (500m).

⑤ At the stone, walk away from the road on the L path to the edge of the plateau (150m) and bear L down the widest path to the first cross path (100m). Go L on this path along the hillside (200m) and on along the boundary fence, round R, to the gateway (100m). ❖

⑥ Join the vehicle track outside the gateway and descend R past houses to the road (400m).

⑦ Walk along the road R to the side path and car park L (400m).

⑧ Take the path from the car park beside <u>Colebrook Lake</u>, past the the bird hide near the bridge (450m) and on to the <u>Blackwater</u> River (250m). ★❋

⑨ Turn R and follow the path along the winding river almost to the next road (1100m).

⑩ At the little sewage works take the side path R to the road (250m). Cross into the field opposite and go L beside the road (70m) then R away from the road. Stay at the L edge to the end of the field (350m).

⑪ Cross the footbridge and turn R between the fields. Go on under trees, past a side path L (250m), ❋ and round R almost to the road and houses of Fair Green (300m).

⑫ Turn L on the footpath outside the end of the last field. Pass over a rise and down to the road (200m).

⑬ Cross to the pavement and walk L to the drive of Rectory Farm and Finchampstead House (150m). Turn R along the drive (200m). Just before Rectory Farm take the footpath skirting R of the buildings (200m), then continue up between fields to the 4-way path junction on top (300m).

⑭ Turn R on the footpath between fields (250m). Cross the tarmac drive and stay ahead up ahead under trees (70m). On top continue on the track then road to the cross-roads below the church (250m).

The **Devil's Highway** was the Roman road from London to *Calleva Atrebatum*, Silchester. It crosses the routes of many walks in this book, often under tracks and roads that are still in use. At Finchampstead it passes beneath the fields just north of the church and was the basis for the suggestion that the church mound had Roman significance. In the parish it changes width from 28' to 17' and contains iron slag and pottery shards of 130-140 AD. A Roman mile stone turned up by a ploughman in 1841 stands in the garden of Banister's.

The first comprehensive survey was made in 1836 by Sandhurst students tracing the road westwards from the Thames at *Pontes*, Staines. It forms parts of the county boundary of Berkshire with Hampshire and Surrey, evidence that it was in use when the counties were delineated. Parish boundaries suggests it issued out of Newgate on the line of Oxford Street. It is the only known great west road from London, perhaps because of difficult forest terrain, so *Calleva Atrebatum* was the hub of all the other Roman western arterial routes. Copies of a Roman gazetteer have survived with lists of distances from main centres of the empire. Places on this road are listed in Iters VII & XV. The document, known as the *Antonine Itineraries*, is thought to be a route planner for itinerant civil servants. *Roman Roads in Britain* Ivan D Margary 3rd edition 1973 John Baker 550pp

8 Colebrook Lake and Wellingtonia Avenue

About 6½km/4 miles with an extension of 3km/2 miles and a short cut of 1km/¾ mile. Good for birds, summer and winter; one short steep hill.
OS maps 1:25000 159 Reading or 160 Windsor, 1:50000 175 Reading.

Start at Horseshoe Lake car park, SU 820 620, near the watersports centre or Simons Wood car park, SU 813 635, off Wellingtonia Avenue. The Ambarrow car park, SU 824 626, is on the extension.

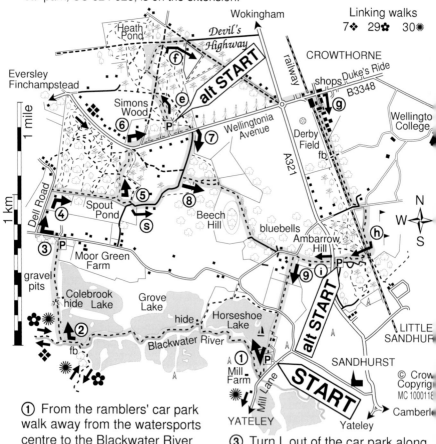

① From the ramblers' car park walk away from the watersports centre to the Blackwater River (150m). ✹ Don't join the road. Turn R along the winding river bank past Horseshoe Lake, the side path R at the hide (600m) and Grove Lake R to the footbridge L (900m). ✿

② Carry on beside the river to the end of Colebrook Lake (100m) ❖ then turn R along the path across the end of the lake, past another hide, to the car park (700m).

③ Turn L out of the car park along the road (200m) and R up Dell Road to the track, R, in the wood after the second house (350m).

④ Go through the wood to Spout Pond L (500m).

Ⓢ *Short cut missing Wellingtonia Avenue: Keep on up to the end of the path (50m) and join the vehicle track. Follow it up L to houses then down and up again (600m).* ➤⑧

(5) At the pond, turn L up the hillside. After the wide cross path take the R steep path up to the road at the R end of the heath on Finchampstead Ridges (450m).

(6) Cross and turn R (100m) then. follow the path, L behind the trees, along Wellingtonia Avenue to Simons Wood car park (300m).

(e) *Extension of 3km/2 miles: At the end of the car park, opposite the road entrance, take the level middle path through the wood to the fork (100m) then bear L down to the junction of path and track at a boundary mound (100m). Walk down the track R (100m), L on the side path to Heath Pond (100m) and R along the edge (200m).*

(f) *At the end of the pond go R on the rising track (Devil's Highway), (150m) and R again on the oblique cross track to the road junction (750m). Cross and continue beside the road into Crowthorne (250m).*

(g) *Immediately after the railway (Reading-Guildford) bridge turn R into St Francis Close (100m). Join the path L of the end building and follow it round to the railway. Keep on beside the railway past the sports field footbridge (400m) to the next bridge (400m). Turn L on the drive from the bridge (40m) then R along the path between fields. Watch out for a gate R just after the start of the wood (400m).*

(h) *Cross the railway lines and fork L on the path away from the railway to Ambarrow car park (250m). Cross the road and take the footpath between the gardens and field (250m). At the lane join the next footpath L (10m). ➔(9)*

(7) Continue down Wellingtonia Avenue to the boundary track of Simons Wood (100m). Cross the road and go up the track past a side track R (330m) and on (40m).

(8) At the very top take the path into the wood along the ridge and drop off the end (250m). Descend between fields and through the bluebell wood to the lane (650m). Walk up the lane L to the first footpath R on the bend (100m).

(9) Go down the R edge of the fields (350m), over the road and on, L of the lake, past the water sports hut, to the car park (300m).

Wellingtonia, *Sequoiadendron gigantea,* has scale leaves. The twigs dangle like clusters of rat tails. The bark is soft (try thumping it) and resists fire. The species is native to California on the western slopes of the Sierra Navada. The jagged skylines around Camberley are caused by Wellintonias at Heatherside, Minley Manor, Hartley Wintney and Tylney Hall.

The two Sequoias are the tallest trees in the world, up to 110m tall. Both are grown in British parks and gardens.

California Redwood, *Sequoia sempervirens,* has twigs that are yew-like though with stiffer pointed leaves, grey beneath. It is native to the sea-board of North California.

x1   x1

9 Crowthorne, Broadmoor and Cæsar's Camp

About 9km/5½ miles with an extension of 2km/1¼ miles. Many variants possible; mainly pine woods; short steep hills; dry under foot. OS maps 1:25000 160 Windsor, 1:50000 175 Reading.

Start from the car park or parking bays in Lower Broadmoor Road at Crowthorne, SU 841 637. Wildmoor Heath car park is near the route, SU 838 630. On the extension there is parking near the A3095 roundabout, SU 655 655.

Linking walks 10❖ 11★

alt START

The Crowthorne Inn
☎ 01344 775886

BRACKNELL

Nine Mile Ride

Cæsar's Camp

Crowthorne Wood

redoubts

Wickham Bushes

plateau

underpass

Transport Research Lab

parking spot

N
W E
S

© Crown Copyr
MC 1000118

Crowthorne Inn

Broadmoor Hospital

Devil's Highway

wall

CROWTHORNE

school

Wildmoor Heath

bog

Sandhurst

Sandhurst

alt START

① From the car park, walk along Lower Broadmoor Road (400m). Just round the bend at Chaplains Hill diverge L into the trees. Keep to the path nearest the road up to the telecommunications mast and flats L then follow the fence ahead to the football field (300m).

② Diverge from the L edge of the field to the exit point at the middle of the far side (120m) then go R along the road towards the high wall of Broadmoor Hospital (70m). Turn L and follow the road nearest the wall (200m). After Club Lane use the tarmac path L of the road (100m).

③ Just over the brow of the hill, at the end of the clubhouse L, take the side path down L in the trees beside the car park to the <u>Devil's Highway</u> track (100m) and turn R.

ⓔ *Extension of 2km/1¼ miles: Almost immediately (30m) take the path L to the forestry track (400m).*

ⓕ *Turn R over the track junction. Go on to the next crossing (400m).*

ⓖ *Turn L to the road (450m).*

ⓗ *Next to the road, turn R along the track R of the ditch. Keep on to the oblique fence (400m). Slip round the end and cross over the culvert but not over the road. Follow the R verge up round to the roundabout and cross into the side road opposite (150m).*

ⓘ *At Crowthorne Wood parking area follow the first path L from the forest track (250m). Go L at the next track, round a R curve to join a major track on the bend (250m).*

ⓙ *Bear L on the other side track down to the end (350m).*

ⓚ *Turn R on the track near the road (<u>Nine Mile Ride</u>) up to the cross track from the road (450m).*

ⓛ *Follow the track away from the road round L & R bends (100m). Go through the fence and up to the <u>plateau</u> then on the level through <u>Cæsar's Camp</u> (300m).*

ⓜ *Just after the converging path joins, turn L on the footpath out to the ramparts (70m) and follow them round R to the vehicle gate through the fence (450m).* ➤⑥

④ Stay on the undulating track and pass under the road (900m).

⑤ After the underpass (50m), turn L on the path between fences near the road (250m). At the end of the fenced section turn R up the wide path. Notice the <u>redoubts</u>. Stay ahead over two cross tracks to the double cross track (750m) and up between fences to the gateway of the <u>Cæsar's Camp</u> fence (250m). Step inside (20m) to see ramparts L & R then return or go right round & back to the gate (950m).

⑥ Emerging at the gate, ❖✤ disregard the track ahead and take the next one R, level & straight (New Town Ride). Stay ahead to the major cross track with power lines (Devil's Highway) at the edge of the plateau (1000m). ★

⑦ Go R on the track and down under the road (600m).

⑧ After the underpass and after the top of the rise (100m), take the downhill side path L to Butter Bottom Ponds (400m). Stay ahead up to the house (100m), along the road to the T-junction (300m) and down the path between woods and fields (300m). In the wood, after the fields (40m), the path bends L up a slope (50m) then R along the edge of the wood (150m).

⑨ At the end of the wood take the path R under trees along the edge of the field (300m) over the lane and on to a path T-junction (400m).

⑩ Go L along the fence down to the corner (250m).

ⓧⓨⓩ *Extension of 900m on map.*

⑪ Turn R along the main path under the trees to the end of the school fields R (800m). If making for <u>Wildmoor Heath</u> car park turn L through the trees (150m). If not:-

⑫ Go up the L edge of the field (200m), out L to the main road (100m) then along the pavement R to Lower Broadmoor Road (400m). Turn R to the parking area (100m).

10 The Look Out and Cæsar's Camp

About 8½km/5¼ miles, an introduction to the main features; many variants possible; pine woods and heath; short steep hills, dry.
OS maps: 1:25000 160 Windsor; 1:50000 175 Reading.

Start from The Look Out car park, SU 877 662, off the B3430, 300m from the roundabout.

Linking walks 9❖ 11✳ 12◇ 45✿

Look Out **Coffee Shop** 01344 354400

❖① From the Look Out parking area, there are gates to the forest at the extremities and the middle. Follow the long straight track from the middle gate to the triangle of three crosstracks (800m).

② Bear R on the 2nd major track, over the rise (350m) and down to the next cross track (450m). Stay ahead to the foot of Surrey Hill (850m) ◇ and up to the gate of the reservoir on the flat top (300m).

③ Turn back R beside the fence and follow it round L, down (county boundary) to a sarsen L and power lines at the bottom (650m). Stay ahead to the next sarsen, the Wishmoor Stone (150m). Pass

20

through the fence to the footbridge at the Wish Stream. ❖ Don't cross but walk away from the fence on the track, ½R from the stream, to the next cross track (250m).

④ Turn R and ascend to the plateau at Lower Star Post, where several tracks meet (600m). Cross the junction straight ahead to the track with the power cables. Keep on to Upper (Roman) Star Post (650m) where the Devil's Highway crosses and there are more reservoirs. Carry straight on to the Cæsar's Camp enclosure (1150m) and along the middle of Cæsar's Camp (300m).

⑤ At the track fork, turn R on the wide side path R along a spur of the hill and down over the ramparts on the flank of the hill (200m). Turn R outside the fence up the path with the boundary mound (300m).

⑥ At the top, the path joins a track at a bend. Go down L to the corner of the farm fence (350m) and on, slightly R, to the end corner of the farm boundary (350m). Disregard the crossing path and bear R to the next major track (150m).Cross and climb the small steep path onto the plateau at Pudding Hill near the trig point (150m).

⑦ Turn L on the main track off the end of the ridge. Descend to the cross path with the Look Out fence visible R (300m) and return, past the **café**, to the car park (200m).

The **Bagshot Sands** (in the original sense) are a mound in the middle of the London Basin, on which stands Camberley. They underlie all the walks in this book though the northern and western walks stray onto the London Clay.

The Sands are a stratum 250 feet thick but are not lithified - turned to rock. The first account of them was read to the Geological Sociey of London by Henry Warburton in 1821. He described his investigations of the sands on the heath around Bagshot and the name stuck. Later on, when correlated with outcrops elsewhere, the Middle and Upper layers were renamed Bracklesham and Barton Sands. In geology *Bagshot* is retained only for the lowest division. The whole thickness is now called the Tertiary Sands or the Bagshot Series.

Chiltern Hills   London Basin   Hog's Back

Sands
London Clay
Chalk
Greensand
Palæozoic

These Sands stretch to the heaths of Dorset and to the Ypres and Paris Basins. Fifty million years ago they were beaches in a large estuary where the earth's crust was slowly sinking. Beach sand is coarse and does not lie in level layers; it grinds sea shells away. The Bagshot and Bracklesham Sands seen in fresh cuttings show current bedding and worm burrows but very few other fossils.

At their thickest, the Bagshot Beds are 130'. The Bracklesham Beds, which form the greatest area of the Sands outcrop, are 70' thick. Within them are sporadic clay beds which cause boggy patches; the clay was dug for brick, tile and pot making, commemorated by names such as *Pottery Lane*. The original thickness of the Barton Sands is unknown; only 50' remain in the tops of Ash Ranges, Bagshot Heath, Chobham Ridges, Yateley Common and the South Farnborough ridge. They yield the heathstone boulders which become sarsens.

11 **Barossa Common and the Devil's Highway**

About 7km/4¼ miles on heath; an extension of 1km/¾ mile and short cut of 2km/1¼ miles may be used together. You may find yourself in the middle of a noisy army exercise! OS maps 1:25000 160 Windsor, 1:50000 175 Reading.

Park near the bend at the north end of the road, Kings Ride, SU 875 621.

Linking walks   9★   10✳   12✳

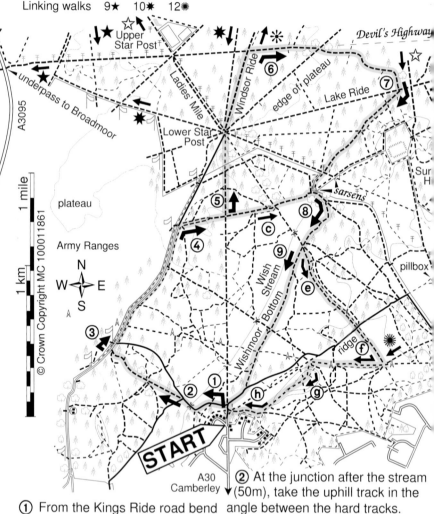

① From the Kings Ride road bend descend the tarmac drive then the track into <u>Barossa Common</u> (120m). Disregard the first side tracks but turn L on the hard track at the major junction. Stay on this track round L and R bends and over the <u>Wish Stream</u> (250m).

② At the junction after the stream (50m), take the uphill track in the angle between the hard tracks. Stay ahead to the boundary road and fence on the <u>plateau</u> (550m).

③ Turn R. Walk on the tarmac or one of the paths beside it (200m). After the power cables keep on to the double side track R, opposite a gate in the fence (800m).

④ Bear R on the double track. After a dip ascend to the cross-roads on the rise (300m).

ⓒ *Short cut of 2km/1¼ miles: Stay on the same track ahead to the bottom of the valley (600m) then turn R outside the fence.* ➜⑧

⑤ Turn onto the track L and keep on, over a wide track to Lower Star Post where numerous tracks meet (550m).★☆✴ Continue on Windsor Ride, the main track R of the power lines, to the level, straight cross track (Devils Highway) (600m). ✳

⑥ Go R, level at first (300m) then descending to the oblique cross track (200m). Stay ahead down round curves LRLR to the next major cross track (600m). ✳

⑦ Cross this major track and turn R up the side track diverging from it. Pass over the rise and down to the cross track at the power lines (750m). Stay ahead, L of the fence, to the next corner (150m), then go out through the opening and L.

⑧ See the Wishmoor Stone at the opening in the fence. Cross the cart bridge over the Wish Stream to the 3-way fork (80m) and take the R track round a R bend to the next cross track (400m).

ⓔ *Extension of 1km/¾ mile: There are three adjacent tracks L. Take the 3rd one up the valleyside to the hard track on the ridge (650m). Go straight down the other side to the power lines (300m).*

ⓕ *Turn R along one of the paths following the power lines past the next pylon (400m).*

ⓖ *On the rise after the pylon (100m), turn L up Saddleback Hill (70m). Stay on the ridge to the end (350m) then descend to the wide path across the foot (50m).*

ⓗ *Turn R down to the hard track (300m) then up L to the starting point (100m).*

⑨ Stay ahead on the track along Wishmoor Bottom, over a cross track (600m), under power cables (150m) to the end (250m). Follow the hard track down R (150m) and turn L up between the houses to the starting point (120m).

The **A30** runs to Land's End. It follows the old road from London which forked at Basingstoke to Winchester and Salisbury - the successor to the Roman road from which it diverged after the Thames and which branched at Silchester.

From Egham to Hartley Wintney, the old road cut up the heath on the Tertiary Sands though not exactly on the present line. It would have been a multiplicity of rutted tracks, not a paved way of Roman type. Road renaissance came with the Turnpike Acts. The heath road was turnpiked from Hounslow to the Basing Stone (the Bagshot boundary, at the *Jolly Farmer*) by an Act of 1728 and from there to Hertfordbridge Hill (*White Lion*, Hartley Wintney) by an Act of 1857.

Medieval roads were the responsibility of Lords of the Manor. Manors became fragmented by land sales and parishes were handed the responsibility in 1555. Parishes overwhelmed by the Great North Road on their clay soils obtained a Highways Act in 1663 enabling them to collect tolls, Wadesmill having the first gate. Earlier turnstiles with pikes to prevent horses passing provided the name.

Turnpike roads became trusts which erected gates and employed toll keepers. They lacked technology at first but had the ruts filled, instigated new roads on better routes and initiated legislation. Many current A-roads were new roads of that period. Later the trusts would appoint engineers like Jack Metcalf, Thomas Telford, John Loudon McAdam, and road building technology was re-born.

12 Bagshot Heath

About 8km/5¼ miles. This is an introduction to some of the main features. Pine woods and open heath; short steep hills; dry under foot; very flinty in places; bluebells in season. OS maps 1:25000 160 Windsor, 1:50000 175 Reading.

Start from near Bagshot Church, SU 905 632. Park near the start of the gravel track a little way into Vicarage Road. No pub but places for picnics.

Linking walks 10✧ 11✳ 13✿

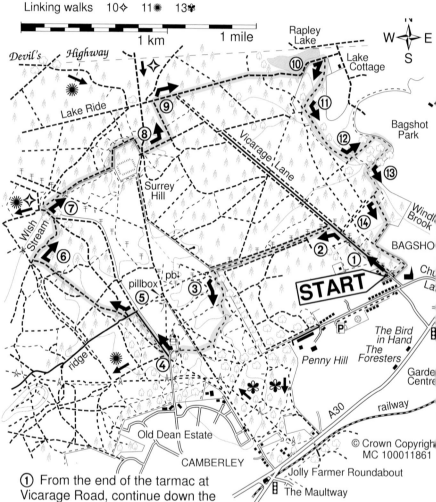

① From the end of the tarmac at Vicarage Road, continue down the gravel track to the stream (300m) and up ahead (150m).

② Turn L on the side path between fences (where power lines cross). Stay on this path, parallel with forest tracks, to the end corner of the boundary mound L (850m).

③ Take the side path L along the boundary mound (200m) ✿ then diverge R up the valley path (60m) and fork L up to the plateau. Follow paths round to the fence of the telecommunications tower and L of it to the gate at the road (500m).

24

④ Join the long straight track which continues ½ L from the road. Follow it, or the small path L of it, out onto the level heath (350m).

⑤ At the major side track turn L to the two side tracks R (70m). ✳
Take the 2nd one over the plateau and down to the T-junction near the bottom of the valley (750m).

⑥ Turn R on the main track. Stay on it round L bends until just over the Wish Stream bridge (450m). ✧

⑦ At the Wishmoor Stone cross the fence and take the path back R (150m). Stay ahead on the track up Surrey Hill (400m) and skirt round the reservoir fence (350m).

⑧ Leave the flat hilltop (plateau) via the track directly opposite the reservoir gate (200m). At the first cross track go L to the long straight track, Lake Ride (300m).

⑨ Follow Lake Ride R, gently down to Rapley Lake (900m). Carry on over the bridge (250m).

⑩ Near the end of the track turn off R beside a fence and follow the path to the 4-way junction (400m).

⑪ Turn down L. Cross a culvert and carry on near (L of) the Windle Brook (500m).

⑫ At the end, take the path L up to the boundary of Bagshot Park (250m). Turn R along the fence under trees (150m) then R down into the bluebell wood (200m).

⑬ After the culvert, go L beside the Windle Brook (200m) then turn R towards the clearing (50m).

⑭ Just before the clearing, turn L along the side path to the boundary (250m). Follow the boundary path R (200m) then L (300m) then R to Vicarage Road (200m).

Bagshot Heath Highwaymen:

Bagshot Heath before the 19th century was a large part of the uninhabited land stretching from the Thames, through Bagshot to Hartley Wintney. The volume of traffic on the great west road (A30) in this wild country made it a profitable work-place for highwaymen, several of whom based themselves nearby.

William Davis, 1627-90, the Golden Farmer, was born at Wrexham. At Bagshot he farmed successfully for 40 years, a pillar of the community with 18 children, concealing his "other job" by operating at night and during travels. He retired to a corn chandler's shop in London in 1685 but came out of retirement and was shot by a coach passenger. It is known he was brought to the *Kings Arms* in Bagshot but there is no record of a trial. Ultimately he was taken at Southwark, executed at Tyburn (Fleet Street) and gibbetted on Bagshot Heath opposite his house. The original pub of the same name may have been his house. Rocque's map of Surrey of 1770 shows the *Golden Farmer* on the north side of the major road at the Maultway junction and in the position of the *Jolly Farmer* (as was) but it may have been on the other side originally. It became *Jolly* in 1823.

The Golden Farmer - Inn and Highwayman George Poulter 1973 18pp

Claude Duval had a house in Lightwater Lane. He came from Normandy in the service of travellers and was a page to the Duke of Richmond before taking to the road. Stories of chivalrous highwaymen appear to emanate from him. He retired but came out of retirement and was captured in London. Several well-born ladies petitioned on his behalf and Mr Justice Morgan threatened to resign if he was reprieved. He was executed in 1670.

Parson Darby was a curate and resident of Yateley. He shot dead a Royal Mail coach driver in 1835 at the Wooden House tavern, Pinetree Hill, and was subsequently gibbetted there. It is said Darby Green takes its name from him.

13 High Curley and Lightwater Country Park

About 8½km/5¼ miles with an extension of 1km/¾ mile to the Heatherside Wellingtonias; heath with long views; short steep slopes, half shady. Part of the route crosses army land with vehicle test tracks. Step into the trees if vehicles approach. OS maps 1:25000 160 Windsor, 1:50000 186 or 175.

Start from the car park, SU 900 617, beside the Maultway 350m from the Jolly Farmer roundabout or from Lightwater Country Park, SU 917 619. On the extension use the Cumberland Road car park, SU 905 598.

Linking walks   12✿   14★   ①✳

The Wheatsheaf ☎ 01276 28744

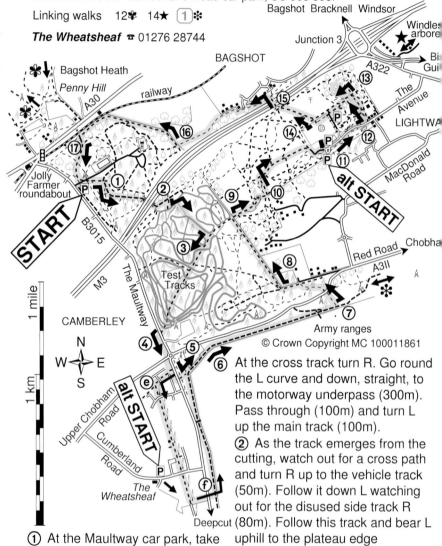

© Crown Copyright MC 100011861

At the cross track turn R. Go round the L curve and down, straight, to the motorway underpass (300m). Pass through (100m) and turn L up the main track (100m).

② As the track emerges from the cutting, watch out for a cross path and turn R up to the vehicle track (50m). Follow it down L watching out for the disused side track R (80m). Follow this track and bear L uphill to the plateau edge (Chobham Ridges) (300m). Where the track curves L on top, step out on to the footpath.

① At the Maultway car park, take the main track away from the road (100m). Under the power cables diverge on the side track R (120m).

③ Turn R. Keep to the path between and across tracks to the road (Maultway) at the edge of Camberley (750m). Cross.

④ Go L on the pavement to the roundabout (150m) and ahead.

ⓔ *Extension of 1km/¾ mile via the Heatherside Wellingtonias: After the roundabout (100m), take the path R between houses and across a road to the avenue of Wellingtonias (150m). Walk along the path beneath the trees to Cumberland Road (600m). (The car park and* **Wheatsheaf** *are 150m R). Carry on ahead (200m).*

ⓕ *At the end of the fields go L to the road, across and through the trees to the military fence (150m). Follow the boundary track back L (600m) and round the corner.* ➔⑥

⑤ After the roundabout (200m) take the path L to the corner of the army fence (70m) and down L of it.

⑥ Keep to the fence (with power lines converging) past the low point with side track (1000m) and pylon L, to the top of the next rise with a path L opposite a gate (100m). ✿

⑦ Take the side path L over the heath (120m). Find the stile and cross the road into the wood (30m) then follow the fire break L up to the boundary (150m). Turn L on the boundary path down to the corner and track junction (150m).

⑧ Go round the corner R and up beside the boundary. Stay ahead to the top of the ridge (550m).

⑨ Follow the ridge path R past the sarsen to the very end of High Curley (220m) then descend the stepped path R (50m). At the bottom of the steps, go L on the 2nd cross path to the end (150m).

⑩ Turn R along the wide path gently down through heath (400m). At the end, curve R on the track which bends L and drops to the Leisure Centre car parks (150m).

⑪ Cross the car parks parallel with the boundary fence R and continue on the path through trees diverging from the fence to the Leisure Centre road (150m). Keep on beside the road to the pond at the bottom corner of Lightwater Country Park (200m). ★

⑫ Turn L after the pond and follow the wide path along the R edge of two ponds (250m).

⑬ At the 3rd pond turn L across the end (70m) (& continue in the same direction to the sports field). Just after the footbridge turn L & R. At the next junction (50m), bear L (10m) then R. Continue on this path to the parking area under the trees (100m), up into the sports field and along the R edge (100m).

⑭ Halfway along the field, exit R over the cartbridge and follow the wide path ahead over the heath to the M3 footbridge (250m).

⑮ Cross the motorway (100m) and take the small path L beside it skirting behind the houses of Bagshot past the end of a road (150m). Continue behind gardens, with a zigzag (100m). After the houses the path converges on the motorway then diverges towards the water tower (400m).

⑯ At the track system, turn R up the boundary path over the rise and down to the railway (Ascot-Ash Vale) (500m). Stay ahead to the bridge (near the A30)(300m). ✿

⑰ Turn L up the path to the car park at the Maultway (300m).

14 Windlesham, village and arboretum

About 6½km/4 miles; through Windlesham arboretum, the village and fields; gentle inclines. The shorter version of 3½km/2¼ miles avoids the village. OS Maps 1:25000 160 Windsor, 1:50000 175 Reading.

Start from Windlesham Church, SU 930 637. The layby at the church holds about 20 cars but fills up during church functions. Trust members may use the arboretum car park, SU 932 627.

The Surrey Cricketers ☎ 01276 472192
The Half Moon ☎ 01276 473329

Linking walk   13★

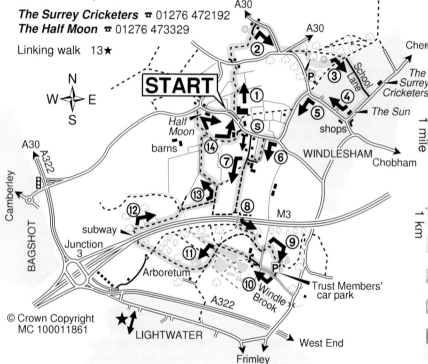

© Crown Copyright
MC 100011861

Ⓢ *Shorter version: Go past the church (100m) and R on Rectory Lane (200m).* ➔⑦

① Take the diagonal path across the middle of the main part of the churchyard then L to the next road (350m). Cross to the house drive, slightly L and carry on on the winding path between fields to the next road (400m).

② Walk along the road R (400m). At the end turn L across the end of the next side road (40m) and take the oblique path L under the trees (100m). At the first opportunity turn R out of the trees to the open sports field and cross the grass to the furthest corner L beyond the children's play area (300m).

③ At the end of the field, turn R along the track between the houses (School Lane) to the road (300m). (The **Surrey Cricketers** is L 100m.) Go R down Chertsey Road to the shops (250m).

④ Turn R and walk up Updown Hill through the middle of Windlesham (350m).

⑤ Take Pound Lane, L, to the main road (350m).

28

⑥ Go R up the main road (100m). Before the houses enter the narrow field L. Follow the L edge to the end (150m) and go R on the track to the lane (50m). Turn L (50m).

⑦ At the end carry on straight ahead (not R) down the track at the L edge of the field (300m).

⑧ Cross the M3 footbridge (100m) but don't continue ahead. Turn L but then fork R away from the motorway on the path into the arboretum (200m). Join the track to the tarmac drive L (50m).

⑨ Cross the drive and turn L on the track diverging from it. Carry on round the trees to the pond (250m) or explore more widely.

⑩ Turn R through the members' car park to the arboretum main drive (100m) and R along the drive to the gates at the house (100m). Take the path ahead through the middle of the arboretum (200m).

⑪ At the crossing path, turn L to pass between ponds and over the Windle Brook (200m). Swing R past the C-shaped pond towards South Farm visible in the distance (400m) ★ and continue on the path under the motorway (200m).

⑫ Follow the footpath beside the motorway R (300m) then bear L and continue ahead along the cart track to the T-junction (200m).

⑬ Turn L along the fenced track (100m). At the R bend, enter the field L. Follow the L edge to the bend and go on along the second side. Continue up the fenced path, bending R to a T-junction (400m).

⑭ Either, go R to the road then L, or, go L to the road then R past the *Half Moon* to Windlesham Church (500m).

Railways in this book:

The **London-Southampton** main line of the L&SWR (London& SW Railway) was one of the earliest public railways to open for long distance traffic. Early railways were private or linked only two stations but gave rise to the notion here and in America of trunk routes. The L&SWR was the 4th of these, only preceded by the Baltimore & Ohio Rail Road in 1830, the South Carolina Rail Road in 1831 and the Grand Junction Railway (Birmingham-Manchester) in 1837. The first L&SWR service ran to Woking in May 1838 - a week before the first GWR train (Great Western) to Taplow. The line was completed in 1839 and the London terminus moved from Nine Elms to Waterloo in 1848.

LSWR a tribute to the London & SW Railway
B Cooper & R Antell 1988 Ian Allan 128pp

The **Reading-Guildford** line opened in 1849 for the Reading, Guildford and Reigate Railway Co (RRGR) and was operated by SE Railways. It used the LSWR tunnel at Guildford to connect with the section along the N Downs.

The **Woking-Farnham** line, a branch of the LSWR main line, was opened in 1870. It superseded the Guildford-Farnham- Alton line of 1852.

The **Staines-Wokingham** railway through Ascot, Martins Herons and Bracknell was built in 1856 by the LSWR as a branch of the Windsor line from Clapham Junction. It joined the Reading-Guildford line at Wokingham and so linked Reading to Waterloo.

The **Ascot-Ash Vale** line was opened by the LSWR in 1878 connecting Camberley and Bagshot to London and Farnham. It was doubled in 1893.

The **Bisley Railway** was a private 1¼ mile spur from the LSWR at Pirbright built for the National Rifle Association in 1890 and extended 3 miles during World War I for the army camps. It closed in 1952 and its bridge (near Lock 15) was dismantled in 1980.

15 **Frimley Green and Deepcut**

About 9km/5½ miles with a short cut of 1km/½ mile; along the Basingstoke Canal and over hilly heath. The heathland is an army training ground where the public are free to wander but shooting (blanks) and thunder flashes may disturb dogs and owners. OS maps 1:25000 145 Guildford, 1:50000 186 Aldershot.

Start from Frimley Lodge Park main car park, SU 888 562.

Linking walks 16✳ 17✿ 35 ✳

Basingstoke Canal Centre 01252 370073

Kings Head ☎ 01252 835431
Rose & Thistle ☎ 01252 834942

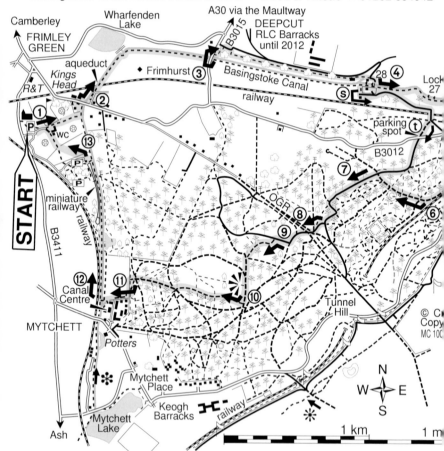

① From Frimley Lodge car park take the track to the pavilion. Go L of it on the path and ahead to the Basingstoke Canal (300m). Turn L on the tow path to the road bridge near the **King's Head** (100m).

② Take the path L up to the road and cross the canal (100m). Turn

into the drive L (30m). Skirt round the garden of Frimhurst Lodge and keep on beside the canal over the railway aqueduct (100m) and on to Wharfenden Lake (300m). Carry on round the bends (as the canal turns out of the Blackwater valley) to the next road bridge (600m).

③ Go under the bridge, R up the steps and R over the canal (100m). At the end of the bridge turn R into the trees (30m) then L to the track (70m). Follow the track away from the road (100m). At the L bend turn R on the path to the edge of the canal cutting (50m). Follow it along the edge of the deep cut to the canal workshop (850m). Pass through the workshop yard and take the track down R to Lock 28 (150m). Cross the footbridge.

ⓢ *Short cut of 1km/½ mile: Turn R along the towpath to the end of the wall (80m) then L up the path away from the canal (80m). At the house turn L along the drive and follow it through the wood and round the R bend over the main line railway (600m).*

ⓣ *After the bridge fork R up the lesser track (100m). Continue over the road, up, round R over a hill, down to a 4-way track junction (500m) and ahead.* ➜⑦

④ Follow the towpath L to Lock 25 at Curzon Bridges (900m). ✪

⑤ Ascend and cross the railway bridge (London-Southampton). Go on to the road, where there is a pillbox (200m). Don't pass under the railway (Woking-Farnham line) but walk along the road R (100m) then diverge on the track L. Disregard the side track under the bridge L (150m) ❉❉ and continue up beside the railway (400m).

⑥ Stay on the same track when it curves R away from the railway up a valley. Keep on to the major cross track just after the top of the ridge (500m). Turn L.

⑦ Follow the track over a ridge. Disregard several side tracks but pass round L & R bends (500m).

⑧ At the next L bend fork R to two major crossing tracks, the second being the Old Guildford Road (100m). Cross the OGR ahead to the track which curves L. Don't turn off from the curve (70m) but keep on to the next junction (100m).

⑨ Turn R with the main track (100m) then take the first side track L descending to meet a larger track (300m). Turn L up onto the ridge (100m). Disregard a wide branch track back down R. See the view and carry on. Turn onto the next major track R (200m).

⑩ Follow this undulating track to a complex junction of tracks and paths (450m) and bear R on the main track, down off the hill (250m). At the bottom cross the wide track and go straight through the trees to the fence (50m).

⑪ Turn L along the fence to the gate (80m) then cross the field ahead to the Canal Centre (200m). Cross the canal swing bridge to the towpath and turn R. This bridge is in use only 11am-4pm. If it is not in use, go L to the road (100m), R over the canal (100m) and back on the other side (100m).

⑫ Follow the towpath to Frimley Lodge Park. The railway L is the Ascot-Farnham line. Keep on as far as the end of the miniature railway track (1000m).

⑬ Diverge from the canal and cross the sports fields diagonally through the middle. Continue on the footpath past the buildings to the main car park L (350m).

16 Tunnel Hill and the army ranges

This walk is often not possible. Most days red flags are flown at entrances to the ranges. Flags stay down some week ends and during holidays at Christmas, Easter and August. The range office is on 01252-325233.

About 7km/4¼ miles; mostly through open heath with hilly paths; best in August or bleak mid-winter. Extensions of 1½km/1 mile and 1km/¾ mile; a short cut of 1½km/1 mile. OS maps 1:25000 145 Guildford, 1:50000 186 Aldershot.

Start from the larger roadside parking area between the road junctions, SU 918 557. Most of the gateways to the ranges have parking spots.

Linking walks
15✳ 17⚙ 35◈ 36✳ 37✦

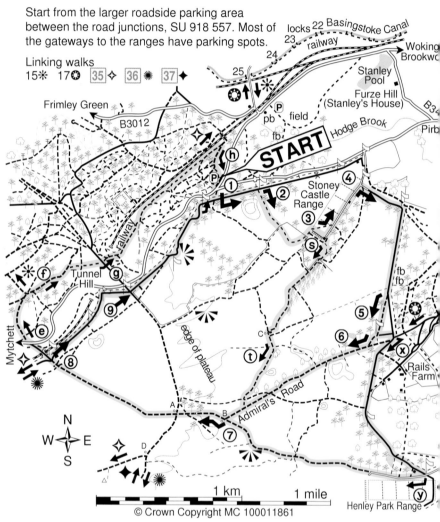

© Crown Copyright MC 100011861

⚙① From the parking area cross both roads (50m) and go out over the heath to the boundary track inside the fence of the army ranges (30m). Follow it down L (350m).

② Take the 1st side track R (400m) eventually curving L to the butts of Stoney Castle rifle range (200m). Follow the track across the front of the butts (100m).

(s) *Short cut of 1½km/1mile: From the end of the sand bank behind the targets drop down the small side path through the trees (50m). At the wider path turn R (100m). Stay ahead at the track (500m).*

(t) *Go round an abrupt L bend then a ½R bend with side track (100m) and descend to the hairpin bend (400m). Use the path ahead to join to the next major track (50m) and go on, R, to an oblique T-junction (150m) then R.* ➜(7)

(3) Walk down the drive beside the range (400m).

(4) Near the bottom turn R on the tarmac side road which soon becomes a track (350m). Carry on round the R bend then along the boundary track until it bends slightly L (600m).

(5) Diverge R up to the top of the hillock (300m).

(x) *Extension of 1½km/1 mile: Turn L down to the boundary track outside the fence (100m) and follow it R to the next rifle range (Henley Park Range) (1000m).* ✦

(y) *Turn back R up the tarmac drive beside the range (400m). After the butts keep on up the track over a rise (350m) (the Hogs's Back is visible far L), up round curves R & L to the side track back R (700m). Keep on ahead.* ➜(7)

(6) Turn R down to the major track from the boundary fence (Admiral's Road). Follow it R through the trees then over a rise. Ignore side paths and keep on up to the oblique T-junction (1100m). Turn R.

(7) Follow the track up onto the plateau, over the 1st cross track (which leads L to a good picnic spot with views) and the 2nd cross track (350m). ✧✳ Keep on ahead over the plateau then gently down to the boundary near the railway (Woking-Farnham) (1000m). ✧

(e) *Extension of 1km/¾ mile: Carry on over the boundary and the railway bridge down to the road (150m). Cross and go up the track opposite which curves R to a complex junction (300m).* ✳

(f) *Take the uphill track ahead skirting the hill R (300m). At the top, fork R then stay ahead to the level straight track over Tunnel Hill (Old Guildford Road) (250m).*

(g) *Cross and take the path ahead soon passing the tunnel mouth (out of sight L). Keep on in the same direction near the railway cutting. Descend the edge of the hill (350m) and skirt round the base of the next hill (300m). When the track bends R into a little cleft, go up the track parallel with the railway, on the little ridge then down L, as if to pass under the railway (500m).*

(h) *At the larger track, 50m before the bridge, turn back R up the valley. Watch out for the side path L (150m) and ascend the valley side through the pines to the parking spot (100m).*

(8) Follow the boundary track up R past the tunnel mouth (550m) and round a R bend to the next cross track, near the road (200m).

(9) Fork L along the boundary on the plateau (Terrace 8) (350m). At the next dip, London buildings may be visible ahead (70°). Either stay on the track looping away from the fence or keep to the fence (350m). Over the next rise, descend to the cross track (100m) and exit L to the road and parking spot (100m).

17 Pirbright and the Basingstoke Canal

About 9km/5½ miles, mainly level, along the canal and over fields; shady. Best when the red flags are down; when they are, a heath extension of 1km/¾ mile on the army ranges. OS maps 1:25000 145 Guildford, 1:50000 186 Aldershot.

Start at Pirbright from the car park on the village green, SU 946 560, or at the larger roadside parking area between the road junctions, SU 918 557.

Linking walks   15❀ 16❀ 35★ 40❀ 1✦ 3❀

The White Hart ☎ 01483 799715   **The Cricketers** ☎ 01483 473198

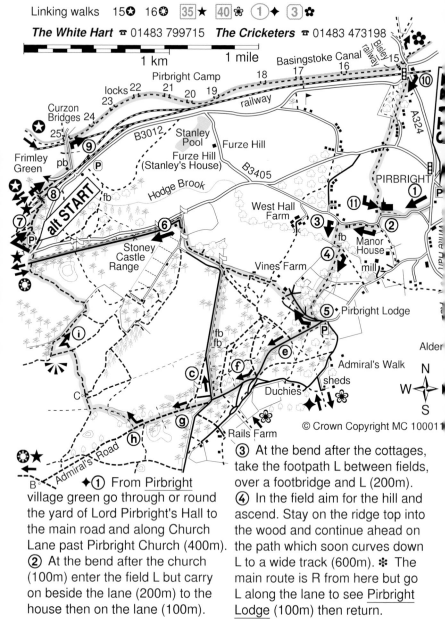

© Crown Copyright MC 10001

✦① **From Pirbright** village green go through or round the yard of Lord Pirbright's Hall to the main road and along Church Lane past Pirbright Church (400m).
② At the bend after the church (100m) enter the field L but carry on beside the lane (200m) to the house then on the lane (100m).

③ At the bend after the cottages, take the footpath L between fields, over a footbridge and L (200m).
④ In the field aim for the hill and ascend. Stay on the ridge top into the wood and continue ahead on the path which soon curves down L to a wide track (600m). ❀ The main route is R from here but go L along the lane to see Pirbright Lodge (100m) then return.

34

(e) *Extension of 1km/¾ mile into the military ranges if the red flags are down: Take the wide level track continuing straight ahead from the end of the tarmac past houses R (200m) and eventually down to a 6-way junction (600m).*

(f) *Bear R on the rising track to the fence of the ranges (400m).*

(c) *If the red flags are flying don't go on but follow the fence R all the way to the road (1400m).* ➜(6)

(g) *The track bends along the boundary. Take the onward track through the fence into the dip and up the next slope (450m). On the brow pass the hillock L and carry on to the hillock R (100m).* ✪★

(h) *Take the path R up the hillock, along the flat top and ahead down to the cross track (350m). Turn R to the sunken bunker (100m). Disregard R turns and stay ahead to the next track (300m).*

(i) *Go L up to the track junction (200m) then down R (300m). At the branch track, fork L and go on round two L bends, down into a dip and up to the fence (550m).* ➜(7)

(5) Go along the curving track over a little rise towards Vines Farm (200m). Just round the R curve, diverge on the path L soon passing between a house and the farm (100m). Keep on outside the fields. A lesser path under the trees avoids winter mud on the track. Eventually the track runs beside the fence of Stoney Castle Ranges to the road (900m).

(6) Turn L and follow the fence of the ranges to the next exit track. If red flags are flying stay outside the fence; if not, use the boundary track inside (1100m). ★

(7) Go out to the road junction and into the trees opposite (50m). Drop straight down into the hollow to a junction of numerous tracks and paths (100m). Either follow the track down the valley R or climb to the next ridge and follow that down R to pass under the railway bridge (Woking- Farnham line) (350m). ✪

(8) Turn R down the track (150m) and keep on ahead at the road (100m). Don't pass under the next railway bridge but turn L near the pillbox along the tarmac track to Curzon Bridges. Cross the bridge over the main line of the London-Southampton railway (200m).

(9) Drop to the towpath R. Follow the Basingstoke Canal passing below Pirbright Camp L.

Pirbright Camp was the depot of the Guards regiments (Scots, Welsh, Irish, Grenadier, Coldstream), infantry units whose duties include guarding the Royal Household. The 3000 acres of wasteland was bought by the Brigade of Guards in the 1870s. Since army reorganisation it has become barracks for training recruits to all regiments.

Just before Lock 15 at the road see the pillars and banks of the former Bisley Railway (2500m). ✿

(10) Join the road at the next canal bridge and go R under the railway. At the road junction, take the footpath R in the angle of the roads through the wood, across a road and on past fields to Pirbright Church (1100m).

(11) Before the road turn L into the churchyard. Go past the church to the other end (the tall lump of granite is Stanley's grave). Join the road and turn L to the village green (500m). ✦

18 Mattingley to Rotherwick

About 8½km/5½ miles with a version 1km/¾ mile shorter, through fields and woods; gentle inclines; lots of stiles, muddy in winter; half shady.
OS maps 1:25000 144 Basingstoke, 1:50000 186 Aldershot or 175 Reading.

Start at Mattingley Church, SU 736 580. For the shorter version start from Rotherwick, parking at the roadside near the church, SU 712 562.

Linking walks 19❇ 21☆ ㉖★ ㉗✷ ㉘❖ ㉙✺

The Coach & Horses ☎ 01256 762542 ***The Falcon*** ☎ 01256 762586
Leather Bottle ☎ 0118 9326371

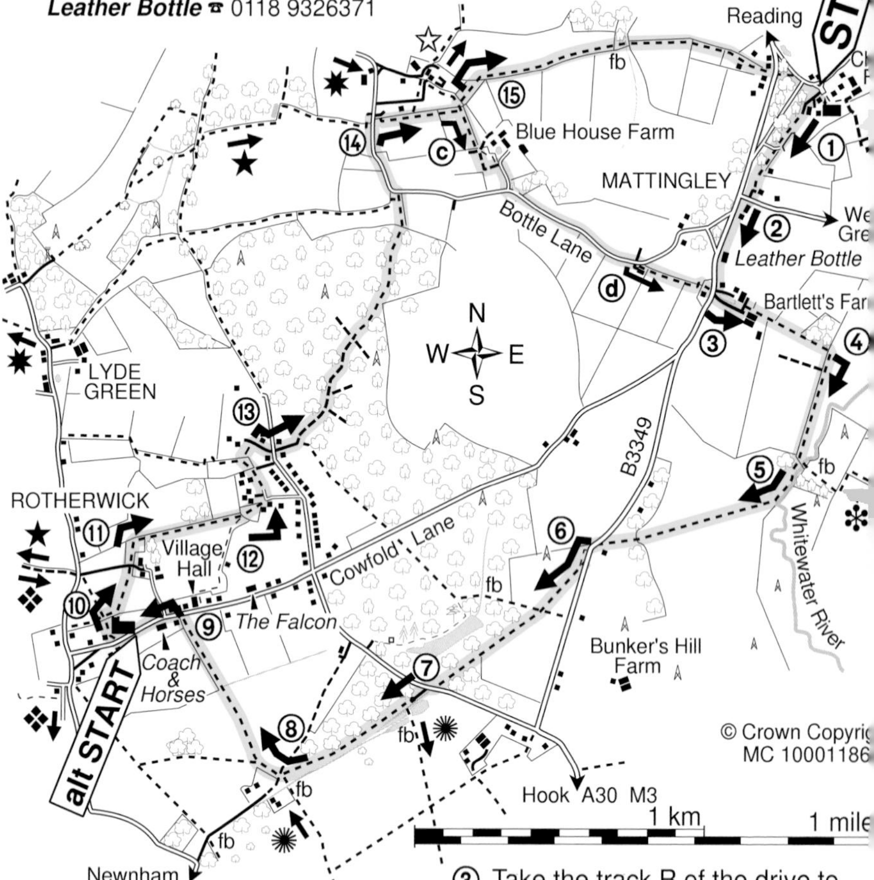

START
Reading
fb
Blue House Farm
MATTINGLEY
Bottle Lane
Leather Bottle
Bartlett's Far
N
W
E
S
LYDE GREEN
ROTHERWICK
B3349
Cowfold Lane
Village Hall
The Falcon
Coach & Horses
alt START
Whitewater River
Bunker's Hill Farm
© Crown Copyri
MC 10001186
Hook A30 M3
Newnham
1 km
1 mile

❇① See Mattingley Church then, outside the churchyard, go L along the house drive and ahead on the path under trees, across another house drive, to the road (450m).

② Over the grass go on along the main road past the ***Leather Bottle*** (200m) to Bartlett's Farm L (120m).

③ Take the track R of the drive to Bartlett's Farm (120m). After the garden and before the barns, turn L on the track (10m) and R down the path between the fields (300m).

④ In the bottom field turn R along the hedge to the end (350m). Just round the corner disregard the footbridge over the Whitewater River.

⑤ Go through the trees, R of the river, into the next field (100m). Continue near the river until it bends L (100m) then turn R up the field. Aim for the 2nd pylon R of the hilltop farm to an indent in the top edge (400m) and go on through the belt of trees to the nasty road crossing (150m).

⑥ On the verge opposite go L round the bend (sometimes there is a path in the field) (100m) then follow the right-of-way diverging R over the field to the corner of the wood, midway along the edge of the field (200m). Stay ahead in the next field at the edge of the wood to the corner (250m) then through the wood to the road (300m).

⑦ Slightly R (15m) take the track opposite. After the anglers' car park keep on beside the trees to the track near houses (550m). ✳

⑧ Cross the track into the field. Follow the garden hedge L to the end (100m) then bear R over the field to the hedge-end (250m) and carry on ahead to the road in Rotherwick (250m).

⑨ Turn L to the **Coach & Horses** (50m) and church (200m). ★❖✳

⑩ Go through Rotherwick churchyard to the field behind (80m). Turn R along the bottom hedge to the end of the churchyard (50m) then up L over the field to the corner of the garden (120m). Continue outside the garden, across the farm track and through the next small field to the hedge (100m).

⑪ Turn R at the hedge and follow it down to the bottom of the next large field. Go out through the small field to the road (450m).

⑫ Turn L to the parking area of Wedmans Place and carry on along the footpath over a drive to the field (100m). Cross the end of the field diagonally (50m).

⑬ Exit along the narrow path over the footbridge and beside the garden (50m) then R on the drive (80m). Cross the road and go on along the track into the wood (100m). Stay ahead on track and path to the far edge of the wood (850m). Cross the end of the field to the road (100m). Go L on the road, round the bend and up to the first house drive R (250m). ☆

⑭ Just into the drive enter the field R. Follow the L edge of the paddocks to the end hedge (300m).

ⓒ *Shorter version: Go R round the corner and along the L edge to Blue House Farm (150m). Skirt round outside the garden to the tarmac drive and exit R (200m). Go L up Bottle Lane (500m).*

ⓓ *When the lane curves L enter the field R but continue in the same direction beside the L hedge (250m). Near the house, cross into the side field L and go out to the main road in Mattingley (50m). (The Leather Bottle is L 100m.) Cross and continue ahead.* ➔③

⑮ Cross into the field L. Along the hedge (20m) turn R into the small side field and exit at the opposite end (80m). Follow the edge R to the end (500m) and cross the little wooded valley (50m). Carry on at the L edge of more fields then between houses (600m). Cross the road and follow the path through the trees. Stay ahead on the road round L to the church (250m).

19 Mattingley and West Green

About 7½km/4¾ miles with a short cut of 2km/1¼ miles; farmland, mainly pasture; muddy in winter, not much shade in summer; lots of stiles.
OS maps 1:25000 144 Basingstoke, 1:50000 186 Aldershot or 175 Reading.

Start from Mattingley Church, SU 736 580, or from the road junction near the *Leather Bottle* (park on the green), SU 733 577, or at West Green (park under the trees beside the road opposite the house), SU 746 563.

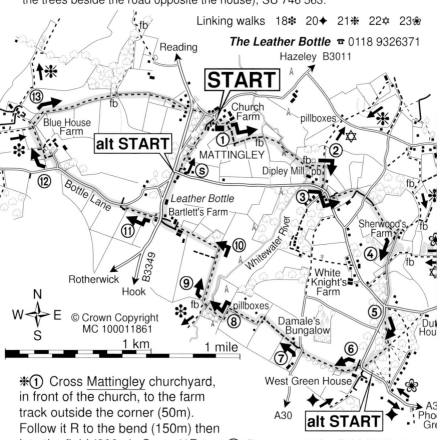

Linking walks 18❋ 20✦ 21❋ 22✿ 23❀

The Leather Bottle ☎ 0118 9326371

❋① Cross Mattingley churchyard, in front of the church, to the farm track outside the corner (50m). Follow it R to the bend (150m) then L to the field (200m). Cross ½R to the bank of the River Whitewater. Stay beside it through the next field to the footbridge L near the buildings of Dipley Mill (350m).
② Cross the river. Go round the pillbox and straight over the field to the hedge (100m) ✿ then R to the road (150m). Turn R along the road to the hump-backed bridge (100m) to see Dipley Mill R.

③ Return past the field (100m) and continue up the road (80m). From the bend turn L into the track and enter the R field. Follow the L edges (150m) and join the track out to the road (80m). Go on along the track opposite. Keep straight on over the field and out to the houses at Sherwood Farm (300m). ❀
④ Go R along the tarmac drive to the road junction (500m).

⑤ Follow the road opposite to the bend (50m) then bear L between the trees to the cross path on the causeway (200m) ✦ and R back to the road near the pond (250m).

⑥ Cross the road at the bend into the field R. Follow the L edge past West Green House, then the line of trees, to the road (400m).

⑦ On the other side, slightly R, continue on the cart track past Damale's Bungalow (350m). At the end enter the field ahead (with pillboxes) and skirt around the L edge to the bottom (300m).

⑧ Turn L along the bottom of the next field (80m). Before the corner cross the ditch R. Diverge from the L edge, cross the Whitewater River and go on to the hedge (200m). ✲

⑨ Turn R along the hedge (300m). Pass the farm track L but turn L on the footpath soon after it (60m).

⑩ At the farm buildings (300m) don't continue into the farmhouse garden but join the farm track L (10m) and go out to the road, R (100m). (The **Leather Bottle** is 100m along the road R.)

Ⓢ *Cut of 2km/1¼ mile: Walk past the pub to the side road R (200m). Just into the side road (30m) turn off on the 1st drive L and continue on the path to the church (450m).*

⑪ Cross the little field opposite. Pass L of the shed and ahead, L of the hedge, through fields (250m) then along Bottle Lane (500m).

⑫ Start along the tarmac drive of Blue House Farm R (100m) but turn off L at the garden wall and skirt L of the homestead (100m). In the first field after it, follow the R fence to the corner (120m). ✲

⑬ Don't turn L on the right of way along the hedge. Go on briefly in the field ahead (30m) then turn R into the small side field and exit at the opposite edge (80m). Turn R and follow the hedge to the end of the field (500m). Cross the small wooded valley (50m) and carry on ahead through more fields, now at L edges, then between gardens to the main road (600m). Cross and follow the footpath through the trees to the smaller road near the church (250m).

West Green House was presented to the National Trust in 1957 by Sir Victor Sassoon.The house is leased but the gardens are open to the public in the summer, 11am - 4pm, Weds, Sat & Sun. The house was bombed in 1990, supposedly by the IRA, but the resident, Alisdair McAlpine, an ex-Chairman of the Conservative Party, had left a week earlier. It was probably a 17th century farm house but was rebuilt for "Hangman" Hawley in the 1740s.

General Henry Hawley, 1679-1759, may have been an illegitimate son of George I. He became a professional soldier and saw action in Ireland and Flanders as a cavalry officer. His renown came from the Scottish rebellion of Bonny Prince Charlie in 1745. His own troopers called him "Hangman" for leaving rebels on gibbets in Edinburgh for weeks after execution. He lost the Battle of Falkirk because he was decoyed to a dinner party at the time of the rebels' attack. At Culloden, the final battle, he was cavalry commander under the Duke of Cumberland and exhorted his men to kill the wounded. He hung deserters and followed the rebel clans to destroy their homes and livestock so they would not rebel again. *Culloden* John Prebble Secker & Warburg 1961 367pp

20 **West Green and Hook Mill**

About 6½km/4 miles with an extension of 1km/¾ mile; undulating farmland.
Numerous stiles. Boggy near the river in winter. Not much shade.
OS maps 1:25000 144 Basingstoke, 1:50000 186 Aldershot.

Linking walks 19✦ 22✿ 23✪ 34✿ ㉙☆

Start near West Green House, SU 746 563, (park under the trees beside the
road outside) or in the side road opposite the *Crooked Billet*, SU 736 547.

The Crooked Billet ☎ 01256 762118

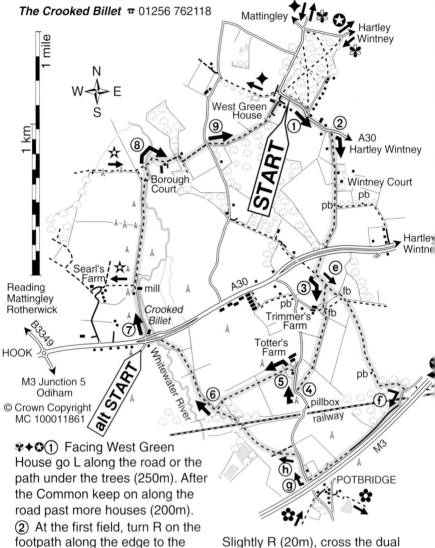

✿✦✪① Facing West Green
House go L along the road or the
path under the trees (250m). After
the Common keep on along the
road past more houses (200m).
② At the first field, turn R on the
footpath along the edge to the
trees (250m). Carry on at the L
edge of the fields and out past the
gas enclosure to the road (550m).

Slightly R (20m), cross the dual
carriageway into the field opposite.
Follow the path diagonally R over
to the path in the trees (150m).

(e) Extension of 1km/¾ mile: Turn L. Stay on the path between the fields past a <u>pillbox</u> *R near the top of the fields (800m) then round L through trees to the end near the motorway cutting (300m).*

(f) Turn R along the disused road (100m). Cross the <u>railway</u> *bridge (London-Southampton) and stay beside the motorway fence all the way down to the road (800m).* ❀

(g) Walk up the road R (200m).

(h) Just before the end of the field L take the path across the corner (100m), over the track and up in the same line to the trees in the corner of the next field (300m). Go under the railway (50m) and keep on to the hedge corner R (150m). ➜⑥

③ Turn L but look out for a bridge R (100m) to the fields. Aim for the hedge corner 100m L of the barns but cross the footbridge L before it (150m). Cross the R corner of the next field (50m) and walk up the fields, R of the fence, over the hilltop. In the last field aim 50m R of the pylon (550m).

④ Join the road and follow it R to Totter's Farm (200m).

⑤ Turn L through the gateway and stay ahead over fences and under power cables (300m). Carry on along the middle of the large field. If the path is obscure aim for the R end of the trees just over the brow (150m) and drop to the hedge corner (70m). Go down the L side of the hedge to the bottom (80m) and round the external corner R.

⑥ Follow the hedge, along the edge of the <u>Whitewater</u> valley (300m). In the next field diverge L from the hedge making for the apparent middle of the end fence (150m), then more L, towards the pub and the road bridge (200m).

⑦ Cross the dual carriageway to the **Crooked Billet** (100m). ★ Walk along the tarmac drive L of the pub (350m). After Mill Cottage L take the narrow path beside the drive. Don't turn L up into the side field (unless you want to look over the hedge which hides Hook Mill in summer) but keep on to the field beyond (100m). Go straight on along the L hedge until it meets the river (500m) then follow the river bank (200m). Don't cross the cart bridge R or diverge on the path along the hedge L. Stay on the river bank round the bends and on to the river footbridge (200m).

⑧ Cross the Whitewater River and bear L over the field (50m) to cross a little bridge then turn R and make your way across paddocks up to the track from the house, <u>Borough Court</u> (150m) and up the slope. Follow the track round R & L bends and up to the road (300m).

⑨ Cross the road and carry on along the path which skirts R of the field then the garden to the West Green car park (600m). Walk out to the road.

Hook Mill on the Whitewater River is probably on the site of one of the eight mills recorded in the Domesday Book for the manor of Odiham. Documents indicate there was a mill here in 1561 but the present building is 17th century. At that time it was a paper mill, the water power being used to pulp cotton and linen rags in alkali. By 1830 the use of water mills for paper making had largely ceased and it was a flour mill until the 1900s. It was converted to a house about 1920.

Hook's Watermill Glynis Wilsdon 1986 12pp

21 Mattingley, Hound Green and Hazeley Heath

About 8½km/5½ miles with a short cut of 1km/¾ mile; undulating fields and heath; lots of stiles; half shady; usually good in winter. The Hazeley Heath paths are confusing. OS maps 1:25000 144 Basingstoke, 1:50000 186 or 175.

Start at Mattingley Church, SU 736 580, or at the roadside opposite the *Shoulder of Mutton*, SU 742 590, just off the B3011.

Linking walks 18☆ 19✳ 22✿ 25★ ㉗✿

Shoulder of Mutton 0118 932 6272
The Leather Bottle 0118 932 6371

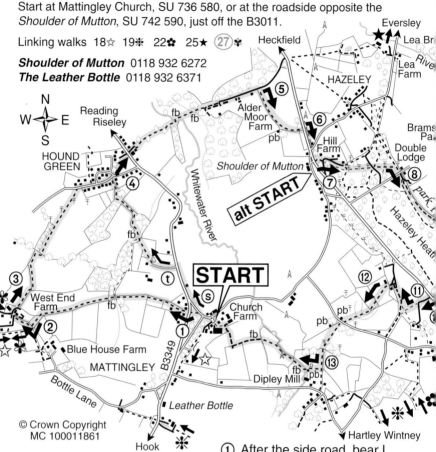

© Crown Copyright
MC 100011861

☆ From Mattingley Church walk out to the road then L (100m).

Ⓢ *Short cut of 1km/¾ mile: Keep on round R to the main road (100m) then R beside it (250m).*

ⓣ *Turn L up the Lynchmere Farm drive (200m). Almost at the house take the path R, between garden and tennis court, down to the brook in the trees (200m) and up between fields and gardens to Hound Green (450m). Turn R.* ➔④

① After the side road, bear L through the corner of the wood (50m). Stay ahead over the main road and between the houses then along the R edge of the fields to the little wooded valley (500m). Continue beside the L hedge in the next field (550m).

② Watch out for a stile L at the curve before West End Farm and cross the little field to the next one (80m). Go R along the edge skirting the buildings and garden (150m).

③ Cross the drive and the track from the road and go on L of the converted barn to the first field L (70m). Follow the R edge to the corner (150m). In the next field skirt round the L edge and exit near the end corner of the wood (250m). Follow the edge of the wood along the next field (200m). When it ends keep on in the same direction to the hedge corner in front of the house (300m). Join the road and continue ahead (250m).

④ At the green cross the grass obliquely to the far L corner (200m). Go over the main road and down the drive next to the garage (50m). Before the last house turn R on the path skirting the garden. Continue between the fields (300m). and over the Whitewater River. Go on across the valley. After the stream ascend through the trees. Stay ahead on the track past the farm buildings (550m). ★

AZELEY HW
OTTOM

⑤ Turn R up the edge of the next field just after the house (50m). Stay beside the fence curving L to the road (550m).

⑥ Cross to the verge opposite and follow the road down R (300m).

⑦ Opposite the side road outlet near the ***Shoulder of Mutton***, climb the stepped path up the bank of the main road (50m). At the track go L round the bend and down the R drive (200m). Just after the house turn R to the power lines (30m) then bear L down the heath path with the power lines (200m). Cross the gravel track and keep on, down to the heath boundary at the Bramshill park pale (200m).

⑧ Turn R to the double lodge and cross the drive (60m). Stay ahead under the trees outside the park pale with views of Bramshill House far L (700m). Cross the grass past the pond to the gravel track at the next house (100m). ✿

⑨ Almost immediately (20m) turn R on the path over Hazeley Heath forking L to the cross path (100m). Stay ahead between low hills along the winding path to the horse track near the (audible) road (200m).

⑩ Turn R on the horse track then almost immediately (40m) L on a narrow curving footpath to the road opposite the drive of Hazeley Court (100m). Go along the drive (100m). When it bends L, keep on ahead down the footpath (100m). ❋

⑪ Halfway down turn R through the wood on the level, converging on the field L. Continue up the bridleway to the cottage L (200m).

⑫ Turn L, past the cottage into the field. Cross to the stile above the bottom L corner and the next field to the L corner. In the 3rd field walk out on the shoulder of the hill then slightly R down to the road, near the pillbox in the hedge (500m). Slightly R enter the field opposite. Diverge from the R edge to the stile and ditch (200m). In the next field follow the L hedge (100m).

⑬ Before the end, take the side path R across the field and over the river (100m). Turn R along the bank through the next field (250m). When the fence bends R, bear L across the field to the gate (100m). Go on along the farm track (200m) and round the R bend (150m). At the farmyard turn L through the churchyard to the car park (100m).

22 Hartford Bridge and Hazeley Bottom

About 6½km/4 miles with an extension of 700m/½ mile to Dipley Mill. Mainly fields but with stretches of heath and oak wood; undulating; lots of stiles; boggy in wet seasons. OS maps 1:25000 144 Basingstoke, 1:50000 186 or 175.

No large parking space. Find a parking spot on the verge in Hares Lane near Hartley Wintney, SU 770 578, or on the verge at Hazeley Bottom, SU 748 579.

Linking 19✿ 20❀ 21✿ 23✹ 27❖

White Lion Tea Rooms ☎ 01252 844000

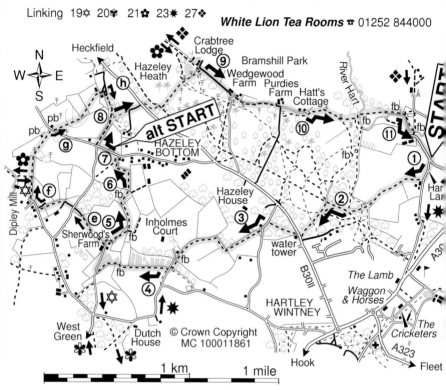

① Follow Hare's Lane from the bend (150m). ✹ Just before Hares Farm take the path up R between fields into trees to the converging major path on the flat top (600).
② Go R on this level path to the concrete track R (180m) and turn L, opposite it, along the path to the road (300m). Cross slightly R (30m) and take the path through the wood to the next road (200m).
③ Turn L along the road to the house (60m) then bear R along the wall to the field (60m). Go down the R edge (<u>Hazeley House</u> R) (250m). In the 2nd field turn R along the hedge into the 3rd field (30m) and go round the R edge to the bottom R corner (400m). Continue ahead either in the next field or on the drive from Inholmes Court (80m). ✹
④ Turn R into the 1st field on the other side of the drive. Follow the R edge to the end (350m) then cross the footbridge and skirt L of the ponds to the drive (150m). ✿ Turn R along the drive and past Sherwood's Farm (200m).

44

ⓔ *Extension of 700m/½ mile to Dipley Mill: At the end of the farmhouse turn L into the field. Go straight over to the trees and out to the road (300m). Continue on the track opposite (70m). Turn L with it into the field then follow the R hedge to the next road (150m).*

ⓕ *Walk down the road R. Just after the side road L is a footpath R (80m). For a view of Dipley Mill stay on the road to the humped bridge over the Whitewater River (150m) then return to the footpath. Follow the R edge of the field. Disregard a path L crossing the field (150m) ✿ and go on to the end (150m). Cross the stream and go straight up the next field past a pillbox to the top corner and out to the road (200m).*

ⓖ *Slightly R, enter the opposite field and, make for the highest point ½R then for the bend in the hedge (150m). Go through to the next field and on in the same direction up the next to exit between barn and house (300m).*

ⓗ *On the heath, up from the house (20m), take the horse track R. Follow it down outside the field to a slight bend (100m) then diverge up the flank of the slope to the cross path (sometimes hidden by fallen leaves) (50m).* ➔⑧

⑤ In the field after the 2nd house go down the R edge into the next field (30m) then aim L for the gate on the other side at the far end (100m). Over the bridge, follow the hedge and stream L (200m).

⑥ Watch out for a footbridge in the middle of the field and cross it to the hedge (100m). Disregard the farm track to the barns above. Go up L of the hedge towards the nearest houses (120m) then turn L, and skirt round the gardens to the road in Hazeley Bottom (150m).

⑦ Walk along the road L (150m). Opposite the Dipley road take the path R (200m). Where it steepens and curves L a little, look for the narrow path up R.

⑧ Follow the path up through the trees away from the fields to the bend in the Hazeley Court drive (100m). Go on to the road (100m). Cross to the heath and follow the path. It bends R parallel with the road briefly then L to a horse track (100m). Go R briefly (30m) then take the path L across Hazeley Heath between the slopes. Keep on, disregarding side paths, to the drive at Crabtree Lodge (400m). ❖

⑨ Turn R along the drive under the trees beside the park pale of Bramshill to Wedgewood Farm (distant views of Bramshill back L) (250m). When it bends R, stay ahead on the bridleway to Purdies Farm (350m) then the drive down to Hatt's Cottage (150m).

⑩ At the end of the tarmac take the path into the trees (20m) and zigzag L,R,L,R (60m). Disregard side paths R, and keep to the main path over the boardwalk and the heath into the trees (300m). Turn L to the River Hart footbridge (30m). Cross and follow the path through the middle of the field, ignoring a river bridge R (300m).

⑪ After the stream, in the next field bear R near the river bank to the next river footbridge (150m) and cross to the road. Walk along the road L to Hares Lane (200m).

23 Hartley Wintney, Winchfield and West Green

About 10km/ 6¼ miles, mainly over fields, gently undulating. OS maps 1:25000 144 Basingstoke, 1:50000 186 Aldershot. Lots of stiles.

Start at the pond at the north end of Hartley Wintney village green, SU 770 569 - roadside parking. Alternatively start at West Green, parking under the trees near the bend in the road, SU 746 563. Winchfield Station is on the route.

The Cricketers ☎ 01252 842166   Linking walks   19✿   20✪   22✳
The Winchfield Inn ☎ 01252 842129
The Phoenix ☎ 01252 842484

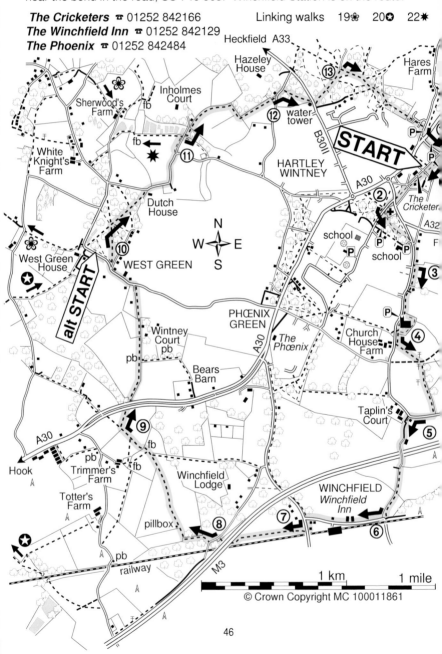

① From the pond, go along the green between the pavilion and the *Cricketers* (300m). Carry on in the same direction over the green and the roads to the church (300m).

② Skirt the churchyard then go ½L up through the trees to the top corner of the green (250m) and on along the road at the edge of Hartley Wintney (150m).

③ Enter the first field L and follow the path along the edge above the road to the old churchyard (300m). Skirt round the L edge to see the grave of Viscount Alanbrooke and the view (200m) then continue on the path above the road down to Church House Farm (80m).

④ Go L diagonally down the field to the bottom (200m). Cross the track and go up the L edge of the field to the next road (450m).

⑤ Walk along the road R to the bend (200m). Immediately after the house take the footpath L then follow the farm track down over the motorway to fields (400m). Stay ahead on the path between fields (150m) then along the R edge of the field to the road (200m).

⑥ Walk up the road R past the *Winchfield Inn* (250m) and Winchfield Station to the T-junction at the main road (400m).

⑦ Go L briefly (70m) then take the footpath R next to the railway fence and cutting (London-Southampton line)(450m). Follow the steps down under the M3 and up the other side (150m). ❂

⑧ Go L briefly on the hard track (50m) then take the track R (60m). Don't enter the field but bear L through the trees (100m) then turn R on the path between fields soon passing a pillbox L (100m). Keep on down. Watch out for side paths L & R (500m) then one L (100m) then the one you want, R (100m).

⑨ Take the R path over the corner of the field (150m). Cross the dual carriageway slightly R and continue on the footpath R of the gas regulator site and up the R edge of the field. Stay ahead to the next road (900m) then go L to the side road at the corner of the tree-covered West Green (200m). ❀

⑩ Turn R into the trees on the downhill path (250m). At the wide causeway path go R, joining the road at Dutch House (350m). Carry on (R) along the road, round the L bend to the R bend (400m) then take the footpath L of the drive of Inholmes Court to the end of the field (100m). ✳

⑪ If boggy continue on the drive (60m) then turn R into the large field. If not, cross R into the field opposite and go L along the hedge (60m). In the large field go up the L edge (300m), R along the top to the stile (120m) then L up the edge of the next field (250m). Exit past the house (50m) and go L on the road. Watch out for a path R (60m).

⑫ Cut through the wood to the main road (200m). Cross to the footpath, slightly R (30m), and stay ahead on it through heath to the start of the concrete track (300m).

⑬ Turn R on the main path (300m). At the next 5-way path junction stay on the main path slightly L and descend through the wood then between houses (500m).

⑭ Go R on the lane to the main road (80m). Follow the side road opposite to the pond (200m).

24 The Blackwater, Farley Hill and New Mill

About 9½km/6 miles with an extension via Riseley Mill of 1¼km/¾ mile and a short cut of 1½km/1 mile. Pine plantations, heath, farmland and quiet country lanes. Lots of stiles. OS maps 1:25000 159 Reading, 1:50000 175 Reading.

Start from the car park beside the Eversley-Heckfield road at Bramshill Common Wood, SU 760 613, or from Farley Hill (kerbside parking), SU 756 642.

Linking walks
1 ✿   25 ★   27 ✤

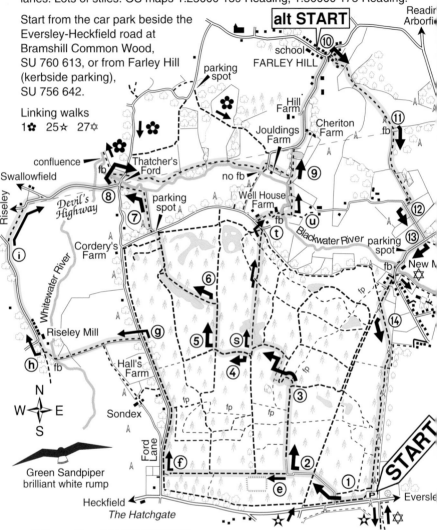

© Crown Copyright MC 100011861

★① From the Bramshill Common Wood car park, go along the track near the road (300m) and turn R on the concrete forest track. Follow it round L bends to a R bend (500m).

ⓔ Extension 1km/¾ mile: Stay on the track ahead to the road (800m).

ⓕ Go R on the forest track beside the road, past a thatched cottage L (450m), another house (100m) and Hall's Farm in the trees (250m).

ⓖ After Hall's Farm (150m), watch out for the bridleway L between the fields and follow it to the end, after the Whitewater River (700m).

ⓗ *Turn R on the track to the road near* <u>Riseley Mill</u> *(80m). Continue ahead on the winding road (750m).*

ⓘ *At the 2nd L curve diverge R on the path between fields (300m) then go R along the next road, over the Whitewater River (600m) to the road bend and ford (150m).* ➤⑧

② Turn R and continue ahead at the end of the concrete to the bend at the pond (600m).

③ Take the side track L round the pond (150m). Just round the U-bend, exit L, over the ditch, to the next path (30m). Turn R to the next track (200m). Turn L to the bend just after the next pond (200m).

ⓢ *Short cut of 1½km/1 mile: Take the horse track R (N) near the pond (450m). Slightly L at the cross path (20m), continue in the same direction to the lane (300m).*

ⓣ *Go along the lane L (80m) and take the footpath R of the tarmac drive of Well House Farm. The path zigzags around the farm and over the* Blackwater *River (250m).*

ⓤ *Soon after the river (50m) enter the field L. Go straight across to the corner (120m) and along the L edge of the next field into the thin end of the 3rd (100m). Don't pass into the next field.* ➤⑨

④ Go round the L bend (40m) and turn R (W) along the next track to the cross track (300m).

⑤ Walk down the track R (300m).

⑥ Turn L along the curving side track (450m). After the long pond stay ahead to the lane (300m).

⑦ Along the lane L (40m) take the footpath R through the trees and along the R edge of the field to the end (300m) then L along the river to the lane (150m). Turn R.

⑧ Facing the ford, take the path L through the field and cross the <u>Blackwater</u> footbridge (70m). ✿ Turn R and cross the lane (100m).

> The **Devil's Highway** (the London to Silchester Roman road) crossed the Blackwater at Thatcher's Ford. The confluence with the Whitewater is at the end of the next field, downstream.

Stay ahead from field to field, along the bottom edge near the river, to the next lane at Jouldings Farm (1000m). Go on through the next field (150m) but turn L in the next.

⑨ Go up the L edge, past the pond, to the lane (200m). Walk up the lane R to the village street in Farley Hill (650m).

⑩ Turn R (30m) and take the narrow path R between gardens. Turn R across the end of the garden then go L down to the field (150m). Cross slightly R to the corner of the wood (100m) and go down the edge of the field next to it (50m). In the next field don't follow the edge but go down the middle of the narrow part then aim for the nearest pylon and pass L of it to the corner of the wood (550m).

⑪ Cross the footbridge and follow the R edge of the wood (150m). Stay at the R edge along the fields until past the house (500m).

⑫ Join the lane (50m) and follow it L to the T-junction (300m).

⑬ Turn R on the lane to <u>New Mill</u> and cross the Blackwater <u>River</u> (300m). ✿ After the ford (50m) bear R on the straight track, past houses and fields to the oblique heath cross track (200m).

⑭ Bear L and stay on the track or the path near the L boundary all the way to the car park (1400m).

25 Around Bramshill Park Pale

About 10km/6¼ miles with a 1km/¾ mile extension; deciduous wood and pine plantations. Dry in winter. OS maps 1:25000 144 + 159, 1:50000 186 Aldershot.

Start from a parking spot in Hare's Lane near Hartley Wintney, SU 770 578, or at the roadside in Plough Lane, SU 754 610, near the Eversley-Heckfield road.

Linking walks 21★ 22✤ 24☆ 26☆ 27✳ 29✳

The Shoulder of Mutton ☎ 0118 932 6272 **The Hatchgate** ☎ 0118 932 6666
White Lion Tea Rooms ☎ 01252 844000

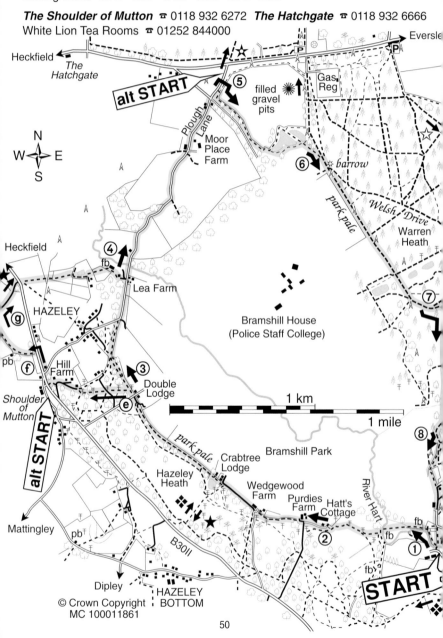

❖① From Hares Lane junction go along the lane away from the main road (200m). At the bend, cross the River Hart footbridge R then go through the paddocks beside the river (150m) and L over a stream. Carry on and cross the next river footbridge (200m). Turn L over the ditch & R out of the trees (50m). Follow the path at the bottom of the slope, ignoring side paths L, and along the boardwalk. Zigzag into the trees to Hatt's Cottage (300m).

② Go up the tarmac drive to the farm (200m). Stay ahead beside the park pale of Bramshill to the next farm (350m), then Crabtree Lodge (300m). ★ Go on past the house, still beside the park pale, to the Double Lodge (850m).

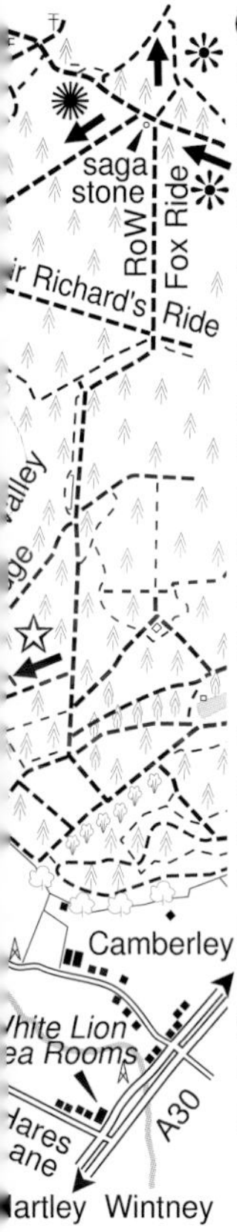

ⓔ *Extra 1km/¾ mile via the* **Shoulder of Mutton**: *Just after the drive (60m) bear L up the path with the power cables (200m), over a track to the top (200m) then R to the house (30m). Go up the drive to the U-bend on top (200m). Just after Hill Farm, take the footpath R down to the road (50m) and the pub.*

ⓕ *Go R along the R verge of the main road (300m). Before the top of the rise take the footpath L along the fence curving R down the large field (550m).*

ⓖ *Go R on the drive to the road (300m) and up the field opposite aiming 100m L of the nearest*

pylon (200m). Follow stiles & gates over to the clump of trees L of the house (200m). Beyond the pond take the path slightly L down into the trees to a long building (100m). Go R beside it and on to the road at Lea Farm (100m). Turn L. ➜④

③ Stay at the Bramshill boundary (300m), round the end R and down (250m), continuing on the road to Lea Farm (700m).

④ Stay on the road which crosses the River Hart (80m) then winds, eventually up to Moor Place Farm (900m) and down past the next road junction (400m). ✫

⑤ After the junction (60m) turn R on the path R into Bramshill Forest (20m). Go R along the fence (50m), L round the corner and on (500m). When fence and path bend L of the the flooded gravel pit, stay ahead R of the water (250m). Bear R on the path from between the pits to the forest track at the power lines and Bronze Age barrow (200m). ✳✳★

⑥ Follow the wide track up R with the cables (1100m).

⑦ Stay on the track when it curves L away from the power lines (200m) and take the next side track R which eventually descends into a valley (700m). Carry on up the flank of the next ridge to the L bend round the end near the top (300m).

⑧ Turn R down the steep boundary track (70m) and R down the cross path to the corner of a field (100m). Stay ahead outside the field (100m), along the track (200m), on tarmac to the L bend (100m) then along the track to the River Hart ford and footbridge (120m). The Hares Lane starting point is L along the road (150m).

(map labels) saga stone · RoW · Fox Ride · Richard's Ride · Camberley · White Lion · ea Rooms · Hares ane · A30 · artley Wintney

26 Bramshill Forest

About 9½km/6 miles with a cut of 1½km/1 mile and extension of 1km/¾ mile; an intricate route to see the best parts of the forest plantations on Warren Heath. Most of the tracks are not public footpaths but the Forestry Commission has an open access policy. Tracks are closed from time to time for forestry operations. OS maps 1:25000 144+159, 1:50000 175 or 186.

Start from the layby, SU 766 614, beside the Heckfield road opposite the side road, a mile from the A327 crossroads.

Linking walks 25☆ 27✪ 29✦ 28✧

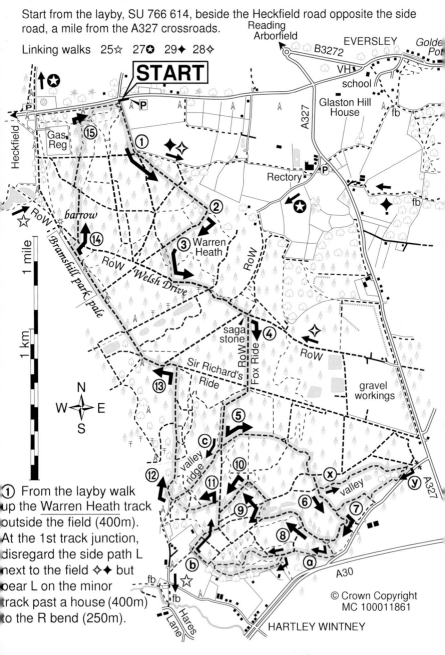

① From the layby walk up the Warren Heath track outside the field (400m). At the 1st track junction, disregard the side path L next to the field ✧✦ but bear L on the minor track past a house (400m) to the R bend (250m).

© Crown Copyright
MC 100011861

② Keep on round the bend and up beside the valley to the side track R on the flat top (400m).

③ Take the path L, opposite the track, round to the next hard track, Welsh Drive (350m) and follow it L to the saga stone R (600m).

④ Bear R on the broad track after the stone, Fox Ride (500m). Cross another track (Sir Richard's Ride) and go on round a R bend then a L bend (200m) and up to the oblique track junction on top (300m).

ⓒ *Short cut of 1½km/1 mile: Bear R on the side track along the ridge and descend to the R bend on the end (500m).* ➔⑫

⑤ Turn back L. Disregard all side tracks and eventually curve round a little valley and up to a T-junction (800m). Slightly L (30m) go down the track opposite (100m).

ⓧ *Extension of 1km/¾ mile: Go L on the valleyside track. Eventually this curves R across the valley and L up to a track junction (650m).*

ⓨ *Turn down R towards the road then follow the winding horse track back near the road to a T-junction (350m). Turn R along the valley side to the major track (300m). Go L up to the curve R (100m).* ➔⑦

⑥ Stay on the track into the valley and up to the R bend (300m).

⑦ Go round the U-curve R and down the winding track (250m).

ⓐ *Alternative of the same length: Turn L up the first side track (100m). Near the road turn R. Disregard the descending track R (250m) and continue to the side path L (80m). Either take the side path which skirts round the S brow of the ridge (500m) or go on to the track bend (100m) and ahead*

round the north brow of the ridge (400m). At the end of the ridge drop to the track (50m) and carry on ahead outside the field (200m).

ⓑ *Go round the corner of the forest and on to the next track junction (200m). Bear L to the steep side track R (100m). Soon after it (70m) turn L.* ➔⑪

⑧ Stay on the track down to the fork after the 2nd pond R (700m).

⑨ Just into the R track (20m), turn R on the little path. Jump the stream and go up past buildings to the next track (100m). Turn R to the track junction and L up the steep side track (200m).

⑩ Go round the L bend on top and down to the T-junction (300m). Turn R (70m) and take the next L.

⑪ Follow the horse track round the flank of the hill. Stay ahead curving R up to the track bend on the shoulder of the hill (300m). ☆

⑫ Go down round the R bend, disregarding side tracks from it. Cross the little brook (250m) and stay ahead up to the plateau and to the T-junction (600m). Turn L.

⑬ Follow the track round 2 curves R (200m) then straight (900m). ✪ 100m before the end of the field L watch out for the small path R halfway between the pylons.

⑭ Cut through to the next track, Welsh Drive (60m). Continue on the other side soon down beside a little valley R (350m). At the cross track turn L up the valleyside (50m) then R to the next cross track (200m). Stay ahead to the path before the power cables (250m).

⑮ Turn R (50m) then converge on the cables & road and follow the track to the parking place (250m).

27 Eversley, Warren Heath and New Mill

About 8km/5 miles or shorter by ¾km/½ mile, through fields and forestry plantations; half shady. OS maps: 1:2500 159 Reading, 1:50000 175 or 186.

Start from the green at Eversley Church, SU 780 609, or the roadside forest car park, SU 760 613 on the Eversley-Heckfield road under power lines.

Linking 6✳ 24✩ 25✴ 26✪ 28✽ 29❀ *The White Hart* ☎ 0118 973 2817

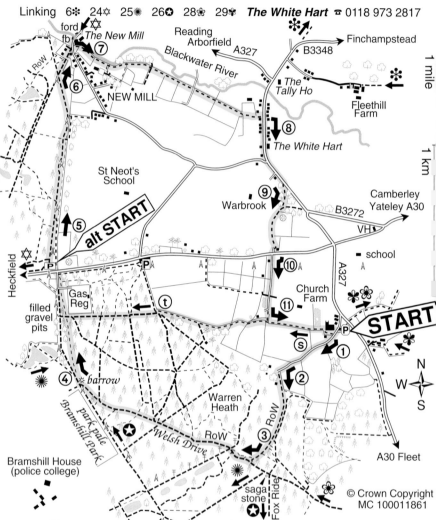

❀✿✽(S) *Short version: Go through Eversley churchyard, round the tower (100m) and out on the path under trees to the fields (50m) and along the L hedge (300m). Pass the footpath R after the first field and stay ahead between fields to* the corner of the wood (200m) then along the edge of the wood (600m). (t) *At the end of the fields R stay ahead on the track through the forest to the boundary track at the power cables (700m) then down R and over the road (300m).* ➔(5)

① Longer version: From Eversley Church walk along the lane past the church and rectory (500m).

② Inside the forest gateway turn L up the bridleway outside the field. Disregard branch paths L and go on to a T-junction (750m). ✳●❂

③ Turn R along the wide track, Welsh Drive through Warren Heath. Stay ahead to the T-junction at power lines and a barrow (1300m).

④ Go R briefly on the boundary track (40m) then diverge R on the footpath and stay ahead, down past the gas regulation station to the road (700m). Cross.

⑤ From the car park follow the track and power lines away from the road along the E boundary of Bramshill Common Wood (1000m) ✿ and round a slight bend L to the oblique cross track (400m)

⑥ Bear R on the hard track. Pass out through the boundary to the road at New Mill (250m) and L onto the footbridge at the Blackwater River ford to see the mill (50m). ✿

⑦ Return along the road from the ford (50m) and turn L into the first field. Follow the footpath at the L edge of the fields all the way to Eversley, joining the road beside Baker's Farmhouse (1400m). ✳

⑧ Walk R along the pavement past the *White Hart*, Warbrook Lane and the house drive (400m).

⑨ After the drive (70m), diverge R on the footpath. See the grand house, Warbrook R. Stay ahead on the track to the next road (500m).

⑩ Cross slightly R and go along the drive (400m). When it bends R to the last house, continue ahead on the short footpath (60m).

⑪ Turn into the field L and follow the hedge all the way to the end (300m) then go on through the trees and churchyard (150m).

The **gas regulation station** steps down the pressure from the 44 bar of the national pipelines to 26, 7 and 2 bar for local distribution - analogous with an electricity transformer. The gas is filtered of dust and rust picked up in the pipes and heated to offset the cooling caused by decompression.

Warbrook is a conference centre and hotel. The house and garden were constructed in 1724 by John James for himself. Born around 1672 he was apprenticed to the Crown carpenter. He was involved in the building of Greenwich Hospital and succeeded Wren as Surveyor of St Pauls in 1723.

The **sarsen** in Eversley Church, under the trapdoor, suggests a pre-Christian religious site. Bede records that Pope Gregory sent Augustine a message in 610 to plant his churches on temples. Sarsens are boulders from the Barton Beds left on the surface when the soft sands are eroded. Their occurrence on the chalkland of Wiltshire indicates it was formerly covered by the Tertiary Sands. Sarsen areas have no other building stone so they have all been put to use as standing stones, henges, boundary marks, foundations, etc.

The Forestry Commission has an open access policy for walkers but sections have to be closed temporarily for logging operations. Small paths suddenly become deep-rutted tracks which after a few years fade away. The Commission was set up in 1919, after World War I, for the strategic supply of timber. It provides policy, advice and grants and has research and commercial divisions, the latter being responsible for educational and recreational uses which includes the provision of footpaths and horse rides.

28 Eversley Church, Up Green & Castle Bottom

About 8 km/5 miles with a short cut of 1½km/1 mile, partly without paths.
Through farmland, heath, woods and Bramshill Forest. OS maps 1:25000
159 Reading + 144 Basingstoke, 1:50000 186 Aldershot or 175 Reading.

Start from the green at Eversley Church, SU 780 609.

Linking walks 25✿ 26✧ 27✿ 29✹ 30✿   *Golden Pot* ☎ 0118 973 2104

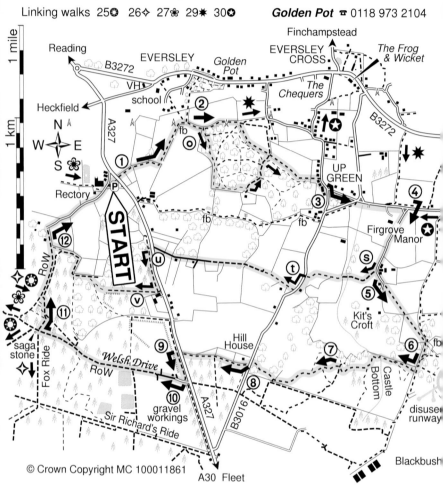

© Crown Copyright MC 100011861

① At <u>Eversley</u> Church, cross the main road from the middle of the green to the footpath through the fields (100m). Stay ahead beside L fences until you meet a hedge (300m) then go L along the hedge (300m) round the end R to the next field (40m) and on to the corner of the wood R (100m). ✹✿

② Either stay on the path around outside the edge of the wood to the houses and road (1000m) or
◉ at bluebell time cross, into the wood and follow paths near the R edge round to the house (600m) then, via the vehicle track, return (L) to the edge of the wood (300m) and follow it R to the road (500m).

56

③ Go R beside the road (70m) and fork L opposite the Martineau Cottages. Stay ahead (200m), over the crossroads, up to the layby opposite the gateway of Firgrove Manor (200m) and along the path L of the road (150m).

④ Take the next side road R to the L bend at Firgrove Farm (450m).

⑤ *Short cut of 1½km/1 mile: Take the track R down into the valley (200m) and continue on the path up to the next road (300m).*

30 ⓣ *Walk up the road L (100m) and take the path R outside the top of the field. Stay ahead to the next road, the path becoming a track then a farm drive (1000m).*

ⓤ *At the end cross the main road into the trees and make your way L below the road (350m).*

ⓥ *At the warehouses, turn away from the road, along the disused forestry track (350m). When the track ends, bear R through the trees down to the edge of the fields then follow the horse track outside the fields round several corners and ultimately down to the forest gateway and lane (650m).* ➜⑫

⑤ Go round the L bend (100m). When the road curves up R enter the field L and cut across the top corner to the ridge at the end of the wood (250m). Continue down the next field diagonally to the furthest corner (200m). Exit over the bridge and fork up R. The path soon follows a boundary mound & fence, and joins a track (200m).

⑥ Follow the track briefly (20m) then take the path R downhill near the fence to Castle Bottom (250m). At the bottom turn L over the brook and go up the valleyside (150m).

⑦ Fork R just before the top. Stay ahead on this undulating, winding track over the top and down into a little valley then up through the wood to the road (900m).

⑧ Cross to the path L of Hill House (30m) and carry on under the trees to the next road (450m).

⑨ Cross the road and join the horse track beside it. Go L to the gravel works gate (300m).

⑩ Walk along the gravel works road and continue on the broad forest track, Welsh Drive, to the saga stone L (1100m). ❍◇✿

⑪ Opposite the saga stone, turn R on the side track. Go round L&R bends and down to the lane (750m).

⑫ Walk along the lane to the church (500m).

Charles Kingsley, 1819-75, was Rector of Eversley. He is remembered for the children's books, *Westward Ho!* and *The Water Babies* but during his life-time was renowned for controversial novels and pamphlets exposing social and public health failings. He claimed to be a Chartist.

The opprobrium and admiration which his writings attracted were contrasts characteristic of his life. His religious doubts did not stop him becoming a parson; he swung between bouts of ill health and depression and periods of energetic outdoor pursuits and reform campaigning; he happily left parochial duties for the grand life of rich in-laws but would sit up at night nursing sick parishioners; gypsies and grandees came to his funeral; it could have been at Westminster but he chose Eversley.

He was a fervent natural historian and geologist, unperturbed by Darwin's *Origin of Species* (1859). While Rector he was also at various times tutor to the future Edward VII, Professor of Modern History at Oxford, a canon of Chester and a canon of Westminster. *A life of Charles Kingsley* S Chitty 1974

29 Eversley Church and Eversley Cross

About 8½km/5½ miles or a shortened version of 5½km/3½ miles, over fields almost level; a bluebell wood. OS maps 1:25000 159 Reading + 144 Basingstoke, 1:50000 186 Guildford or 175 Reading.

Start from the green at Eversley Church, SU 780 609, or the layby opposite Firgrove Manor, SU 799 608, or a pub at Eversley Cross, SU 795 616.

Linking walks 6★ 7★ 8✿ 26✦ 27✸ 28✳ 30☆

The Chequers ☎ 0118 973 2116
The Golden Pot ☎ 0118 973 2104
The Frog & Wicket ☎ 0118 973 1126

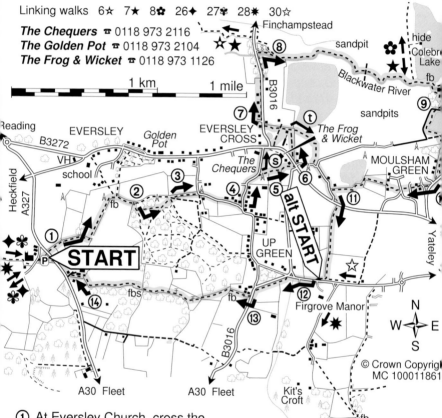

① At <u>Eversley</u> Church, cross the main road from the middle of the green to the footpath through the fields (100m). Stay ahead beside the L fence to the hedge (300m) then go L along the hedge (300m), round the end R into the next field (40m) and ahead to the corner of the (bluebell) wood R (100m).

② Cross the ditch into the wood (40m) and take the side path L to the 5-way junction (150m). Bear L to the corner of the wood (70m).

③ Follow the footpath between fences across the field to the farm (200m). Join the road at the bend and go R along it to the next junction at the houses of Eversley Cross (400m).

④ Walk along the road L, round a R bend to a L bend (250m).

⑤ *Shorter version: Stay on the road to the main road at the* **Chequers** *(200m). Cross the green to the cricket pavilion (200m).*

58

(1) *Behind the pavilion take the footpath R from the corner round to the lane (300m) then go L to the main road (300m).* ➔(11)

(5) At the L bend enter the field R and follow the edge of the fields L to the next road (250m). (The **Frog & Wicket** and the **Chequers** are L along the road, facing the green.)

(6) Slightly L along the pavement (30m) cross to the cricket green. Make for the furthest corner around the edge or via the middle (400m).

(7) Follow the road R to the Blackwater River; the pavement is on the L (300m) then R (200m). The striking timber framed houses are Martineau Cottages. ★☆

(8) Just after the bridge, drop to the river bank R. Follow the path along the river between gravel pits to the side path L (1200m). ✿ Stay ahead, R of Colebrook Lake, to the river footbridge R (100m). ☆

Colebrook Lake is part of Moor Green Lakes Nature Reserve, on gravel pits worked in the 1980s. There are two bird hides for the use of members and more than 200 birds have been seen. The shallows and beaches are profiled to suit the feeding and breeding habits of many waders and swimming birds. Terns and ring plovers nest in summer and there are sightings of rare winter migrants such as red-necked grebe and osprey. The shore vegetation is managed to encourage diversity of land birds and insects. The organisers are the Moor Green Lakes Group which consists of volunteers aided by the extraction company, Cemex.

The gravel represents the Blackwater River floodplain at two Ice Age periods (Terrace 1 & 2 Devensian). The gravel deposits broaden to a mile wide here probably indicating the confluence of periglacial braided streams. Extraction continues in nearby workings.

(9) Cross the river and follow the winding path (either branch) to the road in Moulsham Green (800m).

(10) Turn R (80m). Just after the next side road turn R across the grass (50m). At the next road go R round the bend (20m) then take the footpath L. Carry on in the same line between gardens and over two more roads (250m) then along the L edge of a field (150m). Stay on the footpath which bends L & R to follow the fence round the gravel pit lake to the road (300m). Turn L to the main road (70m).

(11) Cross slightly L to the footpath between the fields (30m). Keep on to the next road, opposite Firgrove Manor (500m). ✳

(12) Turn R along the path beside the road to the layby then continue down the road to the junction (150m). Follow the larger road L or the path behind the trees (250m). At the next road junction bear L past the farm buildings (70m).

(13) Cross the ditch R beside the first field. Carry on into the field and along the R edge (150m) then cross the narrow field to the edge of the wood and follow it L (200m). At the corner of the wood bear L, up past an electricity pole, to the trees at the top of the field (100m) and continue along L edges from field to field, over footbridges near the pond (300m) and on to the end of the last field (350m).

(14) Cross the end of the field to the farm (100m). Outside the field turn L. Skirt L of the buildings, to the main drive then exit to the road (100m). Go down the road R to the green at Eversley Church (200m). ✦✤

30 Yateley and the Blackwater River

About 7½km/4½ miles; with an extension to Eversley Green of 1km/¾ mile; through Yateley village and past bird reserve gravel pits; a few stiles. OS maps 1:25000 159 Reading, 1:50000 186 Aldershot or 175 Reading.

Start at Horseshoe Lake car park, SU 820 620, or one of the car parks on the village green at Yateley, SU 813 613.   Linking walks 6☆ 7★ 8✳ 28✪ 29☆

The Frog & Wicket ☎ 0118 973 1126   **The Chequers** ☎ 0118 973 2116
The White Lion ☎ 01252 890840   **The Dog & Partridge** ☎ 01252 878382

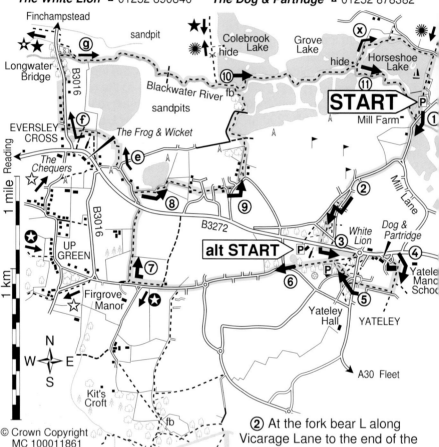

② At the fork bear L along Vicarage Lane to the end of the pond R (200m) then join the path in the trees between the roads and continue to the end road (300m). Go through the belt of trees ahead and over the main road onto the village green at Yateley (100m).

ⓒ *Short cut: Go straight over the grass to the trees (100m) and turn R on the long straight path.* ➜⑥

① At the ramblers' car park take the footpath near Horseshoe Lake away from the watersports centre to the Blackwater River (100m). Go over the road bridge and along Mill Lane to the junction (200m) then round the R bend along Chandlers Lane (500m).

③ Turn L along the edge of the green towards the old village centre (200m). After the green continue beside the main road passing the **White Lion** L (200m).

④ After the **Dog & Partridge** bear R to Yateley Church (100m). Go through the churchyard L of the church (50m) and bear R along the fenced path beside Yateley Manor sports field to the next road (150m). Go R along the path R of the road (200m). When the road bends L keep on ahead to the main road (100m).

SANDHURST

A321

Camberley

⑤ DIagonally R, cross the road, the verge and the side road to the path through the trees (50m). Continue in the same direction over cross paths to the end of the trees (150m). Turn L on the long straight path.

⑥ Stay on the path to the corner of the green near the pond (250m) then continue along Firgrove Road through part of Yateley (500m), over the roundabout and on between fields (150m). After the thatched cottage continue on the path R of the road until level with Firgrove Manor house L (250m). ☆❂

Blackwater

A30

icket Hill
.30 Fleet

⑦ Cross the fields R along the L edge (500m). The hillside ahead is Finchampstead Ridges. At the end, cross the road slightly L and go on along Fox Lane (100m).

ⓔ *Extension of 1km/¾ mile. Stay on the lane round L to the junction (250m) and take the footpath R from the L branch. Follow it round to the pavilion of the cricket green at Eversley Cross (350m). Cross the green, slightly L to the pond (100m).* The **Chequers** and **Frog & Wicket** are over the main road L.

ⓕ *Follow the side road away from the village to the river, past the timber framed Martineau Cottages L. The pavement is on the L (350m) then R (200m).* ★★

ⓖ *Over the bridge, drop to the Blackwater River R. Follow the path along the bank between gravel workings and past a side path L (1200m) ✳ to the footbridge R over the river (100m).* ➔⑩

⑧ Just before the first house, Fox Cottage, turn R to the fields. Follow the path along the L fence (250m), across the end of the narrow side field L (50m) then R along the edge of the next field to the houses (150m). Continue along paths between the houses of Moulsham Green, over two roads to emerge from a house drive near a triangular grass patch (300m).

⑨ Cross the edge of the grass L to the next road (50m) then go L (50m) and bear L to the footpath through the grassy area between houses. Stay on this path which crosses the powerboat club track (250m) then winds round a gravel pit lake to the river (500m). ✳ Over the footbridge, turn R.

⑩ Stay on the river bank to the side path L at the bird hide (900m).

ⓧ *An extra 400m/¼ mile: Turn L and keep to footpaths near the lake, all the way round to the car park, passing through the water sports centre (1200m).*

⑪ Continue beside the river to the road (600m) then take the footpath back L to the car park (100m).

31 Minley Farm and Yateley Heath Wood

Gravel digging will obstruct the western end of this route for some years.

About 7½km/4¾ miles; mainly through well spaced conifers; undulating; many variants possible. OS maps 1:25000 144 + 145, 1:50000 175 or 186.

Start from the little parking area off the Minley roundabout, SU 819 586. Some of the gateways to Yateley Heath Wood have parking spots near the route.

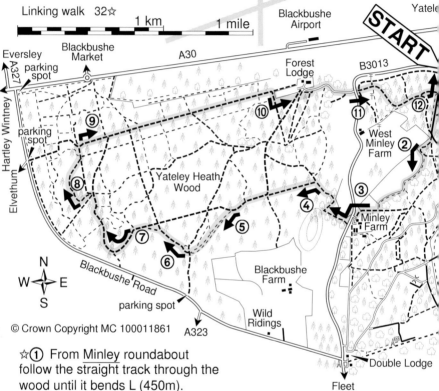

Linking walk 32☆

© Crown Copyright MC 100011861

☆① From Minley roundabout follow the straight track through the wood until it bends L (450m).

② Bear R on the side track then R again (30m) on the track which curves round L to the field (200m). Follow the fence down the edge of the wood to a track between fields overlooking Minley Farm (600m).

③ Go down the track R and round L to the farm (200m). Walk L along the busy road (60m) then R on the disused forestry track (200m). Go round a R bend to the field (100m) then L up to the major track in Yateley Heath Wood (Forestry Commission) (200m).

④ Take the straight track L (350m) and continue on the wider track which joins from R (150m). The track curves down L then R (150m).

⑤ On the R curve bear L on the path to a track junction (400m).

⑥ Continue on the track ahead curving L & R (200m) then fork L to join the wide track (100m).

⑦ Follow the wide track, down round a L curve past a track L (from the road) (300m) then up round the hillock R to the junction with two side tracks L (600m).

⑧ Just into the 2nd side track (30m) take the lesser track L up round the valleyside (400m) then walk up the straight track L (80m).

⑨ Turn R up onto the wide straight track along the plateau. Aircraft noise is from Blackbushe Airfield. Stay on this track until it bends R near a fence (1300m).

⑩ Go round the bend (60m) then turn L through the trees in the original direction parallel with the L

fence past the (ex-)hangar (250m) then join the winding drive and follow it to the road (300m).

⑪ Cross into Minley Wood. Stay on the track ahead which curves R (off the edge of the plateau) down near a field (350m). Disregard the next side track L (80m) but diverge on the next L (100m) up to the straight track (100m).

⑫ Go L to the Minley roundabout parking spot (200m).

Yateley Heath Wood is on the same **plateau** as Blackbushe Airport, Yateley Common and Bramshill Forest. The flat surface is uneven where cut by small streams and it is most obvious at the steep edges. A geological investigation of 1981 suggests it is the 7th terrace of the Blackwater River, formed during the Anglian glaciation. The Ice Age had cycles of cold and warm periods. The best understood glaciations are the Devensian, 13-64 000 years BP, Wolstonian 128-347 000, and Anglian, 440-592 000, but there were others before these.

Plateaus are a feature of the area - all attributed to the Blackwater River and cycles of glaciation. The flint of the hard tops was washed out of the chalk hills of the Weald to lie in great sheets over the surface of the land and wide valley bottoms. At the extremes of glaciation everything was frozen and there was no movement but, during periglacial periods, for thousands of years, the thaws released torrents of water to carry the flints. The tracks are walkable because of the gravel; without it the surface would be soft sand.

During successive periglacials the proto-Blackwater and its tributaries formed valleys within valleys as the waters cut down through the soft Tertiary Sands. After the Ice Age the soft sands continued to be eroded slowly by rainwater but some of the gravel river beds remained in position producing the flat hilltops with steep edges. A neat pattern of symmetrical gravel terraces can no longer be seen because many of the earlier gravel caps have been removed by water action undermining their edges. Interpretation is a three-dimensional jigsaw puzzle using accurate altitude data for the scattered gravel deposits.

There appear to be eleven terraces, more than one per glaciation. The lowest, 1 & 2, are Devensian and do not form plateaus because they lie below the level of the Blackwater River which has lifted itself on alluvium. They are very visible because of the numerous gravel pits along the valley, flooded and made into nature reserves, water sport centres and fishing lakes. Terrace 11, pre-Anglian, forms the plateau with Bracknell Cæsar's Camp on its edge. Above the eleven, the highest and oldest plateau, at 175m, is the one with the Farnham Cæsar's Camp on its edge. It is thought to be much older than the Anglian Glaciation, perhaps 1Ma BP. Its cap is also thicker, up to 6m, and contains larger pebbles.

32 Wyndham's Pool, Hawley Lake and Minley

About 9km/5½ miles; mainly heath and woods. Most of the route is on military land which is open to the public but may have army exercises in progress. OS maps 1:25000 145 Guildford, 1:50000 186 Aldershot or 175 Reading.

Start from Yateley Common (Wyndham's Pool) car park, SU 822 596, or the car park beside the A30, SU 832 592, or Hawley Lake car park, SU 839 577.

The Crown & Cushion ☎ 01252 545253   **The Ely Inn** ☎ 01252 860444

Linking walks   31 ☆   33 ★

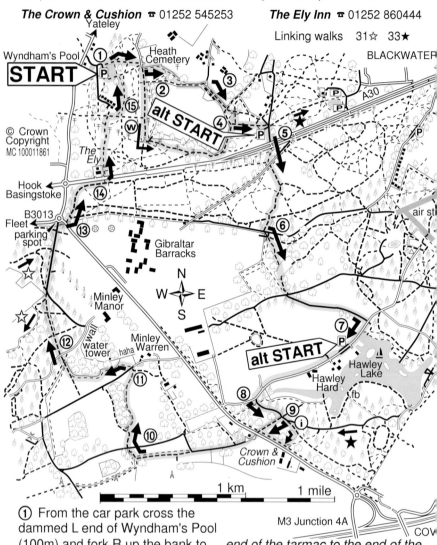

① From the car park cross the dammed L end of Wyndham's Pool (100m) and fork R up the bank to Heath Cemetery (200m). Turn R to the end of the tarmac.

ⓦ *Winter route to avoid bad mud: stay ahead on the track from the* end of the tarmac to the end of the fields L (500m) then go L along the path with the power lines (500m). When they bend R, follow the track L down round a field corner (500m).

Stay beside the field round to the pond (250m) then turn R. ➜④

② Turn L in the trees outside the cemetery fence. Carry on and join the bridleway (300m), going L between fields to the farm (250m).

③ Go R on the drive (40m) and ahead on the track (150m). At the end of the L field go on round the L bend (50m) then turn R past the pond (150m) & L at the next track.

④ Go up the stony slope and on to the 6-way junction near Yateley Common car park (250m). ★

⑤ Go R on the track to the road and cross the dual carriageway (150m). Continue on the path into the heath to the tarmac army road (150m). Stay ahead on the track opposite, which curves R to end at the army hard track (400m).

⑥ Cross into the wood. Avoid the descending paths and follow the level path diverging ½ L from the barracks fence round to the edge of the plateau (150m). Drop to the clearing and cross it slightly R to the exit track (150m). Keep on in the same direction to the hard track junction (150m). Continue on the track opposite to the tarmac army road (600m).

⑦ Follow the army road R down past the Hawley Lake parking area (200m), Hawley Hard and round a L curve (850m).

⑧ On the R bend take the curving track L to the cross track (200m). Either go R to the road (200m) or

ⓘ *If visiting the **Crown & Cushion** stay on the curving track (50m) & fork R (100m) then cross through the beech wood R to the pub. Return along the tarmac path beside the road (250m).*

⑨ Cross the road and continue on the army road which becomes a track (500m). At the first field R, stay ahead on the track or the path near the edge of the field (400m).

⑩ At the end of the field go R on the track (100m). Cross the hard track and carry on up the winding track (100m). When it curves L, bear R on the lesser track round the R edge of the wood (300m). Stay on this track when it diverges from the wood towards the houses of Minley Warren (150m), bringing Minley Manor into view above.

⑪ Over the hard track, aim for the water tower up L in the trees (100m) then follow the edge of the trees L (300m) and round R to the top corner of the field (100m).

⑫ Cross the path at the edge of the wood and continue straight up over the tarmac drive (40m) to the top of the slope (100m).☆ Stay ahead on the plateau to the hard track (350m) and continue on that to the parking area at the road junction (450m).

⑬ Turn R over the road to the corner of the Gibraltar Barracks fence (40m). Take the path to the heath (30m) and turn L on the soft track skirting round the edge (250m). After the end of the curve (100m) watch out for the ***Ely Inn*** L.

⑭ Just after it cross the main road L (50m). Take the path outside the R hedge of the inn. Stay ahead down off the plateau and under power lines (200m) to the cross track (250m), 100m before houses.

⑮ Go R briefly (50m) then bear L down through the trees and keep forking L to the pond (300m). Skirt L of it to the car park (150m).

33 Hawley Woods and Lake

About 7km/4½ miles with an extension of 3km/1½ miles to Yateley Common; woods and heath. Most of the route is on army land which is open to the public but may be military exercises in progress, sometimes noisy. OS maps 1:25000 145 Guildford, 1:50000 186 Aldershot or 175 Reading.

Start at the car park behind Hawley Memorial Hall, SU 851 593, or Hawley Lake car park, SU 839 577. On the extension Yateley Common has two car parks.

Crown & Cushion 01252 545253   ***Hawley Leisure Centre bar*** 01276 35411

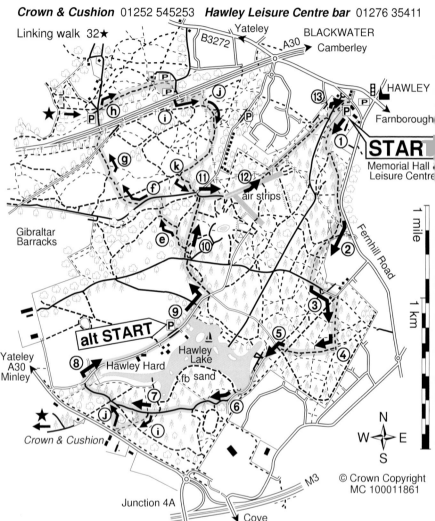

① Behind <u>Hawley</u> Memorial Hall climb to the sports field and cross to the far R corner (200m). Carry on through the wood above the valley track (100m) then curve L to a track (100m). Continue on the L arm from the U-bend soon passing close to Fernhill Road (450m).

② When the track swings R near power lines stay on it to the fence

(200m) then bear L on a side path to the edge of the <u>plateau</u> (100m) and go straight down (300m).

③ On the track at the bottom, turn L to the lodge (200m). Cross the main drive and bear R down through the pine wood to the lowest point (350m).

④ Turn R on the cross track then stay ahead to the tarmac army road (400m).

⑤ From the bend go L on the tarmac, past <u>Hawley Lake</u> and over the outlet stream (450m).

⑥ Disregard the track R just after the bridge but bear R at the next wide side track (70m). Go round bends, over a culvert (200m) and on past the side track R (350m). ★

ⓘ *If visiting the* **Crown & Cushion**: *After the R track (100m), turn L on the next side track (120m). Cross the clearing and another track to find the path to the pub (100m).*

ⓙ *Afterwards, return straight through the trees (no path) to the 1st cross track (100m) then go L to the tarmac army road (500m).* ➔⑧

⑦ Stay ahead on the main track to the tarmac army road (600m).

⑧ Turn R along the road past the Hawley Lake parking area (850m).

⑨ After the sailing club stay on the tarmac road under trees to the side road R (350m). Opposite it, take the track L to the next cross track (300m). Slightly L (40m) up the track on the other side.

ⓔ *Extension to Yateley Common: Up the track (70m) take the first side track L winding uphill (200m). Turn L with the main track at the next junction. Stay on it up to the apex bend (150m) then branch R up to the next cross track (40m).*

Slightly R (20m) go on to the parallel hard track (60m).

ⓕ *Walk L along the hard track (150m) but just round the curve, diverge R on the side path to the cross track (150m). Stay ahead to the curving cross track (200m).*

ⓖ *Turn R to the narrow tarmac army road (200m). Cross it and fork R to the main road (150m). Cross the dual carriageway and continue ahead on the vehicle track to the 6-way junction (100m).*

ⓗ *Opposite the car park track go down the main path R (450m). Continue on the grass, curving R round the pond, and over the car park to the main road (200m).*

ⓘ *Take the little path opposite (30m). Follow the power lines L (150m) then R (100m) to the track.*

ⓙ *Follow the track L, curving R up the slope ⟍⟋ and under the*

Visible across the huge Blackwater valley are Wellingtonia Avenue, the Broadmoor rectangle and Bagshot Heath telecommunications tower.

power lines on top (300m). Go on along the top of the slope to the next major side track L (300m).

ⓚ *Follow the side track (200m) which curves L across the end of the tarmac army road.* ➔⑪

⑩ Stay on this track to the top of the slope (300m) and turn R.

⑪ Follow the level hard track on the brow of the plateau (200m) and continue on the L airstrip (300m).

⑫ Near the end bear L on the hard track which soon descends beside the boundary (700m).

⑬ At the bottom go L on the major track briefly (50m) then take the diverging path R to the road near the Memorial Hall (150m).

34 Poland Mill and the Basingstoke Canal

About 8km/5 miles; farmland and canal, almost flat, boggy in winter; lots of stiles; the extension of 1km/¾ mile to the Waterwitch and short cut of 2km/1½ miles through Odiham Wood (bad in wet seasons) can be used together. OS maps 1:25000 144 Basingstoke, 1:50000 186 Aldershot.

Start from Broad Oak car park, SU 753 520. On the extension, park at Odiham Wharf car park, SU 747 517.

Linking walks 20✿ 35❂
36✳ ▢1 ✳ ㊷ ★

The Waterwitch
01256 702778

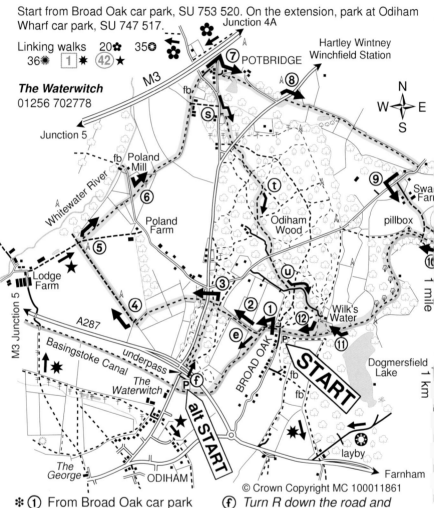

© Crown Copyright MC 100011861

✳ ① From Broad Oak car park cross the Basingstoke Canal (60m) and turn L on the first side path down to the towpath (100m).

ⓔ *Extension of 1km/¾ mile: Stay beside the canal under the main road (600m), past Odiham Wharf car park and up to the road (200m). (The **Waterwitch** is 50m L.)* ★

ⓕ *Turn R down the road and pass under the major road to Odiham Common (100m). Avoid side paths and stay ahead to the end of the trees (500m).* ➤③

② Take the path R of the towpath soon bending away R between fields (450m). At the end of the path turn R, out of the trees (30m).

③ Turn L on the path over the road between the crossroads and the milestone at Frenchman's Oak)

Frenchman's Oak, now propped up by poles, is said to mark the limit to which paroled officers could walk on the London road from the great prisoner-of-war camp at Odiham for the Napoleonic Wars. Presumably the milestone next to it, 40 miles to London, was the real mark.

(50m). Carry on through the trees to the fields (50m) then across the fields from stile to stile (500m).

④ At the last field before the road join the track R in the adjacent field. Follow the track (of Lodge Farm) beside the ditch (750m).

⑤ At the cross track turn R but soon take the side path diverging L from it (almost parallel with the L edge, about 100m from it) (350m). Enter the next field 100m from the corner and go straight on to the tarmac drive (100m). The route is ahead but detour L along the drive, through the garden to see Poland Mill and the River Whitewater (200m) then return (200m).

⑥ Cross the next field to the far R corner (250m). Cross the corner of the next field (20m) and go along the R hedge in the next (100m). Over the ditch, carry on ahead up round the R edge of the field and eventually down past Potbridge Farm (500m). Disregard tracks R and stay ahead though the fields to the road (200m). ✿

Ⓢ *Short cut of 2km/1¼ mile through Odiham Wood: Go along the road R to the first house after the R curve (300m) then skirt round outside of the little field L and keep on to the road (250m).*

Opposite, take the R path soon curving R to a T-junction (150m). Go L, past a cross path (100m) to the next major fork (150m).

Ⓣ *Bear R to the X-junction (150m) then bear L. Keep on to the road (250m). Stay ahead through the wood to the vehicle track (250m).*

Ⓤ *Follow the winding track L to the pond (300m). Turn R.* ➜⑫

⑦ Go up the track R of the house opposite (100m). Pass the house at the end and ascend through the trees (60m). At the road go briefly R (70m) and turn L on the first side track (30m). When it bends to the house take the onward side path R (40m) then cross to the adjacent field L (10m). Turn R across the grass past the end of the pond (60m). Continue in the same line, converging on the drive from the houses. Go on to the road (300m).

⑧ Go L on the road (40m) then enter the field opposite. Aim a bit L across the field for the gate at the far side near a hedge end (250m). Stay ahead at the L edge of the fields to the next road (900m).

⑨ Walk along the road R, round the bends, passing the first house L (200m). Turn L on the track to Swan's Farm. Go up between the buildings and on between fields to the canal (500m). ✿❋

⑩ Don't cross but drop to the towpath R and carry on beside the canal under power cables (1000m) to the end of the fields R (200m).

⑪ After the fields (50m) take the path R (100m).

⑫ Follow the edge of the pond, Wilk's Water, back to the canal (100m) and carry on (R) beside it to Broad Oak Bridge (200m).

35 Odiham and Dogmersfield Park

About 8km/5 miles with an extension of 3km/2 miles across Odiham and a short cut of 1½ km/1 mile. Basingstoke Canal and farmland, boggy at ⑧ in wet seasons. OS maps 1:25000 144 Basingstoke, 1:50000 186 Aldershot.

Start from Odiham Wharf car park, SU 747 517, or on the road before it, at the end of London Road in Odiham. If using the short cut start from Broad Oak car park, SU 753 520 or the large layby, SU 756 512, on the A287 east of Odiham.

Linking walks   34❀   36✳   37❄   1️⃣ ❀   ㊷ ◆

The Waterwitch ☎ 01256 702778
The George ☎ 01256 702081
The Bell ☎ 01256 702282

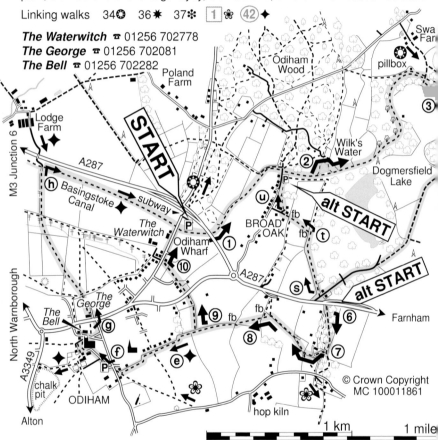

© Crown Copyright
MC 100011861

1 km   1 mile

❀① At Odiham Wharf car park follow the Basingstoke Canal away from the road, under the next road bridge (300m), round L & R curves and past the cart bridge from Broad Oak hamlet (700m).

② After the bridge (220m) take the side path L towards the house. Go round the pond, Wilk's Water, and back to the towpath (200m).

Turn L. Stay beside the canal to the next bridge (1100m). ✳
③ Cross the canal but carry on beside the cutting (200m). At the track turn R. Go past Sprat's Hatch Farm and out on the drive (300m).
④ Round the bend at the start of the road take the path R between fields and carry on along the drive to the bend near Tundry Pond L

70

(450m). ❇ The large house up R is <u>Dogmersfield Park</u>.

Ⓢ Turn back R on the fenced path up the hillside (350m). Join the converging drive and carry on over the top (400m). When the drive bends R, stay ahead on the track down past Dogmersfield Lake (800m) and up through the wood to the twin lodges (400m).

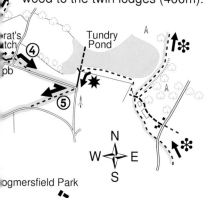

ogmersfield Park

Ⓢ *Short cut to Broad Oak car park: Take the path R after the R lodge through the wood watching out for a stile to the field L (400m).*

ⓣ *Cross the field to exit between the nearest houses (150m).*

ⓤ *Bear R over the grass to the car park near the bridge (250m).*

Ⓢ Continue to the main road (100m) and turn L along the verge (100m). From the layby, cross to the drive of Lothams and take the bridleway diverging L from it into the wood. If boggy follow the drive and, opposite the 1st house take the winding footpath L through the trees to the bridleway (300m). ❁

Ⓢ Watch out for the corner of the 1st field R over a ditch. Cross into it and go over the drive (20m). Stay ahead round the paddocks (200m). In the next field follow the L hedge, almost to the end corner (400m).

Ⓢ Cross the adjacent field L to the next stile (40m). In the next field make for the far L corner at the watercress stream (170m). Cross the fence and the footbridge and follow the R hedge (300m).

ⓔ *Extension of 3km/2 miles across Odiham: Stay ahead into the next field and along the R hedge, which bends several times, all the way to the next road (700m).*

ⓕ *Just up the road R, take the side road L & R to the churchyard (200m). The pest house is at the L corner.* ✦ *Cross past the tower of Odiham Church to the road opposite the* **Bell***. Follow the road R & L to High Street (150m).*

ⓖ *Walk down the drive beside the* **George***. Before the arch turn L to the other side of the wall and follow it R to the fields (200m) where several paths meet. Take the onward diagonal path across to the L hedge (200m). Keep on in the same oblique line over the fields (400m). After the electricity poles, continue ahead on the path beside the hedge, over a rise and down to the canal (300m).*

ⓗ *Cross the cart bridge and follow the towpath R to the next road bridge (1000m). Odiham Wharf car park is just after the bridge (100m).*

Ⓢ Just before the end of the field turn into the adjacent field R and go along the R boundary to the road (250m). Carry on along the footpath opposite, eventually between gardens, to the next road (300m).

Ⓢ Walk along the road R past the **Waterwitch** and over the canal (200m). Drop to the towpath R and Odiham Wharf car park.

36 Dogmersfield and Tundry Pond

About 8km/5 miles with an extension of 1km/¾ mile; almost level throughout; lots of stiles; bad mud after prolonged rain; best at bluebell time; half shady. OS maps 1:25000 144 Basingstoke, 1:50000 186 Aldershot.

Start from the canal car park opposite the *Barley Mow* at Winchfield Hurst, SU 777 538. On the extension, Winchfield Church has a car park, SU 767 536.

Linking walks   34✳   35✳   37✪   38☆   ***The Barley Mow*** ☎ 01252 617490
The Queen's Head ☎ 01252 613531
The Exchequer ☎ 01252 615336

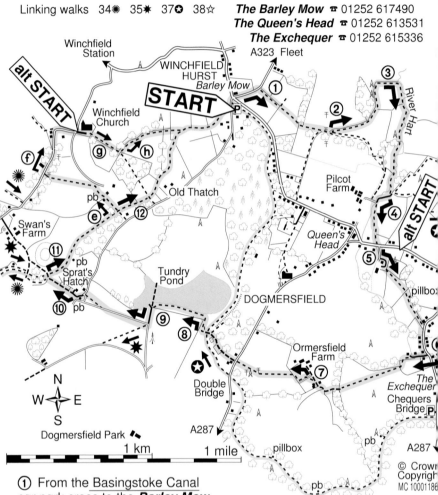

① From the <u>Basingstoke Canal</u> car park cross to the ***Barley Mow*** and go along the side road beside the pub (200m). At the bend enter the field R and follow the path across the paddocks to the trees (250m). Go on through the trees past the end of the next field R (150m) and a bit further (50m).

② Turn into the field L and keep on at the L edge (300m). Bear L round the edge of the wood and past the pylons L (300m).

③ Go round the corner R and on to the River <u>Hart</u> (150m). Keep on near the river along the fields to the footbridge over the river (650m). Cross and follow the river to the end of the field (150m). ❍

④ Go R on the track (120m). Don't cross the farm bridge but continue ahead on the path beside the stream to the road (250m). (The **Queen's Head** is 200m R.) Cross slightly L (20m).

⑤ Walk along the drive of Brookmeadow Farm Stables (80m). Before the house take the track L round the garden (70m). From the corner nearest the power cables take the path through the fields. Diverge very slightly from the L edge to cross into the next field 50m from the corner (200m) and carry on past a pillbox (80m) to the far L corner (200m). Walk along the road R (200m). ☆

⑥ After the 2nd bridge turn along the track R, Stroud Lane (150m). When the track bends to the last house keep on briefly outside the field (50m) then into it. Cross the R corner (40m) to the next large field. Go on, diverging slightly from the R edge, aiming between the pylon L and trees R (200m). Carry on over the top and down towards the gap in the trees (and a distant pylon) (250m). Pass through the belt of trees, along the cart track and up between houses (200m).

⑦ Just after the first houses take the path L across the corner of the little field (20m). Go over more fences, L & R round outside the next field (120m) then diagonally over the large field towards the house. Sometimes the path is direct but the right of way is slightly L and bends towards the house at the electricity pole before the pylon

(400m). Cross the road. Go down the path beside the drive and on along the track at the edge of the wood, round a L bend and over the canal (300m).

⑧ Turn R beside the next field down to Tundry Pond (100m) and go L along the edge (350m). ✳

⑨ Turn L along the track towards Dogmersfield Park (150m) then take the level track R between fields (300m) and diverge R on the path to the trees and buildings at Sprat's Hatch Farm (200m).

⑩ Join the lane but turn L on the farm track and go round the bend. Keep on between fields and over the canal bridge (300m). ✳

⑪ Descend R to the towpath and keep on beside the canal to the next bridge (Badeley's) (700m).

ⓔ *Extension of 1km/¾ mile to* Winchfield Church: *Up on the bridge take the track L. Continue past the large house (Old Rectory) almost to the tarmac drive (250m) then enter the field L and diverge from the R edge across to the gap in the trees (400m).*

ⓕ *Walk along the road R (300m) and round the R bend to the* church *(150m).*

ⓖ *Go through the churchyard (100m) and take the path, exactly in line from the end of the track, at the R edge of the field (200m) and through the belt of trees (30m).*

ⓗ *At the next fields turn L. Go along the L edge (350m), over a narrow field and straight on to the canal (100m). Go L to the car park just after the next bridge (400m).*

⑫ Stay on the towpath under the next bridge (200m), and the next (900m), to the car park L.

37 Crookham and the Basingstoke Canal

About 9km/5½ miles; canal towpath and farmland with lots of stiles, flat, mostly shady; with two extensions, each of ¾km/½ mile.
OS maps 1:25000 144 Basingstoke, 1:50000 186 Aldershot.

Start from the car park at Chequers Bridge, SU 791 517. One of the extensions passes a canal car park opposite the *Barley Mow*, SU 778 538.

Linking walks 35❄ 36✪ 38✦

The Exchequer ☎ 01252 615336   ***The Black Horse*** ☎ 01252 616434
The Queen's Head ☎ 01252 613531   ***The Barley Mow*** ☎ 02521 617490

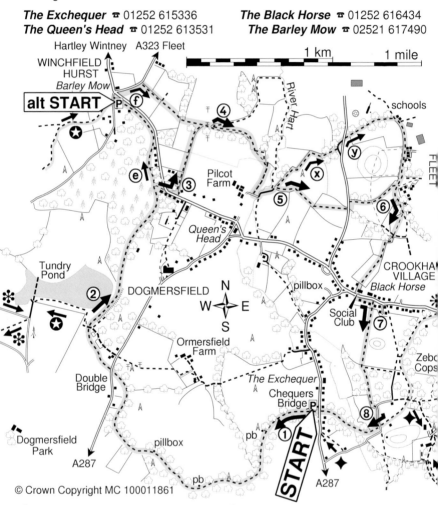

© Crown Copyright MC 100011861

① From the Basingstoke Canal car park, join the towpath and walk away from Chequers Bridge. Go on to the next bridge (2400m). Pass under it and under the next (Blacksmith's)(350m). ❄✪

② Keep on past Tundry Pond L (400m), through the cutting (800m) and round a wide L curve opposite pines. Watch out for a little side path R at the next (slight) R bend of the towpath and canal (150m).

ⓔ *Extension of ¾km/½ mile to the* ***Barley Mow****: Stay on the towpath almost to the next bridge and cross the car park to the pub (950m).*

ⓕ *Go along the side road beside the Barley Mow (200m). At the L bend enter the field R and follow the path across the paddocks to the trees (250m). Go on through the trees to the end of the next field R (150m) and ahead.* ➧④

③ Follow the side path through the trees to the road (80m) and stay ahead to the first side track L (at the sewage pump)(80m). Turn into the track then L on the path through the trees. Carry on past the garden to the fields (100m) and along the R edges to the next trees (350m). At the end turn R.

④ Start along the path in the belt of trees (50m) then turn L into the field and follow the R edge (250m). After the trees, continue round the R edge of the field (150m). Just before the next side hedge L, cross the ditch then continue at the L hedge (100m). In the field after the pond follow the farm track R beside the ditch towards Pilcot Farm (300m). At the farmyard go L on the concrete track over the diminutive River Hart (50m) and turn L on the track through the trees into the field ahead (200m).

ⓧ *Extension of ¾km/½ mile: At the end of the track stay ahead near the L edge of the field and R round the end to the wood (400m). Go through the wood (200m) and L on the track to the road (20m).*

ⓨ *Slightly L (20m) take the path through the trees on the other side Stay on this path round the field with the hillock all the way to the end of the clearing at the edge of the housing estate (part of Fleet) (900m). Carry on along the path R of the houses.* ➧⑥

⑤ Turn R along the hedge (70m). At the hedge-end continue straight up the field to a zigzag in the hedge (150m). Cross the next field to the far L corner and go out to the road (250m). Slightly L (60m) continue through the fields on the other side, outside the hedge of the field with the hillock, towards houses (400m). Turn R on the cross path near the houses.

⑥ Stay on the path skirting R of the trees round the houses (200m). At the field after the pond, cross obliquely to the L end of the wood (150m). Cross the boundary track and follow the track round the narrow end of the wood into the next field. Go up the L edge (200m) then diagonally up the top field and across the club car park to the road in Crookham Village (350m). ✦✳

⑦ Walk L along the road past the ***Black Horse*** (100m). Just after the pub watch out for the path between houses R (30m). Follow this path up between fields and down to the wood (450m). Stay ahead through the wood to the tarmac lane (300m). Go up the lane R to the humped Poulter's Bridge over the canal (150m).

⑧ Don't cross but join the towpath and go R beside the canal to the next bridge, Chequers, and the car park (450m). The ***Exchequer*** is just along the road L from the car park (150m).

38 Crookham Village and Crondall

About 8km/5 miles with extensions to both village centres; gently undulating farmland with lots of stiles; paths very overgrown in late summer.
OS maps 1:25000 144 Basingstoke +145 Guildford, 1:50000 186 Aldershot.

Start from Chequers Bridge car park at Crookham Village, SU 791 517, or, on the extensions, from a pub or roadside parking spot in one of the villages.

36☆ 37✦ 39★ 4❀ 5◇ 6❀ 7☆

Plume of Feathers 01252 850245
Hampshire Arms 01252 850418
Black Horse 01252 616434
The Exchequer 01252 615336

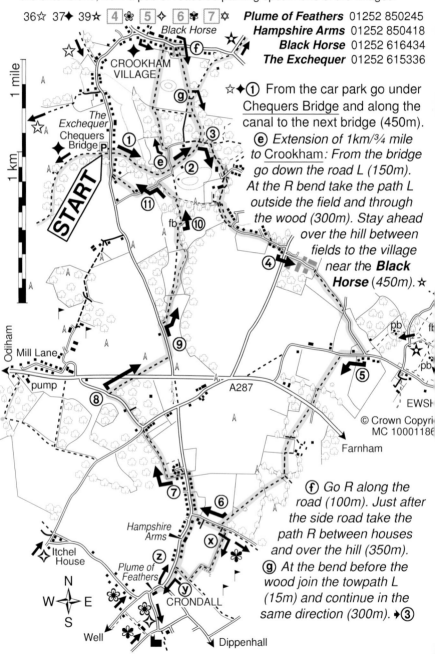

☆✦① From the car park go under <u>Chequers Bridge</u> and along the canal to the next bridge (450m).

ⓔ *Extension of 1km/¾ mile to <u>Crookham</u>: From the bridge go down the road L (150m). At the R bend take the path L outside the field and through the wood (300m). Stay ahead over the hill between fields to the village near the* **Black Horse** *(450m).* ☆

ⓕ *Go R along the road (100m). Just after the side road take the path R between houses and over the hill (350m).*

ⓖ *At the bend before the wood join the towpath L (15m) and continue in the same direction (300m).* ✦③

© Crown Copyri
MC 1000118

② Stay on the towpath (350m). ★

③ At the swing bridge cross to Zebon Copse. Keep to the main track round a R bend (100m) and on between fields (300m). After the tarmac drive of the Community Centre take the path under the trees which bends behind the barn. Stay ahead to the next tarmac crossing (350m). Over the bridge R (20m) carry on as before, now on tarmac, to the road (400m).

④ Cross slightly R and go along the road between the buildings of Redfields Park (200m). At the end carry on along the L edge of the field to the road (400m). Follow the road R to the end opposite Ewshot Lodge (300m). ✿

⑤ Go R along the road out of the hamlet (200m). On the rise and curve, 50m before the next house R, take the path L straight across the field. Look straight over for the nearest large tree. Aim 100m R of the tree then make for the stile (250m). Stay ahead along the hedge to a nasty road crossing (100m). Go straight on aiming 100m R of the farm, over the paddocks from stile to stile, to the hedge (250m). After the hedge cross another paddock then follow the horse track to the next hedge (250m). Just round the bend in the trees, turn R to the next field (30m). Go straight over (120m) and ahead between fields down to the road (350m). ❀

Ⓧ *Extension of 1km/¾ mile into* Crondall. *Join the path opposite, above the road, and go L past the field entrance (50m). Turn R at the golf course and follow the fence, with a zigzag, to the end (500m).*

Ⓨ *At the hedge, go R to the road (120m) and L along the street to the* **Feathers** *(300m).* ✧❀

Ⓩ Return along the same road but carry on past the field, and the **Hampshire Arms** (500m) to the edge of the village (400m). ➔⑦

⑥ Follow the road R to the village street (250m) and go R to the edge of the village (300m).

⑦ Just before the fields R, cross L to the house drive. Go up between houses to the field (120m) and R along the top edge next to the wood (300m). Stay ahead curving L to the road junction (100m). Go on in the same direction down the road with the wood R (300m).

⑧ At the end of the wood take the path R beside the trees to the main road (200m). Cross on the same oblique line and carry on along the path at the edge of the field (300m). At the next road go L (250m).

⑨ After the house L (50m) take the path R in the fields. Don't cross the stream but go L beside it. The right of way is at the middle of the fields but the path usually follows the stream, converging on the wood at the far side (300m), then the R edge of the fields (400m).

⑩ Between the crossing power lines watch out for a footbridge R under the trees and cross the stream (20m) then turn L beside the trees (100m). When the stream and trees bend L, cross to the end trees and go through the gateway to the next field (70m).

⑪ Follow the L edge (150m) then the lane (150m) After the house go R up the path between wood and field (200m). At the road turn R to Chequers Bridge (150m).

39 Fleet, Basingstoke Canal and Ewshot

Longer than usual, about 11½km/7 miles; the towpath through Fleet and heath; gentle inclines. OS maps 1:25000 145 Guildford, 1:50000 186 Aldershot.

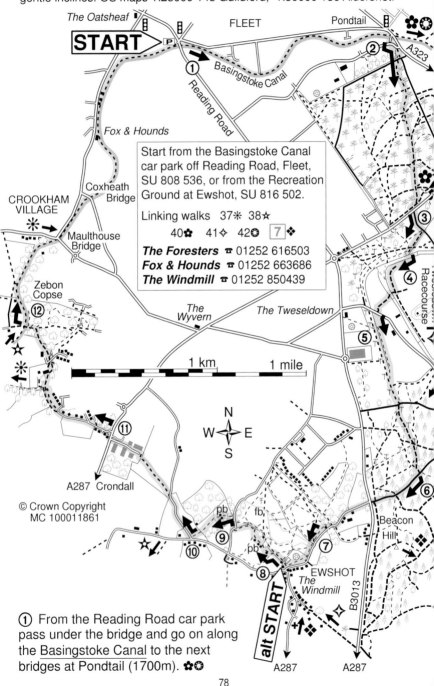

Start from the Basingstoke Canal car park off Reading Road, Fleet, SU 808 536, or from the Recreation Ground at Ewshot, SU 816 502.

Linking walks 37✳ 38★

40✿ 41◇ 42◉ 7 ❖

The Foresters ☎ 01252 616503
Fox & Hounds ☎ 01252 663686
The Windmill ☎ 01252 850439

© Crown Copyright
MC 100011861

① From the Reading Road car park pass under the bridge and go on along the Basingstoke Canal to the next bridges at Pondtail (1700m). ✿◉

78

② Cross the old bridge (40m). Turn L along the road (60m) then R on the track through the trees (50m). At the cross track turn R (20m) then L on the side path (350m). At the cross track after the ditch (40m) take the L path ahead (200m) joining a track to the road (450m). The building 100m L is the **Foresters**.

③ Go R briefly on the track beside the road (40m) then cross to the track opposite and walk away from the road (150m). Turn R along the path beside the fence (and near oil pipeline marks). Disregard the side paths and carry on into Tweseldown Racecourse (200m).

④ Cross the grassy race track and turn R after the hedge. ✧ Follow a horse track near the race track round the bend (250m) and re-cross the race track via the vehicle track to the road (150m).

⑤ Cross the road into the field and go up the R edge. (Outside the field there is a parallel public RoW.) At the end of the field continue on the RoW with power lines to the cross track (700m) and ahead, R of the power lines to the next cross track (300m). Stay ahead to the next cross track (200m). ❖

⑥ Turn R and descend to the road (fast cars) (450m). Follow Tadpole Lane, opposite, past Beacon Hill Farm (150m) and round the little S-bend (200m).

⑦ At the pillbox R climb the bank and go out into the field (30m) then turn L and follow paths round, near the road, to Ewshot Recreation Ground car park (450m). The **Windmill** is 250m up the road L.

⑧ From the car park at Ewshot ascend beside the L fence (50m) and go on through the next field (army land) (80m). Watch out for the first side path L and follow it across the clump of trees, past the pillboxes and round R to the hedge (300m). Follow the hedge down L to the lane (100m).

⑨ Walk along the lane R (80m) and turn L into the first gateway (army land). Follow the path up the field past the pillboxes on top and down (250m). From the middle of the bottom edge cross the next field to the gateway in the trees opposite, to emerge on the road near a T-junction (80m). ★

⑩ Turn R down the road (300m). When it bends R take the footpath ahead to the field and continue at the R edge near the stream. At the end (400m) exit to the industrial estate and walk along the main drive to the road in Church Crookham (200m).

⑪ Cross slightly R and walk along Watery Lane, opposite, to the bend and bridge (450m). Don't continue on the bridleway unless the stream bed is dry but cross the bridge (20m) to the path L which re-joins the bridleway later (200m). ❋ Go on along the bridleway (200m), over the drive of Velmead Community Centre and ahead at the edge of Zebon Copse to the Basingstoke Canal (300m).

⑫ Over the swing bridge turn R and stay with the canal through Fleet: under Malthouse Bridge (700m) and Coxheath Bridge (400m) to the **Fox & Hounds** (600m) and on to the car park at Reading Road wharf (950m).

40 Fleet Pond and Velmead Common

About 8km/5 miles with an extension of 1km/¾ mile; many short cuts possible; heath and woodland; no stiles, fairly shady; passable in winter. OS maps 1:25000 145 Guildford, 1:50000 186 Aldershot.

Start from the heath car park near *The Foresters*, SU 826 527, or Norris Bridge car park, SU 833 536, or one of the streets adjacent to the pond in Fleet.

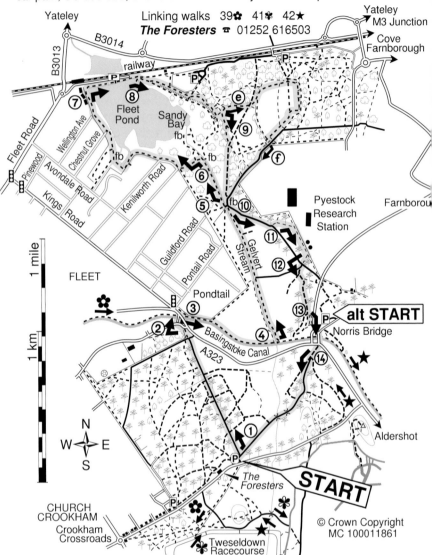

Linking walks 39✿ 41❀ 42★
The Foresters ☎ 01252 616503

© Crown Copyright
MC 100011861

✿① From the heath car park near the *Foresters*, start on the downhill track parallel with the road but, almost immediately (30m), turn L

on the straight side track away from the road. Stay on it to the track junction near the main road at the end of the heath (850m).

② Continue on the path ahead to the minor road (70m). Go L to Old Pondtail Bridge and cross (80m).

③ Drop to the towpath R, pass under the main road and carry on beside the <u>Basingstoke Canal</u> to the sluices (550m).

④ Cross the overflow weir and turn L down to the Gelvert Stream which emerges from under the canal. Stay on this footpath to the bridge at the junction of several paths and tracks (1100m).

⑤ Cross the stream but carry on beside it (350m).

⑥ Just after the next footbridge turn L to the road (200m). Follow the boundary path R, curving L then round R & L bends and over a footbridge (600m). Stay ahead to the corner near the (London-Southampton) <u>railway</u> (550m).

⑦ Cross the end of <u>Fleet Pond</u> next to the station car park (350m).

⑧ Bear R on the path round the corner of the pond (50m). When the high & low paths split, diverge L up the bank then stay near the top of the bank until the path passes the corner of the field L (650m). Turn L out of the trees (20m).

ⓔ *Extension of 1km/¾ mile: Keep to the edge of the trees L. Follow paths beside the wood round the end of the fields and back along the top edge to the crossing hedge with trees (1000m).*

ⓕ *At the hedge cut L through the trees to the hard track (30m). Keep on in the same direction (R) down past the bridge (500m).* ➜⑩

⑨ Go R on the path up beside the trees to the vehicle track (250m). Follow the track R past the bridge at the track junction (400m).

⑩ Stay on the main track, now diverging from the stream (300m).

⑪ On the R bend watch out for a side path L and ascend, forking R, to the fence of <u>Pyestock</u> Research Station (150m). Follow the fence R and find a path down R, just after the two circular tanks (250m).

⑫ Descend back to the main track (80m). Start along the side track opposite (30m) and fork L Disregard the side track diverging R and climb to the top (300m). ★

⑬ When the track bends downhill R, take branch paths L to the road (100m). Go R along the pavement over the canal (100m).

⑭ Cross the main road and go up the heath path to the track junction on top (100m). Disregard the track ahead and the track L and bear L on the track between them down the slope and round a R curve (200m). Stay on this track, over the culverted Gelvert Stream (300m) and up to the car park (350m). The uphill track behind the car park leads to the *Foresters* (100m). ✤

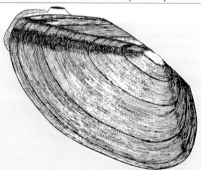

Swan Mussels, up to 10cm/4" long, live in the mud on the bottom of Fleet Pond and used to be eaten. They draw in a current of water from which they filter planktonic food. The larvae travel and feed embedded in the skin of sticklebacks as parasites.

41 Beacon Hill, Ewshot and Tweseldown

About 9km/5½ miles with two extensions of 1½km/1 mile to Cæsar's Camp and the *Foresters*. Mainly heath; short very steep slopes. Avoid Tweseldown on race days. OS maps 1:25000 145 Guildford, 1:50000 186 Aldershot.

Start from a Bourley Road car park, SU 831 510, in a dip near Bourley Lane or from the recreation ground car park at Ewshot, SU 816 502

The Windmill ☎ 01250 850439   **The Foresters** ☎ 01252 616503

Linking walks
39◇ 40❊
42❊ 44⊙
7 ❊ 8 ☆

ⓔ *Extension to Cæsar's Camp: From the highest corner of the car park take the path diagonally R over the grass. After the line of trees continue diagonally into the trees and along near Bourley Road. Watch out for Bourley Lane opposite (300m) then a large track (100m).*

ⓕ *Cross and go up the track (80m). Take the 1st side track L, curving R over the rise. Stay ahead to the pebbly top on* Cæsar's Camp *(500m). The best view point is 200m L near the* plateau corner.

ⓖ *Turn R. Keep to the edge until it fades into the hill (400m). Just round the L bend turn R through the ramparts (40m).*

ⓗ *Turn R immediately down the hill (200m) and fork down L past reservoirs R (500m).* ➔③

© Crown Copyright MC 100011861

82

☆♣ ① Cross Bourley Road via the path in the trees from the top of the car park. Go up the track on the other side. Continue on tarmac over crossroads (200m) up to the Army Waterworks reservoir (150m).

② Turn R and skirt round the edge (350m). Just before the footbridge fork R past the top pond to the track (200m). Turn R.

③ Keep on over a 5-way junction (80m) and ahead up round the bend to the next pond L (200m).

④ At the fenced pond, pass the 1st side track R (50m) but turn up the 2nd R. Stay on it, winding ever upwards, to the top near the road (400m). Turn L to the gate (100m).

⑤ Cross the road slightly L (30m) to the track. Follow it down to the **Windmill** in Ewshot (550m). Keep on to the road junction (200m). ✧

⑥ Go R on Tadpole Lane or along the fields beside it to the pillbox at the bend under trees (500m).

⑦ Just after the S-bend take the path R up round the edge of the fields (250m). At the house go R to the road - nasty crossing (100m).

⑧ Slightly R (10m) go through the trees opposite to the track (60m). Cross it and follow the water duct (150m). After the R curve (50m), at the cross path, turn R and climb to the flat top of Beacon Hill (100m). A track comes past the trig point to end on the plateau corner. Drop off this corner steeply down over a runnel, to the hard track (150m).

⑨ Walk down the track L, over a 4-way junction (100m), past the pond L (250m) and round L & R curves to a T-junction (200m).

⑩ Go L on the track up round a U-bend to the cross track (250m).

⑪ Turn R. The track drops then rises through forestry plantations and bends on the top (250m). Continue down into a dip (200m) and up the other side (100m).

⑫ Just over the brow, take the 1st path R down to the road (250m). Cross into the trees and go L to Tweseldown Racecourse (30m).

⑬ Cross the race track and make for the tower on the hilltop (400m).

ⓧ *Extension to The Foresters:*
Go on beside the race track (300m) and round the top bend (150m).

ⓨ *Cross to the fence outside the race track and, after the high point (100m), take the diverging path L to a path junction (50m). Continue ahead to the cart track (150m). Go L to the road (100m) and R on the track on the other side (100m). ❈❊*

ⓩ *From the parking area opposite the **Foresters** drop to the heath. Follow the path away from the road skirting L of the hillock to the hard track after it (400m). Go L to the junction (250m)*

ⓝ *Turn R on the sandy test track to the intersection (350m) then bear R on the hard track (200m). ❖⑮*

⑭ Turn R down the ridge towards Farnborough Airport (100m) then turn R and make your way over to the ponds (300m). Cross the race track to the gate near the jump and follow the path through the trees to the track junction (150m). Turn R.

⑮ Continue on the hard track over the rise and down to a low point (300m) then round a slight R curve to a rising tight L curve (80m).

⑯ At this bend take the side path R over the ditch and ahead to the end (200m). Turn R to the field and the car park (200m).

42 Claycart, Long Valley and Basingstoke Canal

About 8½km/5¼ miles with extensions of 1 km/¾ mile and ½ km/⅓ mile: canal towpath and heath, undulating: mainly army land where you may pass through a military exercise. OS maps 1:25000 145 Guildford, 1:50000 186 Aldershot.

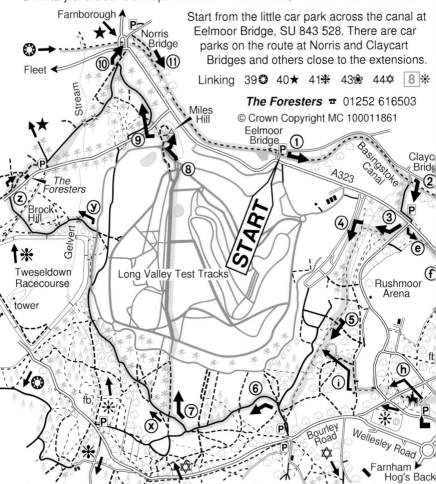

Start from the little car park across the canal at Eelmoor Bridge, SU 843 528. There are car parks on the route at Norris and Claycart Bridges and others close to the extensions.

Linking 39 ✪ 40 ★ 41 ✻ 43 ✸ 44 ✿ 8 ✻

The Foresters ☎ 01252 616503

© Crown Copyright MC 100011861

① From Eelmoor Bridge drop to the Basingstoke Canal and walk L along the towpath (1200m). ✸

② Cross Claycart Bridge and aim L over the grass for the exit of the car park at the top (250m).

ⓔ Extension of 1km/¾ mile to Bat's Hogsty: *Walk up the side road opposite the car park (30m) then cross through the wood L to the fence and follow it down to the* road (150m). Go on (R) along the pavement to the bend (200m).

ⓕ *Bear R along the track by the fence (100m). When it curves R, go L into the wood, over a culvert and up to the sports field (200m). Cross the R corner to the end of the trees (200m).*

ⓖ *Continue on the track between fields (300m). Cross the little road and go on along the fields on the path or on the grass or through the splendid wood (300m). After the next road cross the sunken field to the furthest corner (200m).* ✳

(h) *From the Garrison Church car park, go over the knoll R of the* Wellington Statue *and down to the road behind (150m). Opposite a gateway go on through the wood (50m) then turn L at a right angle (no path)(150m). If you hit the road in the wrong place, look for a fence corner on the other side at the bend. Follow the path away from the road beside the fence (80m).*

(i) *Turn R down the track beside the fence (150m) then L down the curving side track (150m). Just round the L bend, fork R briefly then cross the fence R into Bat's Hogsty. Make your way (no paths) to the bottom L (100m) then more steeply to the Claycart Stream (50m). Turn L.* ➜(5)

Camberley
Farnborough
A325
hotel
(g)

(3) Opposite, walk up through the trees (no path) R of the side road until level with the vehicle track L from the road (200m). Turn R down the small path from the road and cross the Claycart Stream (150m) .

(4) At the rise turn L. Go along the shady path at the foot of the bank (or along the grass on top) (300m). Curve L with the path to a cross track (150m). Go on along Claycart Stream to the cross track after the R curve (300m). Cross the stream and continue on the other side.

(5) Stay beside the stream to the next track (650m) then go R (100m) (or ahead if making for the Crossways parking area ✿).

(6) At the junction take the main uphill track curving L. Continue over the top, ahead at the cross-track (650m), ✳ down round the R bend in the defile (100m) and over to the next cross track (150m).

(x) *Extension of ½km/⅓ mile to the* **Foresters***: Stay ahead on the winding track and along outside* Tweseldown *Racecourse, visible L through the trees (1400m).* ➌

(y) *Turn L at the side track after the racecourse, up to the road (700m).*

(z) *On the other side follow the track R to the pub (150m).* ★ *Pass behind the pub down to the heath car park (100m). Take the downhill track (650m) and stay on it winding to the flat top of a hill (200m).* ➜(10)

(7) Go down the side track R to the the Long Valley test track complex at the bottom (400m). Stay ahead to a very wide track (100m), beside it to the end (1200m) and over the broad curving cross track up to the smaller boundary track (50m).

(8) Turn L (100m) then R on the next cross track (20m) and R up the knoll, Miles Hill, overlooking Farnborough Airport (150m).

(9) Drop back L off the knoll via the track opposite the trig point (70m) and turn ½R on the little path to the road (nasty crossing) (100m). Over it, go R on the rising track (500m).

(10) From the 4-way junction drop to the main road at Norris Bridge (150m). Cross the canal via the R edge of the R bridge. Turn R on the 1st side road to the track R (80m).

(11) Go down the track which converges on the canal (200m). Carry on (L) along the towpath past the end of the runway to Eelmoor Bridge (1300m).

43 Around North Camp

About 7½km/4¾ miles, along the Basingstoke Canal and the Blackwater River and through the military town; level; suitable for wheel chairs. The extension of ¾km/½ mile uses more canal but has a long road section. OS maps 1:25000 145 Guildford, 1:50000 186 Aldershot.

Start from the army car park on Queen's Avenue, Aldershot (near the canal), SU 867 522, or North Camp car park, SU 873 534, or the service road near North Camp Station, SU 880 537, or Lakeside Road car park, SU 889 518.

Linking walks   42❀   35 ✳   36 ✳

The Old Ford ☎ 01252 544840   **The Standard of England** ☎ 01252 325539
The Swan ☎ 01252 325212   Aldershot Military Museum ☎ 01252 314598

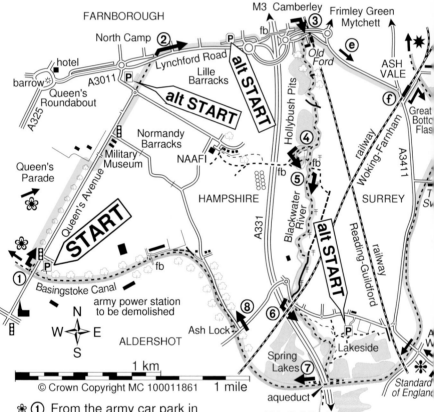

❀ ① From the army car park in Aldershot go through the trees to the canal (50m) Pass under the iron bridge then up R to open fields (Queen's Parade). Carry straight on over the grass or under the trees parallel with Queen's Avenue (opposite the army sports centre) to the end of the fields (900m). Go on along the grass or the pavement, past the Military Museum, opposite (500m). When the road bends L stay ahead past the pond into Farnborough (200m).

② Cross the main road to the service road and turn R. Follow the road past the North Camp shops and down (700m). Cross the long footbridge over the A331 (150m). Stay on the service road to the end (50m) then turn R under the main road to emerge near the station and the *Old Ford* pub (100m). ✳

ⓔ *Extension of ¾km/½ mile: Cross the railway and go on along the main road to Ash Vale (800m).*

ⓕ *Walk under the railway bridge and L up past the station to the canal (200m). Follow the towpath R to the aqueduct (2600m).* ➧⑦

③ Find the footbridge over the Blackwater River and follow the winding footpath beside it (900m).

④ After the last of the Hollybush Pit lakes, fork R up the small hill (100m). Pass over the top then L back to the original path (50m).

⑤ Cross the footbridge and keep on beside the winding river until the path joins a wider track (750m) then go R to the road (300m).

⑥ Cross the road to the path behind the emergency pumping station. Pass under the railway (Woking to Farnham & Alton) and over the river (100m). Carry on (300m) and join another path. Go R between gravel pits (300m), up the ramp to the Basingstoke Canal (100m) and R onto the aqueduct over the dual carriageway (100m).

⑦ See contents of box below then continue along the canal on the embankment under the railway bridge (600m) to the road (200m).

⑧ Go under or over the road to Ash Lock and on beside the canal to the next road, Queen's Avenue (1800m). The side paths before the iron bridge lead to the car park.

The view from the Basingstoke Canal aqueduct:

Beneath, are the A331, the Hampshire/Surrey county boundary and the infant Blackwater River much re-channelled for the building of the road. The length of the canal embankment shows how broad the Blackwater valley is compared with the trickle of the present river. Southwards the Hog's Back is visible over Ash Church. Below, the mound is an artificial bat cave built as part of the road building plan. Gravel Extraction (Terraces 1 & 2 Devensian Glaciation) during the 20th century left the flooded pits. They have a low pH, contrasting with the Basingstoke Canal which receives most of its water from springs in the chalk tunnel at Greywell with a high pH. Thus there is a rich aquatic flora in the area.

The A331, Blackwater Valley Relief Road, passing under the aqueduct was completed in 1996. It follows the marshy valley, crossing the old Hampshire/ Surrey border repeatedly. Troughs sunk in the London Clay 15m below the water table take the road under the canal and railway. They are weighted with extra concrete to stop them floating up. The 60cm thick plates are set in a dihedral under the road with neoprene hinges at the middle and edges so that, if the road sinks, the centre is raised, forcing the sides out to lock the structure in the ground. The troughs have emergency pumps. The county boundary is now along the middle of the road.

44 Blackwater Source and Cæsar's Camp

About 7km/4¼ miles with an extension of 2km/1¼ miles to the Wellington Statue; confusing heath and wood with stony tracks and short very steep sections. As well as getting lost, you may find yourself in an army exercise with rifle shooting (blanks). OS maps 1:25000 145 Guildford, 1:50000 186 Aldershot.

Start at Rowhill car park, Cranmore Lane, Aldershot, SU 848 500, or Crossways car parks, Bourley Road, SU 844 509. On the extension, start from the car park at the Welllington Statue, SU 853 511.

Linking 41❂ 42✿ 7 ✳ 8 ✦ *Bat's Hogsty*

The Royal Arms 01252 310708

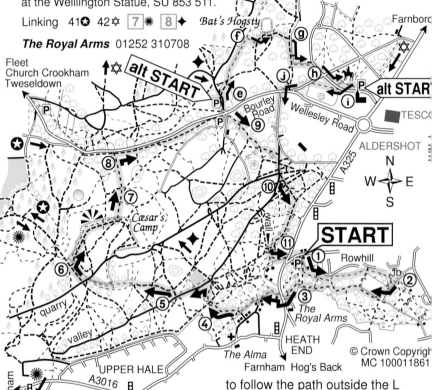

① At Rowhill car park, Aldershot, follow the track next to the house away from the road (100m). Just after the last garden (10m) turn L down the steps (100m). Cross a brook, the infant Blackwater River, and go on (100m). At the R bend turn L down the side path to the brook and continue beside it to the *tarmac* path from the bridge (500m).
② Turn R up the path (100m) & R up steps to the field. Cut across it to follow the path outside the L edge. Keep on round R & L bends to the pond (550m) and up to the source of the Blackwater (150m).
③ From the bend, zig-zag up the steps (30m) and turn L to the road (150m). The **Royal Arms** is 80m L. Crossing is hazardous. Look over the main road for the path at the R end of the garden wall then cross to it (40m). Climb the steep path and continue along the garden fences to the wide cross path from between the gardens L (350m).

④ Turn R up through the trees and stay ahead over the ridge track to the edge of the valley (300m). Drop down the steep path to the corner of the pond (80m). ✦ Turn L up the main valley track L to the junction after the pond (250m). ✳

⑤ Turn R on the side track (80m) and L up the cross track. When the track shrinks (250m) keep to the path ahead (150m) and past the ramparts in the trees R up to the next hard track (200m). Continue on the other side, 20m L, still outside the ramparts (150m). ◯

⑥ At the edge of the plateau turn R through the Cæsar's Camp ramparts and follow the little path at the L edge (300m). Go round a bend overlooking the circular reservoir (Army Waterworks) and on to the corner of the plateau (300m) facing the N Downs.

⑦ Go back (50m) then down the very steep path through the pebble layer, over the water duct (100m) to the track junction (100m). Stay ahead down between knolls almost to Bourley Road (250m). ✿

⑧ Turn R on the path near the road and keep to it all the way down to the Crossways parking area - tracks with parking spaces on both sides of the road (850m).

ⓔ *Extension of 2km/1¼ miles to the Wellington Statue: Walk up through the parking area on the N side of the road (120m) and bear R on the next side track (120m). After the cross track follow the little path beside the Claycart Stream. Watch out for a little water chute then a pipe crossing the stream (300m).*

ⓕ *After the pipe (15m) take the little path R up to the track (100m).*

Go L on the track round a R bend (near Bat's Hogsty) (100m) and up to the boundary track (200m).

ⓖ *Go R on the track to the corner of the fence (200m) then L on the path beside the fence (150m).*

ⓗ *Walk R along the road (100m), over the crossroads (100m) then L up the knoll to the statue and down towards the church (100m).*

ⓘ *From the car park walk over the grass L of the knoll with the statue (100m) then cross the road and go through the football field to the gateway at the far end (200m). Go L up the road (200m) and R on the verge of Bourley Road (80m).*

ⓙ *Cross the road to the concrete track and follow it up the boundary (300m). When it curves L at the top, fork R on the hard track up over the little ridge (200m). ✦⑩*

⑨ From the parking area on the S side of the road cross the ditch (Claycart Stream) to the adjacent army road. Immediately after the cattle grid turn L up the side path. Avoid R forks and keep on to the major hard track on top (450m) Turn R over the little ridge (100m).

⑩ Go on down to the junction with the hard track R (100m) then turn L over the open space with several tracks to the uphill track. Ascend onto the ridge - traffic is usually audible (200m). Follow the ridge track R up to a complex of tracks at a short concrete wall (400m).

⑪ Over the summit bear L down the straight sunken path (80m) and turn L on the first downhill side path to the road (100m). Cross the main road and go down the side road. Cross to the car park beside the first house R (100m).

45 Englemere Pond, Swinley Park and Lily Hill

About 7½km/4¾ miles; heath, forest and public parks at the edge of Bracknell with an extension of 2½km/1½ miles in Swinley Forest and a short cut of 1½km/1 mile. OS maps 1:25000 160 Windsor, 1:50000 175 Reading.

Start from the roadside parking area on Swinley Road, the B3017, 100m S of the railway bridge, SU 900 681, or from Englemere Pond car park 100m N of the bridge. Free car parks at Lily Hill Park and Longhill Park are on the route.

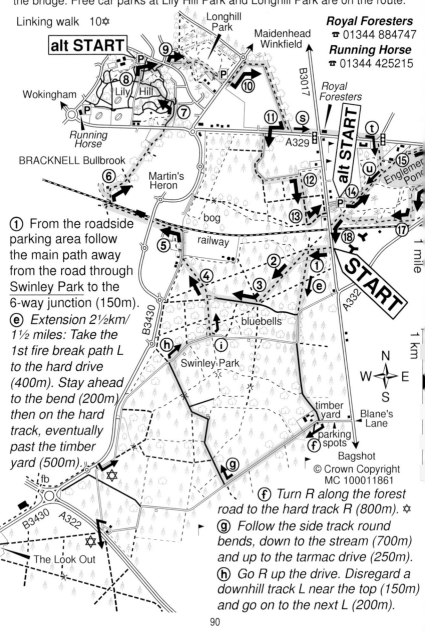

Royal Foresters
☎ 01344 884747
Running Horse
☎ 01344 425215

① From the roadside parking area follow the main path away from the road through <u>Swinley Park</u> to the 6-way junction (150m).

ⓔ *Extension 2½km/ 1½ miles: Take the 1st fire break path L to the hard drive (400m). Stay ahead to the bend (200m) then on the hard track, eventually past the timber yard (500m).*

ⓕ *Turn R along the forest road to the hard track R (800m). ✿*

ⓖ *Follow the side track round bends, down to the stream (700m) and up to the tarmac drive (250m).*

ⓗ *Go R up the drive. Disregard a downhill track L near the top (150m) and go on to the next L (200m).*

© Crown Copyright
MC 100011861

① *Descend L to the cross track (250m). Continue ahead.* →④

② Take the 2nd firebreak path L to the major junction (500m).

③ Bear R along the hard track to the cross track (350m) and turn R.

④ Stay ahead to the gateway near houses at the edge of Bracknell (300m) then follow the lane R to the railway (150m).

⑤ Go round the L bend then on beside the railway (200m), under the road bridge and past Martin's Heron station to the cross path at the Bull Brook (300m).

⑥ Turn R under the railway. Stay on the tarmac path round the R bend (100m) and up to the main road (550m). Cross into Lily Hill Park and go up the hard path near the edge (200m).

⑦ After the L bend on the ridge, turn down the path R of the grassy valley to the drive (300m).

⑧ Turn R (100m). At the curve below the car park, take the hard path R winding up the end of the hill. Between L & R bends near the top, turn L down to the road opposite Badgers Way (200m).

⑨ Turn R along the pavement (50m) then L along Milman Close to the end (100m). Continue on the path through the trees (30m). After the cross track climb the bank into Longhill Park and follow the path curving R at the edge of the grass to the car park and road (300m).

⑩ Slightly L (20m) cross the road and follow the footpath in the trees beside the road (150m). Go round the corner of the fence R and stay ahead to the main road (500m).

Ⓢ *Short cut of 1¾km/1 mile: Walk along the pavement L to the cross*

*roads at the **Royal Foresters** (200m) and carry on to the next road junction (400m).*

Ⓣ *Cross the main road R and take the footpath away from the road to the pond (200m).*

Ⓤ *Turn R on the long straight path and keep on (passing near the car park R) to the road (500m).* →⑱

⑪ Walk along the pavement R (200m). After the wall and fence of the last garden opposite, cross the road into the corner of the wood. Follow the boundary path away from the road curving round a hillock (300m). After the hillock turn L, continuing beside the boundary fence until it zigzags LR (250m).

⑫ Turn R. Go down the firebreak through the pine plantation into a dip and up to the track junction just before the railway (300m).

⑬ Turn L along the main track to the road (150m). Slightly L (30m) carry on to the car park (70m).

⑭ From Englemere Pond car park take the path away from the road to the long straight heath path (100m) and follow it L to the pond (250m).

⑮ Carry on round the end of the pond and back on the other side to the end bend in the garden fence L just before a footbridge (600m).

⑯ Take the side path L diverging from the fence. Keep to the same direction to the railway (200m).

⑰ Turn R on the path parallel with the railway. Stay on this path round the zigzag opposite the house and eventually curve R to the straight cross path just before the car park (500m). Turn L to the corner of the wood near the railway (100m).

⑱ Join the road and cross the railway to the footpath R (150m).

Aldershot became the home of the British Army when the Government bought large tracts of heath in 1854. It was part of Domesday Book Crondall but is first heard of as the hamlet, *Alreshute*, in a list of 1316. The medieval church, St Michael, probably derives from a chapel of Crondall which existed before 1400.

Ambarrow Court was a large house. It has been demolished and the grounds, with the hill, belong to the National Trust. During World War II it was a secret RADAR countermeasures research station of the Royal Aircraft Establishment.

The **Arboretum** at Windlesham is a charitable trust and allows free access to pedestrians during the hours of daylight. Near the brook, excavation yielded Saxon, Roman and Iron Age finds, including a coin of Addedomarus, of about 20 BC, King of the Trinovantes (an Essex tribe). The arboretum was the brain-child of Major William Spowers 1925-2009, and the product of his own physical labour and scavenging. He was an Australian who served in the Australian, British and Indian Armies in North Africa, Italy, India and Burma and started the Book Department at Christies. He bought Old House Farm in 1957, added land from the former nursery, started planting in 1960 and turned marsh into ponds.

Arborfield is not a Domesday Book manor. It was probably detached from the Bishop of Salisbury's Sonning estate in the 13th century which would account for it being an enclave of Wiltshire until the 19th century. The manor house is featured anonymously in *Our Village* by Mary Russel Mitford. The Church, St Bartholomew's, an airy Victorian building (1863) replaced the earlier crumbling church. Points of interest: flint façade; reclining alabaster figure of William Standon, d 1639, who claimed to be an Atrebate. The Arborfield Army Camp, mainly in Barkham Parish. started as an army remount depot before WWI, collecting and distributing large numbers of horses. It is now the HQ of REME and the REME school for electrical and aircraft technicians. It has a museum.

The **Army waterworks** were constructed around 1865. Ceramic and brick runnels around Cæsar's Camp and Beacon Hill catch run off and delivery it to ponds. From the treatment plant it was pumped to the round covered reservoir.

Ash Lock (29) is at approximately the mid point on the Basingstoke Canal and is the highest lock, the canal being level from here to Basingstoke.

Bagshot was part Windlesham until 1874. The village probably derived from inns on the great west road to Winchester, Southampton, Salisbury and Exeter. The earliest inn recorded by name was *The Crown,* in a rental of 1515, but a John Hostiller of Bagshote was plaintiff in a theft case in 1417. A guild was licensed in 1480 to fund St Mary's chapel at Bagshot as a cooperative chantry. The church, St Anne, was built in 1884. Records are bedevilled by use of the name Bagshot for the village, parish, medieval manor, royal park and Surrey bailiwick of Windsor Forest. It is not in the Domesday Book, it was *Bagshete* in the 1164 pipe roll, possibly from Bacga's shete: *Bacga*, a Saxon owner and *shete,* water channel. *A History of Bagshot & Windlesham* Marie Eddle 1977 Phillimore 262p

Bagshot Heath of old was a large wild area on the corners of Berkshire, Surrey and Hampshire straddling the main road to Exeter (now the A30) between the Thames and Hartley Wintney. In 1722 Defoe wrote: *I took the Winchester coach .. dined at a small village called Egham and from thence through the worst heathy country I ever saw...18 miles to Farnham.* William Cobbett described a spot in the New Forest in 1822 as *more barren and miserable than Bagshot Heath.* Much of the heath has disappeared under Camberley, Farnborough, Fleet, Yateley and forestry plantations. The large remnant between Camberley and Bracknell is the 19th century commons of Windlesham and Frimley and Crown Land which was heath in the Swinley Bailiwick of Windsor Forest. There was a World War II prisoner-of war-camp on Old Dean Common where the housing estate is now.

Bagshot Park is a crown estate of 320 acres with 81 acres of parkland. It was the site of a medieval royal hunting lodge. The earliest record is the grant of the keepership to William Mitchell in 1486. The Stuart kings made frequent use of the lodge but, after Charles II, its resident rangers were royal relatives or officials of state. The present Tudoresque house, red brick and Portland Stone, is the residence of HRH The Earl of Wessex. It was built in 1857 for the 3rd son of Queen Victoria, the Duke of Connaught (1850-1942). He was a professional soldier who rose from cadet at Sandhurst to C-in-C, Aldershot in the 1890s and was Governor General of Canada. It was the Army Chaplains' HQ 1946-96.

Barkham first appears as BEORCHAM in 952 in a grant by Eadred, king of Wessex. The present Manor House, now apartments, was built around 1700. It has Georgian and Victorian additions. The ornamental water was the stewpond for storing live fish and may have been a moat. George Washington's mother, Mary Ball, came from a Barkham family. There is a record of sale for The Bull alehouse in 1749. Barkham's last Court Baron (manorial land board) was held there in 1846. The Church, St James the Apostle, consecrated 1861, was built by John Walter III of Bearwood who bought Barkham Manor in 1874. It is the latest in a long line of churches on this spot since Norman times. No church is listed in the Domesday Book; the earliest record is for the advowson in 1220. The anonymous wooden figure may be Agnes de Nevile whose ownership of the manor was disputed in the 1330s. David Davis, rector 1782-1819, figures in social history. He grew up in Barbados and gave evidence against slavery; as champion of farm workers, he wrote the treatise *The Case for Labourers in Husbandry Stated and Considered*. The moat near the church was probably for the medieval manor house.   *Barkham, 952-1990* Richard Noble 1994 38pp

Barkham Brook drains westward to the River Loddon.

Barossa Common is part of Bagshot Heath which had its commoners' rights extinguished for the army training area. The Surrey part was Frimley Common and the Berkshire part was Windsor Forest. The fenced part has rifle ranges.

The **Basingstoke Canal** is 37 miles long. It starts at Byfleet where it joined the Wey Navigation in 1796 at the apogee of the British canal building period. It did not pay for itself. Agricultural produce was conveyed to London; coal and horse dung brought back. The last large contract was to carry bricks from Up Nateley for re-building Aldershot army camp at the end of the 19th century. No barges reached Basingstoke after 1910. It is now owned jointly by Surrey and Hants County Councils. Cut by the M3, it is navigable only as far as Odiham Castle.
          London's Lost Route to Basingstoke P A L Vine 1968 David & Charles 212pp

Bat's Hogsty is a curiosity amongst walkers because of its name and because they cannot find it; amongst archæologists because they cannot decide what it was for. It is a rectangle of about ¾ acre enclosed by four mounds with three ditches between them, externally 300' x 270', in total about 1¾ acres.
          The Bat's Hogsty Earthworks D Westlake Aldershot Hist & Arch Soc 1983 & 84

Beacon Hill is on similar terrain to Cæsar's Camp. The trig point was erected in 1951 at a cost of £11 10s 9d. Two beacons are shown on the hill in Norden's map of 1595. This beacon site, in Crondall parish, was part of a county network fanning out from the Isle of Wight. Beacons told of the fall of Troy in 1084 BC but the first record of English beacons appears in 1324 when Edward II made ready for invasion by his queen. From Dogmersfield, Edward IV ordered the beacons to be maintained in 1468. A French report in 1539 attributed deterrent value to these beacons. Walsingham obtained an analysis of the forces mustered when the beacons were lit for the Armada in 1588. The last-known record is for a trial of beacons in Devon in 1638. Early beacons were piles of timber. Later, a barrel of pitch was specified and funding for constructing beacons and keeping watch was assigned to the parishes. Symbols on an old map show beacons as iron baskets on poles but these may have been small ones for short distances. The word comes from the Saxon *beacnian*, to beckon, but some place-names like Beaconsfield derive from *Beca*, a Saxon man's name.   *The Beacon System in Hampshire* H T White Proc Hants Field Club Vol X 1931 28pp

Blackbushe Airfield is a civil aviation complex for small aircraft. It opened as RAF Hartfordbridge on its plateau (Terrace 7) in 1942. It was used for glider trials by the Royal Aircraft Establishment before the runways were ready then a succession of squadrons flew Mustangs, Tomahawks, Blenheims, Lockheed Venturas and Mosquitos. The Free French Lorraine Squadron made daylight bombing on V-I sites. Mitchell bombers flew to the bridge too far, at Arnhem. Spitfires shot up the Calais area as a feint prior to D-Day in Operation Starkey. It was renamed RAF Blackbushe 1944-46 and became a civil airport in 1947. Silver City moved in in 1947 and RAF Transport Command flew Dakotas for the Berlin Airlift in 1948. Aircraft used to be towed to hangers across the A30.
Hampshire Airfields in the Second World War R Brooks 1996 Countryside Books 192pp

The **Blackwater** River flows into the Loddon at Swallowfield. It was the main river in ancient times. During the Ice Age the source was the chalk mountains of the Weald probably near Hindhead; the great valley and masses of flint gravel provide the evidence. Its present puny form is due not only to climate change but also to the capture of its headwaters by a branch of the Wey. It flowed to the sea through the London area in a valley which was subsequently joined by the Lower Thames. The present-day Blackwater rises on Rowhill at Aldershot, and forms a few miles of the Hampshire boundary with Surrey and Berkshire. All of its water comes out of the Tertiary Sands with low calcium. The A331 sweeps through the original Ice Age Blackwater valley.

Borough Court is ancient. The core of the building is a 5-bay timber framed hall of about 1480. John Fielder bought it in 1561 and added the tall chimneys.

Bracknell was a small village until the middle of the 20th century, its earliest church being the present one of 1850. The Greater London Plan of 1944 proposed 10 new satellite towns and Bracknell was assigned as one in 1949. Its Development Corporation functioning until 1982. The scheme created self contained estates with shops, schools, etc. The first three were Priestwood 1951, Easthampstead 1957 and Bullbrook 1957. Lily Hill and Martin's Heron were houses with large grounds which became part of Bullbrook.

Bramshill is said to be the finest Jacobean house in Hampshire. It was the Red Cross HQ for World War II and residence of the King of Romania in exile. The Home Office purchased the estate in 1953 and made the house into the Police Staff College for England and Wales. BROMSELLE was the name of two Domesday Book manors belonging to the Norman Baron Hugh de Port of Basing. The estate has had many occupants and was emparked around 1350. Edward Zouche, 1556?-1625, 11th Baron Harringworth built the present house using the foundations and walls of earlier houses. He was a minor government official under Elizabeth I but became more prominent under James I. The long building period, 1605-1625, and mean plan suggest he was not over-wealthy. A keen horticulturalist, he is sometimes credited with or blamed for introducing the Scots Pine to the south of England. Jonson's masque *Lovers Made Men* was written for Bramshill in 1617 - said to be the first operatic performance in English. During a visit to consecrate the Bramshill chapel, George Abbott, Archbishop of Canterbury (tomb in Holy Trinity, Guildford), went hunting and shot the gamekeeper. Peter Hawkins lost his life; the Archbishop lost face.

Bramshill Forest is a Forestry Commission name for plantations on the estate and elsewhere, nearby. Above Bramshill Park is the western edge of Yateley Heath plateau (Terrace 7, Anglian Glaciation, 47-59 000 years BP). Sand and gravel workings have scalped the lower parts, some of the pits used for landfill.

Broadmoor Hospital is one of three institutions for the dangerously insane in England with about 260 patients (male only since 2007) and 1500 staff. Most patients arrive as a result of criminal trials but some are from other psychiatric hospitals. In 1800 James Hadfield tried to shoot George III but was denied his wish to be hung, drawn and quartered for treason, being found to be mad. This precedent ultimately led to an Act of 1860 establishing the Broadmoor Criminal Lunatic Asylum. The secure part was 10 acres for men and 3½ for women with 150 acres of farmland. The main buildings in "Prison Romanesque" were by Sir Joshua Jebb. Broadmoor remained under the Home Office until 1948 thereafter being the province of the Ministry of Health. Since 1960 it has been called Broadmoor Hospital. Useful alumni were Richard Dadd the painter (42 years) and Dr Minors, the Oxford Dictionary scholar (around 1900).

Cæsar's Camp, near Bracknell, is an Iron Age hillfort of about 700 BC on a promontory (of Terrace 11), fortified by two banks and ditch with an extra bank & ditch at the level S end. Between here and the Devil's Highway at Wickham Bushes, Roman pots and a brick floor have been found, possibly a mansio.

Cæsar's Camp near Farnham: View near the corner in line with the tower of Farnborough Airport below and the Old Dean TV Tower on the skyline: Just R of this line are the arch of Wembley Stadium and the tall buildings of London. The North Downs are ½R . Guildford Cathedral stands in front of the notch in the Downs where the River Wey crosses the ridge. Visible through the notch is St Martha's Hill. Far R are the South Downs. L of the Old Dean Tower on the end of plateau 11 is Broadmoor. Further L, are the wind turbine at Reading and the Didcot Power Station or its smoke. Underfoot is a thick pebble bed capping the plateau. This is Terrace 12 of a pre-Anglian glaciation perhaps 1m years ago, 60m/200 feet above the present-day source of the Blackwater River. West of the ramparts, flints were quarried and are seen in local Victorian buildings.

Cæsar's Camp is an Iron Age promontory fort of 28 acres The flat parts have double and treble ramparts but the steep scarp was probably not fortified. The straight mound across the middle is the county boundary and has post holes of the 12th century pale of the Bishop of Winchester's Farnham deer park. The Battle of Farnham (Anglo-Saxon Chronicle 893) is said to have taken place below. Alfred the Great had already made peace with settler Vikings but a raiding group came to Kent after several years in France. He brought them to battle here, won and recaptured booty, then chased them over the Thames.

California Country Park was a holiday camp in the 1920s & 30s with ballroom, zoo, speedway and steam railway, said to be the inspiration for the Pontin camps. Longmoor Pond started as a claypit for brick-making in the 1850s.

Camberley was a 19th century spontaneous new town on the uninhabited heath of Frimley Manor. The impetus was Sandhurst Royal Military College for which construction workers' houses were built in 1802. The Duke of York Hotel, built for visitors, became a nucleus for other service providers. When the Staff College opened in1862, the Duke of Cambridge Hotel was built for its visitors and became another nucleus - hence Yorktown and Cambridgetown. The GPO devised the name *Camberley* in 1877 to avoid confusion with Cambridge. Much of the land sold from Frimley Manor was large plots for large houses and the modern housing estates have arisen by the redevelopment of these, which infill still continues.   *The Story of Camberley 1798-1987* Gordon Wellard 1989 134pp

CEDAR is the Centre for Dairy Research, part of the Department of Agriculture of Reading University and one of the world's leading research centres on bovine health. It is funded largely from research contracts and a levy on milk producers. There are 645 hectares of grazing and forage land and 450 cattle. On the same site is the Veterinary Epidemiology & Economic Research Unit.

Chequers Bridge takes its name from the nearby pub which accommodated workers and horses during the building of the canal. The car park occupies the Crondall wharf. The house nearest the bridge is thought to have been the original office of the canal company. From here to Blacksmith's Bridge are several WWII pillboxes and large concrete blocks for obstructing the canal.

Crondall was the Domesday Book Hundred of CORENDEL with the manors of Crondall (CRVNDELE), Cove, Itchel, Farnborough, Long Sutton and Badley. It appears in Alfred the Great's will, drafted around 885, as a bequest to Ethelm, his nephew. *He* passed it to St Swithun's Abbey, Winchester. At the Dissolution in 1539, it was granted to the Dean & Chapter of Winchester Cathedral. The village roads reflect the Saxon layout with houses of all periods after 1475. The *Plume of Feathers* occupies a prime site and was probably always an inn. The jettied part dates from about 1500; the middle part would have replaced an earlier hall house a bit later. Externally, under the jettied corner, is the end of the dragon beam of the front parlour which supports joists for jettying on two sides. It is said Cromwell stayed here in October 1645, on his way to the siege of Basing House. The church, All Saints, was built when styles were changing in the 12th century with Norman round arches in the nave but slightly pointed arches in the chancel. The clerestory arches are Victorian brick restorations. Features of interest: the east end of the aisles distorted by the original central tower (replaced by the brick north tower in 1657 for £428), the slanting chancel arch pillars, the possible Saxon font, a large brass of about 1380 in the chancel floor. *Medieval Houses in Crondall* M A Jeffries *Crondall Society News*

Crookham was part of the great Domesday Book estate of Crondall, belonging to the monastery in Winchester from the Saxon era. The name first appears in writing in 1257 when the Prior and Convent of St Swithun granted to *Henry called the hunter our bailiff ... land ... in Crokeham formerly held of us in villeinage* - for 30 marks down + 60 shillings pa. It was a hamlet and tithing of Crondall until the parish was detached in 1842 with the new Christ Church. Crookham and Fleet became civil parishes in 1894 with the canal as their boundary.

Crowthorne developed on empty heath, at the building of Wellington College and Broadmoor in the 19th century. The name first appears in Norden's map of 1607 where it seems to label a tree, perhaps a boundary mark, at the juncture of three forest walks (Bigshot, Sandhurst and Easthampstead) and four tracks. The area was part of the Windsor Forest and the only ancient records are the proceedings of the swainmote (Forest court) at Wokingham which go back to 1586. The forest was broken up in 1800 when allotments were made to local landowners. Most of the village lay in the ancient parish of Sandhurst. The Church, St John the Baptist, was consecrated in 1873 and Crowthorne became a parish in 1874. The Road Research Laboratory was hived off from the National Physical Laboratory Teddington in 1953 but is an independent company now, TRL. It does research on all aspects of land transport, statistical as well as vehicle testing and road construction. It occupies 253 acres. *The Crow on the Thorn* Martin Prescott 1975 347pp

Curzon Bridges are on the line of the pre-railway road from Frimley to Guildford. The wall below on the east side was required under the railway Act to prevent canal horses being frightened by steam engines.

Deepcut village takes its name from the canal which was cut through the hills in the late 1780s before the era of power tools and vehicles. Most of the sand removed went to build the embankment across the Blackwater Valley. Deepcut army depot is the home of the Royal Logistics Corps (until 2013). The track in the wood on the north side of the canal follows the line of the army railway, the WWI extension of the Bisley line which crossed the canal near lock 15.

Devil's Highway Roman road - see box on page 15.

Dipley Mill is a picturesque dwelling best seen from the road bridge over the River Whitewater. It may be on the site of the Mattingley mill recorded in the Domesday Book The last miller was William White who worked it from 1905. It had two undershot wheels and was converted to a house in 1921. The garden shed is a pillbox and there are World War II blocks at the road bridge.
Water & Wind Mills of Hampshire & the IoW Ed Monica Ellis Southampton Univ Ind Arch Gp 1978

Dogmersfield was the Domesday Book manor of ORMERESFELT which was taxed for 100 pigs @100 shillings. It was given to the Bishop of Durham in the time of Henry I. From the 12th century until bought by Henry VIII it belonged to the Bishops of Bath & Wells, who lived there. The medieval church was near the house but was pulled down in 1806. The present village is a fusion of Pilcot and Chatter Alley hamlets with a Victorian church, All Saints. Pilcot had a mill.

Dogmersfield Park is a Queen Anne mansion built in 1728 but much restored after a serious fire in 1982. It is now a hotel but has been a college of the de Salle Brothers and HQ of the US computing company Amdahl. Henry VII rode with his son, Arthur, to the Tudor bishop's palace here to greet Catherine of Aragon on her arrival in England, hence the *Queen's Head* in the village.

Eversley was part of Edward the Confessor's founding endowments of Westminster Abbey, around 1060. A translation of the charter is displayed in the church. The Domesday Book indicates EVRESLEI had been four manors with two mills. In the 15th century its dues consisted of a sparrow hawk. The name may derive from Anglo-Saxon *Eofresleah*, boar's clearing or the man's name, *Eofor*. The church, St Mary, is not mentioned in the Domesday Book but a valuation of the benefice (£8) exists from 1235 and a sarsen under the trap door near the font suggests a pre-Christian site of worship. The chancel dates from about 1500 and the nave from 1735. Charles Kingsley was rector 1844-1875. Points of interest: the barrel vaulting of the roof (1876); the chancel screen (1730), the only 18th century one in Hampshire; the brass memorial cross of 1502 in the chancel floor; the south window of the chancel, 1942, with two water babies and fishing rod; Charles Kingsley's grave (white marble) near the road wall; the Wellingtonia potted as a seed in 1875 by his daughter.

Ewshot was hived off as a parish from Crondall and Crookham in 1886. It first appears in records of 1279 as land of the Bishop of Worcester - a Giffard. The church, St Mary's, suits this period but is Victorian (1873). The flint pebbles of *Windmill*'s walls would have come from the quarry near Cæsar's Camp.

Farnborough Airport is now largely civil being used by air taxis and private owners. It was the Royal Aircraft Establishment, 1918-1991, which originated as an army balloon factory built in 1905. By WWI it was the Royal Aircraft Factory but changed to RAE when the RAF was created in 1918. It went on to be world leader in aluminium alloys, carbon fibre, radio, aviation medicine and crash investigation and still has a defence research presence. The airfield was a fighter base in WWII. The Farnborough Air Sciences Trust Museum is chiefly about research and development and occupies the Balloon School building. Farnborough itself straddles the Portsmouth branch of the great western road. It was FERNEBERGA in the Domesday Book and has a 12th century church.

Finchampstead was FINCHAMSTEDE in the Berkshire folios of Domesday Book. It is also mentioned in the Anglo-Saxon Chronicle for 1098 and 1103 (repetition error?): *in the Summer a pool of blood welled up in Finchampstead out of soil*. Finchampstead was a bailiwick of Windsor Forest responsible for the red deer walks of Sandhurst, Bigshotte, Bearwood and Easthampstead. The old village has always been at Fair Green, some way from the church; a 3-day Whit fair was granted in 1458 (Henry VI). The mound on which the church stands is likely to be an Iron-age fort which may have been used by the Romans.   *Finchampstead, past present & future* S Paulden Finchampstead Soc 1977 72pp

Finchampstead Church, St James, has Norman walls modernized with Tudor windows and pointed chancel arch. Features of interest: Norman or late Saxon font with a round stem of 1855; rare apsidal sanctuary; 1½ slit windows in the N wall of the nave; brick tower of 1720; brasses for Henry Hinde, Tudor Royal Purveyor, 1580 and Elizabeth Blighe d.1635; list of rectors from 1299. Samuel Marsh broke the quill in 1645 when obliged to sign the Solemn League and Covenant during the Civil War leaving the parish without a rector for 15 years.

Finchampstead Ridges were acquired by the National Trust in 1911 when John Walters III sold the Bearwood estate to aid the finances of the *The Times*. The road was constructed in 1863 and the Wellingtonias were planted in 1869 by John Walters II. The ridges are the heath-clad edge of a gravel plateau (Terrace 8, Anglian) above the huge valley of the small Blackwater River.

Firgrove Manor is now apartments. It is a Georgian house, built in 1736. The design and date suggest the architect was John James, who built Warbrook for himself in Eversley village. The last Lords of the Manor of Eversley lived here - the Copes who also owned Bramshill until they had to sell up in the 1930s.

Fleet was a 19th century new town that grew up on the almost uninhabited heath, common land of the tithing of Crookham in the Parish of Crondall. The first mention of the name is in the Crondall Customary of 1567, a *parcell of grounde now inclosed called Fleate Pond*. In the same document Widow Cawett had a croft near the pond, *Le Flete*. Fleet Pond Station interpolated in 1847 by the LSWR put the place on the map and the arrival of the army at Aldershot in 1855 provided jobs. Faster trains brought Fleet into the London commuter belt and the army spawned the Royal Aircraft Establishment - a major employer. All Saints Church was consecrated in 1862 and Fleet became a parish.

Fleet Pond is a nature reserve owned by the borough and maintained by the Fleet Pond Society to produce a diversity of habitats. Reed warblers, bitterns water rails and cormorants are regular visitors. The main feeder is the Gelvert Stream which drains the area around Cæsar's Camp. The pond was managed for fish stocks possibly from the Anglo Saxon era to the 19th century. In an indenture of 1505 the prior of St Swithun leased *La Flete* to William Gifford, Knight of Itchell for 23s 4d plus 100 fish per annum but retained the right to fish himself! The Latin text changed to English for the fish names : *pykes, tenches, perches, bremes* et *roches*. The railway split the pond. Fleet Pond Station was for London excursion trains - picnics in summer; skating in winter.

Frenchman's Oak, now propped up by scaffolding, is said to mark the limit to which paroled officers could walk on the London road from the great prisoner-of-war camp at Odiham during the Napoleonic Wars. The milestone next to it, 40 miles to London, was, presumably, the real mark.

Frimhurst was the home of the suffragette and composer Dame Ethel Smyth, 1858-1944, whose music is performed more in Germany than in Britain. At a boathouse opposite the lodge, Harmsworths hired out rowing boats, 1901-38.

Frimley is not a Domesday Book village but the name gets its first airing in a charter of 933 as FREMELEY, suggesting derivation from *Fremma's clearing*. It was on the edge of Windsor Forest whose boundary was the Blackwater. On its heath and common land arose Camberley.

Gibraltar Barracks was founded in 1976 and replaced Southwood Barracks in Cove at a Royal Engineers Depot. The officers' mess is Minley Manor.

The River **Hart** starts from Crondall village pond and joins the Whitewater at Bramshill. It gives its name to Hart District (Fleet, Yateley and Hartley Wintney).

Hartley Wintney is a large village whose charm lies in the jumble of styles and large green with duck pond and cricket pitch - the Cricket Club dates from 1770. It is not in the Domesday Book probably being then part of the great Royal manor of Odiham. Its first mention is in a 13th century will bequeathing it to the Cistercian Priory. On dissolution the priory's estate went to Henry VIII's cellarer. It was a coaching stop on the London to Exeter road with several inns and farriers. William Cobbett rode by in November 1821 and noted the planting of the oaks on the green. The old church, St Mary's, has a 19th century tower and transepts appended to the 13th century nave and chancel. "Hangman" Hawley and Field Marshall Viscount Alanbrooke are buried there. The new church, St John's, was built in 1870 when the village had moved down to the turnpike road. Before Camberley arose, the *White Lion* (now with Tea Rooms) was the first sign of habitation after Bagshot. General Walker had his Cavalier HQ here in 1644 during the Civil War. The present building dates from about then. In 1776 it was the venue for the public meeting which first proposed the Basingstoke Canal; as the eastern part would pass through heath, most of the interested landowners lived between Crookham and Basingstoke.

The Old Village of Hartley Wintney David Gorsky 5th ed 1995 HW Preservation Soc 73pp

Hawley was a hamlet and medieval tithing of Yateley. It had 16 dwellings in 1567. The village was enclosed from the heath in 1817. Hawley Hill is the same plateau as Blackbushe. Hawley Woods and the heath extending to Fleet Pond were part of Minley estate acquired by the War Department in 1936. They are used by army for troop training, route marches, logistic support and attack. The wood and lake are also used by film makers. The air strips are of unknown origin. They are in the position of a the old army balloon training station and may subsequently have been used for training army spotter pilots. The author would welcome definite information.

Hawley Lake is used by the army for aquatic exercises. The Royal Engineers training site is Hawley Hard. There are myths about the digging of the lake by WWI soldiers. The first OS 1" map, of 1816, has a pond a furlong long in an area labelled Peat Moor. The Yateley tithe map of 1846, has *Hawley Pond* without creeks, 560 yards long. The first OS 6" map, 1871, shows it at its present size and shape. There was much landscaping in the late 1850s by Raikes Currie of Minley Manor and the dam may have been raised then.

Hazeley Bottom is a hamlet of old cottages. It was originally home to the artisans brought by Lord Zouche to construct the Bramshill house in 1605.

Hazeley Heath is a private common on a ridge of plateau gravels (Terrace 6, Anglian) between the farms of the Bramshill estate and those around it, on the Tertiary Sands. Until 1850 there was a race course between Hazeley House and Purdie's Farm, patronised by the owners of the many large houses nearby.

Hazeley House is a late 18th century house, the family home for generations of the Singleton family from the time of George III until World War II (see the Celtic cross in Mattingley churchyard). The garden is now a private arboretum.

High Curley is a promontory of the plateau (terrace 11, pre-Anglian) whose edge forms Chobham Ridges on which runs the Maultway. The army tracks are now used for training drivers on difficult terrain; until 2003 they were used for testing army vehicles. Maultway may derive from the Anglo-Saxon *molt*, sheep. Farmers on the more fertile soils of the North Downs may have sent flocks this way for the summer to the great expanse of Surrey common land later called Bagshot Heath. Heatherside was the name given to his house and 300 acres by the Swiss botanist Mongredien. He planted the Wellingtonias.

Lily Hill Park was a private garden for the house originally in Windsor Forest in an area later made fashionable by racing at Ascot. The 19th century owners landscaped it, continuing the Georgian fashion. The estate was bought for house building by Bracknell Development Corporation in 1955, the landscaped grounds being retained as a public park. The house was later sold.

Lily Hill House a family history V G Hunt Bracknell History Society

Lock 15 of the Basingstoke Canal is the start of the Deepcut series of locks, 15-28, the main ascent, where the Basingstoke Canal climbs 29m/95 feet.

The River **Loddon** rises from the chalk in Basingstoke and joins the Thames near Wargrave. The area enclosing its tributaries is the Loddon Basin.

Long Valley has been a cavalry and tank training area. The test tracks are now used for cross country driver training and, by the Army Trials and Development Unit, for testing wheeled vehicles.

The **Look Out** is a recreational centre for Bracknell on Crown Estate land, managed as commercial forest. The area is a remnant of Windsor Forest that stretched north to the Thames, west to the Blackwater and south to the Downs.

The **Martineau** Cottages were built by John Martineau 1834-1910 to improve the living conditions of farm workers. He was a household pupil of Charles Kingsley. Homilies are incised on the timbers. The houses are owned by a trust; there are several groups around Eversley and more in Suffolk.

John Martineau Pupil of Kingsley Violet Martineau 1922 Edward Arnold.

Mattingley is MATINGELEGE in the Domesday Book, a small manor with mill in Holdshott Hundred. The church is a delightful timber frame building with oak pillars and herringbone brickwork - thought to be early Tudor but with aisles added and the roof cunningly extended in 1867. The bricks in the old part were shaped to fit the frame. It was a chapel of ease to Heckfield. The pope did not license it for burial of the dead until 1425. The Celtic cross in the churchyard marks the graves of the Singleton family of Hazeley House; nearby is a rare cob wall.   *The History of a Hampshire Parish Heckfield & Mattingley* W J James 58pp

The **Military Museum** in Aldershot has an outdoor display of fighting vehicles and, inside, shows how the garrison developed - lots of uniforms. Museums of the Army Physical Training School and the Airborne Forces are nearby.

The **miniature railway** at Frimley Lodge Park started running in 1991. The 3000 feet of rails have three gauges 7¼", 5" & 3½". On 1st Sundays, March-November, the club is open to the public and train rides are available. 3rd Sundays are club members' running days. Wednesdays are maintenance days. The operators are the Frimley & Ascot Locomotive Club.

Minley was the small Domesday Book manor of MINDESLEI in Holdshott Hundred held by Alfsi who was also lord of the manor of Mattingley. In the 18th century the estate belonged to the Tylneys, great Hampshire land-owners, then to the Wyndhams. It was purchased by Raikes Currie, the banker, in the mid-1850s and it stayed in that family until the banking crisis of the 1920s. The War Department bought the estate as a training area in 1936.

Minley Manor - the house - was built 1858-60 on the site of an earlier house as a retirement home for Raikes Currie, the banker. The architect was Henry Clutton, author of *Domestic Architecture of France in the Middle Ages*, and the house is said to owe much to the Chateau de Blois. It was enlarged by Raikes' son and grandson. In *Victorian Country Mansions,* Mark Giraud described the house as "highly Victorian anarchy". When the War Department bought the estate, the house became part of the Staff College. On completion of College extensions in Camberley in the 1960s it was assigned to the Royal Engineers and became the officers' mess. It is now under consideration for sale. It has been used for several films and the TV *Jeeves & Wooster*. The Wellingtonias in the garden form a landmark from afar. *The Manor of Minley* Brian A Myers 1984 38pp

Minley Warren, the Jacobean fore-runner of the present house, was the home of Captain Blood. Despite attempts on the Crown Jewels and the life of the Lord Lieutenant of Ireland, he was saved from execution and had his Irish lands restored to him by Charles II. Historians have hypothesized that while serving with the Roundheads he may have been aiding the king.

Moulsham Green, now a housing estate of Yateley, is mentioned as Mules Fen, a boundary marker of Crondall in King Edgar's charter of 975.

New Mill, hamlet and restaurant on the Blackwater, are probably on the site of one of the Domesday Book mills listed for Eversley. The mill building of 1577 has the wheel and grinding mechanism still in working order. It ground corn until the beginning of the 20th century but has also been a saw mill.

Nine Mile Ride, now a tarmac road, was one of the paths cleared through Windsor forest at the behest of George III.

North Camp was the part of the camp north of the Basingstoke Canal built when the army came to Aldershot in 1855. The Iron Bridge over the canal replaced an earlier pontoon bridge in 1870. Shops and banks sprang up on the edge of the parish of Farnborough which also became known as North Camp and was the main commercial area of Farnborough until the 1960s. The army camp was originally tents and wooden huts but re-building in brick took place in the 1890s. Some of the red brick buildings still stand but modern houses and blocks have risen since the 1970s. North Camp Station was only for army use until 1858. It is on the Reading-Guildford line which opened in 1849.

Odiham has a delightful wide High Street with buildings of many periods, all listed in its own book. The settlement is very ancient. This was a Saxon royal hunting area. Odiham was a Hundred and the first place listed for Hampshire in the Domesday Book - a great royal manor of 78½ hides. Conveniently sited halfway between Winchester and Windsor or London, there are records of many visits by medieval kings. There seems to have been a palace before and after King John's Castle was built. Parliament met in Odiham in 1303 and Elizabeth I held Privy Council meetings here in 1569 and 1591.

Odiham High Street Ed Sheila Millard The Odiham Society Ed2 1994 57pp

Odiham Church, All Saints, is mainly of 13th century flint construction on the site of the Saxon Domesday Book church but much rebuilt. Points of interest: the piscina which may be Saxon; the 14th century pillars of the 3-arched north aisle contrasting with 15th century pillars in the 4-arched south aisle; several brasses now on the walls, one above the lectern of 1498 for William Goode, priest; the heavily carved Jacobean pulpit; the RAF window in the tower arch. Two French gravestones outside the south wall date from the Napoleonic Wars. Outside the gate are the stocks. The pest house, at the SW corner of the graveyard, was built under a bequest of 1625 as an isolation hospital particularly associated with plague. It was used as an alms house 1780-1978.

Odiham Wharf opened in 1793 and expanded to 3 acres with warehouses, offices and workshops near the present car park. Land owners met at *The George* in Odiham to finalise the sale of land for the canal in 1788. The sons of John Pinkerton, the canal's engineer, lived in Odiham to supervise the building.

The **oil pipelines**, indicated by wayside marks, are owned by ESSO and were built in the 1960s. They run from the refinery at Fawley and branch near Alton to Heathrow and Gatwick. The 10" pipe carries only aviation fuel. The 12" pipe carries different products at different times for distribution in the London area.

A **park pale** noted on a map may be visible on the ground as a mound which marked the boundary of the emparked area and originally had high wooden palings. Parks were private enclosures for deer keeping licensed by the crown, mostly medieval in origin. The deer were captured by driving them against the fence (reserves for pursuit hunting were chases). Many were disparked several centuries ago but the name lingered. Houses with *Park* in the name hark back to emparkment real or imaginary. The real ones were usually manor houses.

The Bishop of Winchester's Deer Parks 1200-1400   Proc Hants Arch Soc Vol 43 1988

Pirbright is not a Domesday Book village but was probably cut from Woking Manor by Henry I for his son Robert, Duke of Gloucester. The marriage portion of Katherine of Aragon included Pirbright. The Manor House dates from the 16th century but there are records of a house in 1302; part of its moat is still visible. The mill, next-door, ground corn until the 1930s. The church, St Michael and all the Angels, is Georgian but a church as early as 1200 is deduced from a charter signed as witness by Jordan, parson of Pirefricth (facsimile in church). The grave of Stanley the explorer, BULA MATARI, is in the churchyard.

Pirbright Lodge was the home of Admiral John Byron, 1723-86, who explored the Pacific rather badly, fought a French fleet rather easily and became a grandfather poetically. As midshipman he was shipwrecked in Patagonia for six years; story has it that he set off to retire there but, coming to Pirbright, found it wild enough and stayed. The lane was the Chertsey-Farnham coach road.

The Day before Yesterday - the Story of Pirbright   Helen Yool 1973 56pp

The **pillbox**es were part of the GHQ line between the Thames and Severn estuaries to protect London and the Midlands in the Second World War. The line linked geographical barriers such as the North Downs, River Wey and Basingstoke Canal. Pillboxes and tank traps were at weak points .

Pillboxes - a study of UK defences 1940   H Wills 1985   Secker & Warburg 98pp

Plateaus - Ice Age terraces of the Blackwater: see box on p 63.

Pudding Hill is a promontory of the main plateau (Terrace 11). The trig point was built in 1950 at a cost of £15-14s. It was a 2nd order survey point in the third triangulation of Britain, initiated 1936. Tree cover must have been absent.

Pyestock research station was the National Gas Turbine Establishment 1946 - 91, which tested engines for aircraft and ships and was central to the early development of jet engines. The engine was first proposed at Farnborough in 1926. Frank Whittle, an RAF officer, started his designs independantly in 1927 and patented them in 1930. Power Jet Ltd was set up in Lutterworth to develop Whittle's engines and the prototype flew in 1941. Farnborough designed an engine in 1939 which flew in 1942. The site was founded in 1941 to bring together the Farnborough and Power Jet teams.

Queen's Parade, now used for sport, was where Queen Victoria reviewed the troops. There was a race course around it in the 1870's before Tweseldown was laid out. It was used for trials of early observation balloons for the army.

Railways of the area: see the box on page 29

The **redoubts**, humps on the heath, were defences for guns at the great army training exercises of 1792. About 7000 soldiers participated, infantry, cavalry and artillery. George III inspected and the Reading Mercury reported 200,000 spectators were present at the arrival of the regiments. The camp was lampooned in the London theatres.   *Bastions of Berkshire Berks CC 12pp*

Riseley Mill is the lowest of eight mills on the Whitewater River - late 18th century in origin. It ceased to operate when the mechanism failed in 1910.

Rotherwick was part of the large, royal Saxon manor of Odiham. The name most likely derives from the Saxon *hrither*, cattle, so it may have been the dairy farm for the Royal estate. It became part of Greywell Manor when that was detached from Odiham around 1240 and a manor in its own right in the 16th century which was bought by Richard Tylney in 1629. The village hall, despite its antiquated timber-framed form, was built in 1932 as a memorial for the son of Henry de Forrest, an American, who had leased Tylney Hall for shooting visits. The church was a chapel of ease to Heckfield parish church. The late 13th century chancel is the oldest part. The 15th century nave had timber frame walls (like Mattingley) which can be seen in the gables internally.

Sarsens - see box on page 55.

Sir Henry Morton **Stanley**, 1841-1904, of "Dr Livingstone, I presume" fame retired to Furze Hill in Pirbright Parish, hence the African names on OS maps. Brought up in a Welsh workhouse he fought in the American civil war and became a *New York Herald* journalist. His great *coup* was the expedition to central Africa to find Livingstone who had been "lost" trying to establish that Lake Tanganyika was the source of the Nile; they met at Ujiji, November 1871. He continued Livingstone's work in a second expedition, following the Lualaba River down to the Atlantic to find it was the Congo, not the Nile. Employed by the Belgian king to set up a chain of trading stations Stanley became the creator of the Congo (now Zaire) and a catalyst for the carve up of Africa by the European powers. His last expedition saved Emin Pasha from the Mahdi.

Surrey Hill is a little plateau (Terrace 11, pre-Anglian) traversed by the Surrey/Berkshire boundary. The reservoir holds 42 000m3/900 000 gallons. It serves Yateley, Sandhurst & Crowthorne and parts of Camberley and Fleet. The water comes from the Thames at Bray through a new 900mm pipe.

Swinley Park was the grounds of Swinley Lodge where the royal staghounds were kennelled at the head of Nine Mile Ride.

The **telecommunications** tower at Old Dean belongs to BT and is 100m tall. It was built about 1965 for colour television distribution to transmitters for which copper cable was unable to handle the frequencies up to 11 gigaHertz. Many of the antennae on the lattice-work belong to site sharers who are able to rent space on the tower. The plateau it stands on is Terrace 10.

Tundry Pond is a quiet stretch of water with kingfishers, sandpipers and herons. The causeway bridge was built for the carriages of Sir Henry Paulet St John when the canal cut his normal route from Dogmersfield Park.

Tweseldown Racecourse was the army racecourse laid out soon after the army settled in Aldershot in 1855. It is now leased to a private company and is used for point-to-point racing and other equestrian events.

Warren Heath is managed by the Forestry Commission as part of Bramshill Forest. It is used as a venue for cross country motor sports.

Welsh Drive is an ancient drove road, the route by which drovers from Wales brought meat on the hoof to medieval markets at Blackwater and London.

The **Wellington Statue** arrived at its present site in 1885 - 40 tons of bronze from guns captured at Waterloo. It was always controversial. There were objections to commemorating Wellington when it was erected in 1846 and when it was removed from Hyde Park corner for road widening in 1882. Current objectors believe such a splendid statue should stand in a more public place. *The Wellington Military Memorial 1885-1985* Tim Childerhouse Southern Books 1985

Wharfenden Lake is the site of the Lakeside Country Club and was the HQ of ENSA during World War II. "Every night something awful" said the soldiers.

The River **Whitewater** River which joins the Blackwater near Thatcher's Ford rises from chalk springs near Greywell Mill and flows over the London Clay. It has a much richer fauna and flora than the Blackwater. It had eight mills.

Wildmoor Heath is greatly valued in Berkshire as one of its few heaths. It is an assemblage of various bits of land mainly heath and bog put together as a reserve managed by Berkshire, Buckinghamshire & Oxfordshire Wildlife Trust.

Wilks Water pre-dates the canal. The ornate house (huge facade, little house) appears to have been built as a folly for Dogmersfield Park around 1770.

Winchfield Church, St Mary's, is Norman. The chancel arch and south door of about 1150 are elaborately decorated and well-preserved. The nave was Gothicized with larger pointed windows in Victorian times but the chancel retains its Norman form with narrow windows (some restored) and thick walls. Winchfield was gifted to Chertsey Abbey in a charter of 675 but the Domesday Book contradicts this. The modern village is far away near the railway station.

The **Windle** Brook issues from Rapley Lake and drains the eastern heights of Bagshot Heath. After Windlesham it becomes the Mill Bourne in Chobham.

Windlesham became a village in the 19th century. Before, perhaps because of its forest origin, it was scattered hamlets, one of which was Bagshot. The great western road (now A30) formed the N boundary of the parish. Windlesham is not in the Domesday Book. There were several early land holdings. One was part of Edward the Confessor's endowment of Westminster Abbey. The church, St John, the Baptist, was rebuilt in 1874 but has the medieval nave as the south aisle and the tower of 1838. Church documents date back to 1189.

The **Wishmoor Stone,** a sarsen, was *Wysshemorestone* in the perambulation of Godley Hundred of 1446. It appears to mark where the county boundary takes off from the Wish Stream over Surrey Hill. Five civil parishes meet here: Winkfield, Bracknell, Crowthorne, Frimley & Camberley and Windlesham.

The **Wish** Stream drains the western part of the heath and joins the Blackwater near the Meadows roundabout. It is the county boundary throughout its length.

Yateley was probably part of Domesday Book Cove which found itself in the medieval parish of Yateley. From the 10th century it was Winchester church property so many old records survive. The houses of the medieval village - seven in a rental of 1287 - probably lay on the old Reading road opposite the green. The "big house" was probably on the site of the present Yateley Manor School near the church. The parish had a scattering of hamlets and houses and the 20th century village resulted from filling the gaps. The population is estimated to have been about 300 in 1287, was 470 in 1801 and is around 22,000 in 2010. The church, St Peters, was badly burnt (arson) in 1979 when the Norman arches collapsed. The timber tower of about 1450 survived. The damage enabled archæologists to investigate the north wall which was found to have a blocked Anglo-Saxon window (now restored). The sarsen L of the porch at the NW corner of the Anglo-Saxon walls may indicate a pre-Christian religious site. *Yateley, a mediæval village* Derek Doherty 1982 Yateley Society 21pp

HOW
TO BE A
MATHEMAGICIAN

ADVANCE PRAISE FOR THE BOOK

'This book will make you fall in love with several topics—exponentials, for example. What I like most about its contents is that it not only explains the concept concisely, but also enlists real-life applications of the same. This is handy and provides clarity to students so that they can see where they will actually apply this knowledge once they are out of the classroom. Give it a read. You will be glad that you did!'

—H.S. Anand, zonal director, Akal Academies

'Just like magicians performing tricks with a wave of their wands, Aditi and Sudhir have turned maths into a fascinating "world of wonder" with their new book. Becoming a maths wizard is now astonishingly easy with their interesting tricks and amazing mathematical facts. Just go through the pages, and amaze and impress your friends and audience with your superpowers of the mind! It's as easy as abracadabra!'

—Sharon Galstaun, academic head, St Karen's High School and
St Karen's Secondary School, Patna

'Aditi and Sudhir Singhal's book *How to Be a Mathemagician* is for those who love maths as well as for people with maths-phobia. They have a knack of making this subject interesting and easy. Their sincere efforts and dedication in this field have given them a place among renowned and recognized authors of a subject that is of great value for today's student'

—Goldy Malhotra, director, Academic Staff Training College and
Administration, Manav Rachna International Schools

'This book will make maths understandable to all learners. It will help students prepare for any entrance examination where arithmetic has weightage, and teachers and mentors will find it very useful. I congratulate Aditi and Sudhir on making learning maths fun'

—Lalit Sharma, president and principal,
FCS Foundation School, Punjab

'*How to Be a Mathemagician* is a brilliant piece of work to strengthen and expand mathematical notions. It is a wonderful resource for teachers who want to increase active participation of students in maths lessons. Magic tricks, problem-solving methods and calculation techniques are specially beneficial for the students'

—Sharmila Singh, principal, Pioneer Montessori Inter College, Eldeco-I, Lucknow

'*How to Be a Mathemagician* is a wonderfully entertaining and interesting book for adults and children alike. It kept my children engrossed for hours. They enjoyed learning the concepts and doing the magic tricks with their friends. It's written in a way that is easy to understand. The best part is that children don't even realize they are doing maths while having so much fun. I would highly recommend this book for all ages'

—Sona Sood, professional photographer

'This book is a treat for both children and adults alike. It is a collection of engrossing tricks that will keep you on your toes all throughout. This book is especially helpful in gaining insight into new ways of teaching some difficult concepts to children in a more friendly manner. I extend my heartfelt congratulations to both the authors of this book for creating a marvellous mathematical journey for us to experience'

—Ashima Gupta, PhD, economics

ADITI SINGHAL
SUDHIR SINGHAL

HOW
TO BE A
MATHEMAGICIAN

EBURY
PRESS

EBURY PRESS

USA | Canada | UK | Ireland | Australia
New Zealand | India | South Africa | China

Ebury Press is part of the Penguin Random House group of companies
whose addresses can be found at global.penguinrandomhouse.com

Published by Penguin Random House India Pvt. Ltd
7th Floor, Infinity Tower C, DLF Cyber City,
Gurgaon 122 002, Haryana, India

Penguin
Random House
India

First published in Ebury Press by Penguin Random House India 2017

ISBN 9780143427483

Typeset in Adobe Garamond Pro by Manipal Digital Systems, Manipal
Printed at Replika Press Pvt. Ltd, India

www.penguin.co.in

To the
Almighty God,
the Supreme father of all souls and
the source of true knowledge

Why do children dread mathematics?
Because of the wrong approach.
Because it is looked at as a subject.

Shakuntala Devi

CONTENTS

INTRODUCTION

Mathematics is not just a subject but a part of our lives. Whether you are a child or a grown-up, a student or a professional, a musician or a magician, maths plays an important role in your daily routine. You can even find mathematical patterns in spiderwebs or honeycombs.

Learning maths can be made enjoyable if it is taught through activities, puzzles and games right from an early age. Many a time, we find that some students solve complex maths problems in minutes while some take a long time to solve even the basic ones. Contrary to popular belief, it's not their level of knowledge that leads to this difference but the way they apply their knowledge.

This book is written with the aim of enhancing the power of reasoning, critical thinking and the problem-solving ability of the reader. It is intended for students, teachers and parents alike, as the learning of mathematics is not restricted to any age. For students who find themselves afraid of the subject, we have attempted to make it fun to learn and give them the confidence to approach each problem with a fresh perspective. We have also written this book for teachers, who can use many of the activities mentioned to make their classes livelier and show their students that maths need not be a dreaded subject. Parents can also pick up this book to make it easier to explain complex concepts to their children and help them develop a strong base in the subject. It contains mind-bending questions with unusual solutions, logic-related maths problems, interesting maths facts and proofs, and calculation tips that highlight the almost magical simplicity of the subject. These are effective methods that help in day-to-day application of mathematics, while reducing one's dependency on gadgets as well as providing good practice for the types of questions that are asked in examinations and interviews.

The other section of this book contains some amazing magic tricks and enthralling activities—just flip the book to find them!

You might find some parts of the book challenging even after reading and rereading the solutions. If so, keep going. Even without necessarily understanding every detail, you will be surprised how much of the overall picture you are able to absorb by simply moving ahead.

So forge ahead, work your brain and unravel the secrets and mysteries of mathematics.

PART A

PROBLEMS WITH
SURPRISING SOLUTIONS

1

WHICH PIZZA DO YOU PREFER?

Once I went to a restaurant with my kids, where they ordered a 12" pizza. After sometime, the waiter came and told us that they had, by mistake, served our order at another table. He apologized for the mix-up and offered us two 8"pizzas instead of one 12".

My kids were ecstatic when they heard this as they thought they would have more to eat and enjoy. But to their disappointment, I refused to accept this deal and insisted on our original order even though it meant a wait of another ten minutes.

The kids thought that I was making a mistake.

If you were in my place what would you have done?

Deal or no deal?

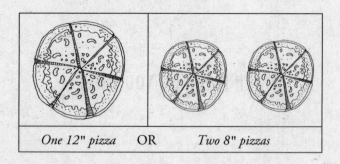

| One 12" pizza | OR | Two 8" pizzas |

SOLUTION

We all know that the area of a *circle* is πr^2, i.e. pi × radius^2
The radius of an 8-inch pizza is 4 inches,
And the radius of a 12-inch pizza is 6 inches.

Area of two 8-inch pizzas = $2 \times \pi \times (4)^2 = 32\,\pi$ sq. inches
Area of one 12-inch pizza = $\pi \times (6)^2 = 36\,\pi$ sq. inches

So in which case are you getting more pizza?

Mathematics is not only to score marks in exams—mathematical concepts can be of great use in our day-to-day life if we apply them properly.

2

EXPONENTIAL MYSTERY

Through the following experiment, we will lead you to a fact that is difficult to believe when you hear it for the first time. Therefore, we have also shared the mathematical explanation. So go ahead and surprise others as well.

Experiment:

1. Take an A4 sheet (i.e. 8.27 × 11.69 inches) and fold it in half. Now the paper is twice as thick as before.
2. Fold this paper in half again, it will be four times as thick as the original paper.
3. Fold it a third time.
4. Try folding it a few more times and see how far you can go.

It will be difficult to fold a normal paper more than seven or eight times.

You must have observed that the thickness of a folded paper is doubled each time it is folded, i.e. the number of layers of paper doubles with each fold. So you start with a single layer, then you have 2 layers, then 4, then 8, then 16, then 32, and 64 layers after six folds. After seven folds, you get 128 layers, as thick as a notebook.

The current record for folding a paper is twelve times, held by Britney Gallivan.

Let's assume that we are able to fold the paper as many times as we want. In that case, after 23 folds, the paper would be 1 km thick.

Sounds unbelievable, doesn't it? Let's do some calculations to see how this is possible.

Consider a ream of 500 A4-size sheets of normal quality (i.e. 75–80 gsm). It is approximately 5 cm thick. So, we can say one A4 sheet would be around 0.01 cm or 0.1 mm thick.

Let us calculate the thickness after 27 folds:

$$0.1 \text{ mm} \times \underbrace{2 \times 2 \times ... \times 2}_{27 \text{ times}}$$

= 13421772.8 mm
= 13.42177 km, which is much more than the height of Mt Everest.

It would take *30 folds* to reach the equivalent of 100 km above us:

$$0.1 \text{ mm} \times 2^{30} = 107374182.4 \text{ mm} = 107.4 \text{ km}$$

Similarly, it only takes *42 folds* of paper to get from the earth to the moon.

It's hard to imagine getting from here to the moon in 42 folds. This is because our brain is inclined to think linearly, not exponentially.

If you fold a sheet of paper in half, fifty times,
how thick, do you think, the resulting paper will become?

The thickness will be 3/4 of the distance
from the earth to the sun.
Unbelievable, isn't it?

Thickness at 50 Folds

$$0.1 \text{ mm} \times \underbrace{2 \times 2 \times ... \times 2}_{50 \text{ times}}$$

$= 112.589990 \times 10^6 \text{ km}$, which is over 112 million km.

This is about three-fourths of the earth–sun distance, which is 149.6 million kilometres. With 51 folds, you would burn in the sun.

This is the incredible power of an exponential, that small numbers can become huge by simply compounding what you have over and over again.

See the following table showing some more calculations of thickness per fold:

Folds n	Number of folded layers 2^n	Thickness (in km) $(0.1 \times 2^n \times 10^{-6})$
1	2	0.2×10^{-6}
2	4	0.4×10^{-6}
3	8	0.8×10^{-6}
4	16	1.6×10^{-6}
5	32	3.2×10^{-6}
6	64	6.4×10^{-6}
7	128	12.8×10^{-6}
8	256	25.6×10^{-6}
9	512	51.2×10^{-6}
10	1024	0.1×10^{-3}
11	2048	0.2×10^{-3}
12	4096	0.4×10^{-3}
13	8192	0.8×10^{-3}
14	16384	1.6×10^{-3}
15	32768	3.3×10^{-3}
16	65536	6.6×10^{-3}
17	131072	13.1×10^{-3}
18	262144	26.2×10^{-3}
19	524288	52.4×10^{-3}
20	1048576	104.9×10^{-3}
...	.....	.....
30	1073741824	107.4×10^{0}
35	34359738368	3.4×10^{3}
40	1099511627776	109.9×10^{3}
45	35184372088832	3.5×10^{6}
50	1125899906842624	112.5×10^{6}

Paper-Folding Record

Britney Gallivan from California created a record by folding a paper 12 times. She took a long piece of paper (a single roll of toilet paper) that measured 4000 feet (1.2 km) and folded it.

She also provided an equation that yielded the width or the length of the paper necessary to fold a piece of paper in a single direction:

$$L = \frac{\pi.t}{6} \cdot \left(2^n + 4\right)\left(2^n - 1\right)$$

Where, t represents the thickness of the material to be folded, L represents the length of a piece of paper to be folded in only one direction and n represents the number of folds desired.

This equation is also known as the paper-folding theorem.

Use of Exponential Thinking in Real-Life Situations

Such situation-based questions are often asked in interviews and exams.

Q: You are offered a job that lasts for seven weeks and given two options to earn your salary.

Option 1: Take ₹100 for the first day, ₹200 for the second day, ₹300 for the third day and so on. Each day, you are paid ₹100 more than the day before.

Option 2: Take 1 paisa for the first day, 2 paise for the second, 4 paise for the third and 8 paise for the fourth day. You are paid double the amount of what you were paid the day before.

Which do you choose?

If you have fully grasped the above mathematical fact, you will choose the second option.

Let's explore the solution:

- In the first, add ₹100 to the previous day's amount each day.
- In the second, start with 1 paisa and double the amount with each passing day.

Check the progress weekly.

By the time you reach the fourth week, it will be clear to you that the second option is better, as shown in the table below:

Weeks	Option 1 (Adding ₹100 each day)	Option 2 (Doubling each day)
	Amount (in ₹)	Amount (in ₹)
1	2800	1.27
2	7700	163.83
3	12600	20,971.51
4	17500	2,684,354.55
5	22400	343,597,383.67
6	27300	43,980,465,111.03
7	32200	5,629,499,534,213.11
Total	**122,500**	**5,673,826,302,198.97**

3

SMART BUSINESS

Mr Kumar is a self-made man who made his small business reach great heights with his sharp intellect and quick thinking. His three sons, Jayesh (the oldest), Amit (the second) and Arjun (the youngest) are equally smart and diligent. One day, Mr Kumar thought to test his sons' analytical thinking and business skills. He called his three sons and gave them this task:

'Here are 90 apples for you to sell in the market,' said Mr Kumar. 'Jayesh, you will take 50 apples; Amit, you will take 30; and Arjun, you will take 10. All of you must sell your apples at the same price. For example, if Jayesh sells his apples at ₹15 per piece, you two will have to sell yours at the same price. And if Jayesh sells his apples for ₹10 each, you two will have to do the same. But no matter what price you pick, each of you must end up with the same amount of money from your individual apples.'

'The other terms and conditions are that you cannot share your apples with each other. Jayesh must sell 50 apples. Amit must sell 30 and Arjun must sell the 10 apples that remain,' Mr Kumar reminded them.

The task given by Mr Kumar seemed impossible. The amount collected from the sale of 50 apples will definitely exceed the amount earned from selling 30 or 10 apples at the same price.

But the three young men took on the challenge. They discussed among themselves for a while and went to the market and sold their apples as instructed. Jayesh sold 50, Amit sold 30, and Arjun sold 10 apples, all at the same price and each one of them earned exactly the same amount. Mr Kumar felt proud of his sons when they told him how they managed to do it.

Can you guess the solution?

SOLUTION

Jayesh started selling his apples at a price of 7 apples @ ₹10. He sold 49 of his apples at this price, but retained 1.
Amit sold 28 apples at this price, i.e. 7 @ ₹10, and kept 2.
Arjun sold 7 of his apples at this price, and retained 3 apples.

Then Jayesh sold his last apple for ₹30. In accordance to the rules set by their father, Amit also sold his remaining 2 apples for ₹30 each, and Arjun sold his 3 apples at ₹30 each.

Their earnings are summed up in the following table:

Jayesh's sale	Price	No. of apples sold	Amount earned
First Sale	7 apples for ₹10	49	₹70
Second Sale	1 apple for ₹30	1	₹30
Total		50	₹100

Amit's sale	Price	No. of apples sold	Amount earned
First Sale	7 apples for ₹10	28	₹40
Second Sale	1 apple for ₹30	2	₹60
Total		30	₹100

Arjun's sale	Price	No. of apples sold	Amount earned
First Sale	7 apples for ₹10	7	₹10
Second Sale	1 apple for ₹30	3	₹90
Total		**10**	**₹100**

We can see that each of the brothers earned the same amount by selling different number of apples at same price. That's called smart business.

Special Tip

Try to find the solution if the three men were asked to sell 25, 15 and 10 apples respectively.

4

THE INVISIBLE THIEF

Two brothers, Raju and Mohan, brought watermelons from their respective fields to sell in the city market. When they reached the market, they got to know that only one stall is available. They decided to sell their stock together from a single stall. They had 30 watermelons each. Raju decided that he would sell his watermelons at ₹25 for 3, so that he would earn ₹250. Mohan decided to sell his watermelons at a higher price of ₹25 for 2 to earn ₹375.

However, they were confused whose watermelons to sell first. If they were to sell the expensive ones first, they would not get many customers, and if they sold the cheaper ones first, it would be difficult to sell the expensive ones later.

Finally, they decided to sell their watermelons in batches of 5—3 @ 25 and 2 @ 25, i.e. 5 @ 50

By the end of the day, all 60 watermelons were sold in 12 batches of 5 each.

They earned: $12 \times 50 = ₹600$ in total.

Then came the time to divide their earnings.
Mohan gave Raju ₹250 as his 30 watermelons were sold at 3 for ₹25.
He himself was left with ₹600 – ₹250 = ₹350
But he had calculated his earnings to be ₹375, by selling 30 watermelons at 2 for ₹25.
He wondered where the remaining ₹25 went. He was sure that he had sold the entire stock without making any mistakes in calculation. So who took away the ₹25?

Can you help him in finding his lost ₹25 and to find the invisible thief?

SOLUTION

If the brothers had sold their products individually,

- Raju would have sold 10 batches of 3 watermelons each. Each lot would have earned him ₹25. The total would have been ₹250.
- Mohan would have sold 15 batches of 2 watermelons each. Each lot would have earned him ₹25. The total would have been ₹375.

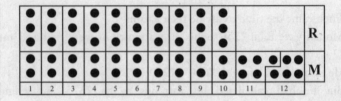

Understanding the above figure will solve the mystery of the *missing* ₹25.

'R' represents Raju's 30 watermelons, which were to be sold at 3 for ₹25 and 'M' represents Mohan's 30 watermelons to be sold at 2 for ₹25. The numbers in the last row correspond to the batches.

These 60 watermelons were divided into 12 batches of 5 each, sold for ₹25.

If you look at the last two batches, you will notice that these are not same as the other ones.

When the watermelons were sold in batches of 5 each, Raju's 30 watermelons were sold off in the first 10 batches.

All the remaining watermelons were Mohan's. They should have sold these at the price that Mohan wanted, i.e. 2 for ₹25.

$$(2 @ ₹25) \times (5 \text{ batches}) = 25 \times 5 = ₹125$$

Whereas, they sold these 10 watermelons for:

$$2 \text{ batches} @ ₹50 = ₹100$$

Thus, there was a difference of ₹25.

5

THREE IN A RACE

A, B and C are in a 100 m race, each running at a uniform speed.

If A beats B by 10 m and B beats C by 10 m, by how much distance does A beat C?

If you are thinking that C is 20 m behind A or at the 80 m mark, then think again. Solving it mathematically can get you the correct answer.

SOLUTION

When A crosses the 100 m line, B is at the 90 m mark, as it is given that A beats B by 10 m. Thus, we can say that B covers 9 m for every 10 m of A.

Similarly, since B beats C by 10 m, C covers 9 m for every 10 m of B.

So, when B is at the 90 m mark, C has covered nine-tenths of 90 m, which is 81 m.

Finally, when A crosses the 100 m line to win, B is at the 90 m and C at the 81 m mark. Thus, A beats C by 19 m and not 20 m as it seemed in the beginning.

6

CLEVER SALESMAN

An insurance salesman knocks on the door of a home. When a lady answers, he asks, 'How many children do you have?' She replies, 'Three.'

When he asks, 'What are their ages?', she decides that he is too intrusive and refuses to tell him. On his insistence she says that she can give him a hint about the children's ages. She says, 'If you multiply the ages of all three, you get 36.'

He thinks for a while and then asks for another hint. Then she says, 'The sum of their ages is the number on the house next door.' He then immediately walks to the house next door and comes back, saying, 'I need one more hint.' The lady replies, 'I have to go, my eldest son is sleeping upstairs.'

The salesman said, 'Thank you! I now have everything I need.' He then knows their ages. *Do you?*

SOLUTION

First hint:

The lady said that the product of the ages of her three children is 36.

So let's find all possible ways of representing 36 as the product of three factors:

1) $36 = 12 \times 3 \times 1$
2) $36 = 6 \times 3 \times 2$
3) $36 = 4 \times 3 \times 3$
4) $36 = 36 \times 1 \times 1$
5) $36 = 9 \times 4 \times 1$
6) $36 = 18 \times 2 \times 1$
7) $36 = 9 \times 2 \times 2$
8) $36 = 6 \times 6 \times 1$

At this stage, the information is not sufficient to guess the ages of three children. It can be any of these combinations.

Second hint:

The sum of their ages is same as the house number next door.

If we add up the combinations of factors given above, we get the following totals:

16, 11, 10, 38, 14, 21, 13 and 13.

If the number of the house next door was 16, 11, 10, 38, 14 or 21, the salesman would have guessed the ages without a doubt. But he still wasn't sure. That means the house number is 13, as there are two combinations for that total, i.e. '9, 2 and 2' and '6, 6 and 1'.

Third hint:

The lady said that her *eldest* son was sleeping upstairs.

That means the older siblings are not twins and she has an eldest child.

That's how the salesman guessed the children's ages as 9, 2 and 2 years respectively.

7

SOLVING QUESTIONS WITHOUT ALGEBRA

Sonia bought 3 cupcakes and 2 doughnuts for ₹157. Anisha bought 1 cupcake and 2 doughnuts for ₹113 from the same shop. If all cupcakes cost the same and all doughnuts cost the same, how much does each doughnut cost?

₹ 157   ₹113

We can easily solve such problems using algebra by considering the unknown quantities to be x and y and creating and solving two equations according to the given condition. It can still be solved if someone has not been introduced to algebra yet or is unclear about the concepts.

Can you determine the solution without using algebra?

SOLUTION

The difference between the amount paid by Sonia and Anisha is ₹44.

This is the price of 2 cupcakes.

As all cupcakes cost same, the price of each cupcake is ₹22.

Anisha bought 1 cupcake and 2 doughnuts for ₹113.

Cost of 2 doughnuts = 113 – 22

= ₹91

As all doughnuts cost same, the price of each doughnut is

$\frac{91}{2}$, i.e. ₹45.50.

8

COMPARING MOVIES

Percentages can be deceptive at first glance and reveal interesting statistics if understood properly. Consider the following example:

A movie 'A' is shown to a group of 90 people, out of which 63 people like it.

So the percentage of people who like 'A' in this group is

$$= 70\% \left(\text{i.e.} \frac{63}{90} \times 100 \right)$$

The same movie 'A' is shown to another group of 10 people, out of which 4 people like it.

So the percentage of people who like 'A' in this case would be

$$= 40\% \left(\text{i.e.} \frac{4}{10} \times 100 \right)$$

Another movie 'B' is shown to the same first group of 90 people, out of which 45 people like it.

So the percentage of people who like 'B' in this group is

$$= 50\% \left(\text{i.e.} \frac{45}{90} \times 100 \right)$$

The same movie 'B' is shown to the second group of 10 people, out of which 8 people like it.

So the percentage of people who like 'B' in this case would be

$$= 80\% \left(\text{i.e.} \frac{8}{10} \times 100 \right)$$

Based on this information, which movie do you think is liked by the most people? Movie A or Movie B?

MOVIE A			MOVIE B		
Group	Liked by	Percentage	Group	Liked by	Percentage
90 people	63	70%	10 people	8	80%
10 people	4	40%	90 people	45	50%

SOLUTION

MOVIE A			MOVIE B		
Group	**Liked by**	**Percentage**	**Group**	**Liked by**	**Percentage**
90 people	63	70%	10 people	8	80%
10 people	4	40%	90 people	45	50%
Total:			**Total:**		
100	67	$\frac{67}{100} \times 100$ $= 67\%$	100	53	$\frac{53}{100} \times 100$ $= 53\%$

Hence we see that although at first glance movie 'B' seems to be more popular, it is actually movie 'A' that more people like.

To get the actual result, we need to calculate the percentage by taking both the cases together, as shown above.

9

MATCHSTICK PUZZLES

These puzzles test your ability to think logically. As the main props, i.e. matchsticks, are easily available, it is also very easy to practise. So go ahead and don your thinking caps. Time yourself while solving the puzzles, and see if you get faster as you go along.

1. **Move one matchstick and make a square.**

2. **Take only two matches away to leave behind two equilateral triangles.**

3. Use 11 matchsticks to make 9.

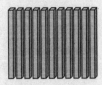

4. Take away two matchsticks to leave two squares.

5. Take away six matches to leave 10.

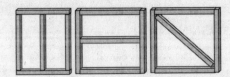

6. Move one match to make the house face the opposite direction.

7. **Remove 8 matches to leave just two squares.**

8. **Take away three matches to leave only three squares.**

9. **Arrange four matchsticks and a coin as shown below to represent a glass containing a ball. Can you move the ball out of the glass by just moving two matchsticks?**

10. **Change position of only one matchstick and make the following equation correct:**

$$5 + 5 + 5 = 550$$

11. Move one matchstick to make four triangles:

MATCHSTICK EQUATIONS

The equations given below are incorrect. Can you rectify them by just moving a single matchstick?

Note: 'X' and '+' are made using two matchsticks only.

1. XI – V = IV

2. X + V = IV

3. L + L = L

4. VI = IV – III

5. XIV – V = XX

6. IX – IX = V

7. X = VIII – II

8. VII = I

9. VII = III + II

SOLUTIONS

1.

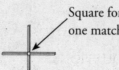

Square formed at the centre by moving one matchstick upwards.

2.

3.

4.

5.

TEN

6.

7.

8.

9.

10.

5+54 5=550

11.

4△

MATCHSTICK EQUATIONS SOLUTIONS

1. **XI – V = IV**
    X – VI = IV
    or
    XI – V = VI
    or
    XI – VI = V

2. **X + V = IV**
    IX – V = IV
    or
    X – VI = IV

3. **L + L = L**
    ⊏ – L = L
    or
    L + I = LI

4. **VI = IV – III**
    VI = IX – III
    or
    VI = IV + II

5. **XIV – V = XX**
    XV + V = XX

6. **IX – IX = V**
    IX – IV = V

7. **X = VIII – II**
    X – VIII = II

8. **VII = I**
    square root of 1
    (i.e. $\sqrt{1} = 1$)

9. **VII = III + II**
    VI = III + III

10

OBSERVATION-ENHANCING PUZZLES

The latest gadgets and advanced technology have made our life simple, but at the same time they have affected our mental abilities by adding numerous distractions. As a result, reduced attention spans and observational skills are a common problem. These fun-filled puzzles are meant to help fix that.

Calculate the value of each item given in the pictures and find the value of missing number.

PICTURE PUZZLE 1

PICTURE PUZZLE 2

$$\text{rabbit} + \text{rabbit} + \text{rabbit} = 24$$

$$\text{rabbit} + \text{carrot} + \text{carrot} = 16$$

$$\text{carrot} - \text{boots} = 2$$

$$\text{boot} + \text{rabbit} + \text{rabbit} \times \text{carrot} = ?$$

PICTURE PUZZLE 3

$$\text{flower} + \text{flower} + \text{flower} = 30$$

$$\text{flower} + \text{leaves} + \text{leaves} = 20$$

$$\text{leaves} - \text{leaves} = 3$$

$$\text{leaf} + \text{flower} \times \text{leaves} = ?$$

PICTURE PUZZLE 4

PICTURE PUZZLE 5

SOLUTIONS

Picture Puzzle 1:

First row: 3 mangoes = 60, so the value of each mango is 20.
Second row: 1 mango + 4 bananas + 4 bananas = 28, so the value of each banana is 1.
Third row: 4 bananas – 2 pears = 2, so the value of each pear is 1.
In the fourth row, observing the number of items carefully and substituting the values, we get:
1 pear + 1 mango + 3 bananas = 1 + 20 + 3 = 24.

Picture Puzzle 2:

First row: 3 rabbits = 24, so 1 rabbit = 8.
Second row: 1 rabbit + 2 carrots + 2 carrots = 16, so 1 carrot = 2.
Third row: 2 carrots – 2 shoes = 2, so 1 shoe = 1.
In the fourth row, observing the number of items carefully and substituting the values, we get:
1 shoe + 1 rabbit + 1 rabbit × 1 carrot = 1 + 8 + 8 × 2
= 1 + 8 + 16 = 25.

Picture Puzzle 3:

First row: 3 flowers = 30, so 1 flower = 10.
Second row: 1 flower + 5 leaves + 5 leaves = 20, so 1 leaf = 1.
Third row: 5 leaves – 2 buds = 3, so 1 bud = 1.
In the fourth row, observing the number of items carefully and substituting the values, we get:
1 bud + 1 flower × 4 leaves = 1 + 10 × 4 = 1 + 40 = 41.

Picture Puzzle 4:

First row: 3 pastries = 30, so 1 pastry = 10.
Second row: 1 pastry + 1 ice cream + 1 ice cream = 20,
so 1 ice cream = 5.
Third row: 1 ice cream + 2 fries packs + 2 fries packs = 9,
so 1 fries pack = 1.
In the fourth row, observing the number of items carefully
and substituting the values, we get:
1 ice cream + 1 fries pack × 1 pastry = 5 + 1 × 10 = 5 + 10 = 15.

Picture Puzzle 5:

6 + 6 + 6 = 18 (sum of numbers shown on the top of each die)
3 + 3 + 3 = 9 (sum of time displayed in the clocks)
3 × 3 − 3 = 6 (3 books in each pile)
2 × 3 − 2 = 6 − 2 = 4 (observe the number represented by each
item in the row)

PART B

CALCULATIONS WITHOUT CALCULATORS

11

HOW LONG DOES IT TAKE TO DOUBLE YOUR MONEY?

A penny saved is a penny earned. With so many options available to invest your hard-earned money in, it is often hard to decide what to choose to get the maximum returns. Even if we know the rate of interest, we have to depend on calculators to decide the tenure of our investment, making it confusing and time-consuming. But the magical numbers 72 and 115 can help you estimate how long it'll take to double or triple your investment.

Magic of 72

To estimate the number of years required to double your investment at a given interest rate (compounded annually) you just have to divide 72 by the interest rate. It will give you an approximate answer. For example, if you want to know how long it will take to double your money at 12% interest per annum, divide 72 by 12. The answer is approximately 6 years.

Years required to double investment = 72 ÷ interest rate compounded annually

This formula is more accurate when the interest rate is less than 20%. You can compare the estimated answer arrived at by using 72 and the actual calculation from the following table:

Rate of interest	Years needed to double investment (magic of 72)	Actual number of years needed
1%	72	69.661
2%	36	35.003
3%	24	23.450
4%	18	17.673
5%	14.4	14.207
6%	12	11.896
7%	10.286	10.245
8%	9	9.006
9%	8	8.043
10%	7.2	7.273
11%	6.545	6.642
12%	6	6.116
15%	4.8	4.959

Rate of interest	Years needed to double investment (magic of 72)	Actual number of years needed
18%	4	4.188
20%	3.6	3.802
25%	2.880	3.106
30%	2.4	2.642
40%	1.8	2.060
50%	1.440	1.710
60%	1.2	1.475
70%	1.029	1.306

This formula is useful for financial estimates. If you want to know the interest required to double your money in a specific time period (compounded annually) then divide 72 by the number of years.

Interest rate required to double investment = 72 ÷ number of years

For example, if you want to double your money in six years, divide 72 by 6, to find that it will require an interest rate of about 12%.

Thus the magical formulas are:

$$T = \frac{72}{R} \text{ and } R = \frac{72}{T}$$

T and R are the time period of the investment in years and the annual interest rate, respectively.

Special Tip

To know the approximate time period required to triple your money, use the following formula:

Years required to triple your investment = 115 ÷ interest rate compounded annually

For example, if the compound interest rate is 10%, it will take 11.5 years to triple your investment.

?

Riddle Time

Can you guess the word which is pronounced wrong by every mathematician?

Wrong.

12

DETERMINING THE UNIT DIGIT AT A GLANCE

In competitive exams, some questions require you to find the unit digit of the answer resulting from complex calculations, e.g. find the unit digit of:

$$(743)^{85} - (625)^{37} + (986)^{67}$$

Such calculations are very time-consuming if you don't know the trick to solve it. In this chapter, we will discuss and understand the secret to solve such complex questions.

We will see the pattern in the unit digit of the powers of all the numbers from 0 to 9 first.

A. Finding the unit digit of any power with bases 0 and 1

The unit digit of 0^n and 1^n will always remain 0 and 1 respectively.

B. Finding the unit digit of any power with base 2

The following table shows the possible unit digits of 2^n:

Power	Unit digit
$(2)^1$	2
$(2)^2$	4
$(2)^3$	8
$(2)^4$	6
$(2)^5$	2
$(2)^6$	4
$(2)^7$	8
$(2)^8$	6

The above pattern of unit digits repeats itself after interval of 4.

To get the unit digit of 2^n, follow these steps:

Step 1
Divide the exponent by 4.

Step 2
If there is any remainder, consider that to be n, i.e. the new exponent. Determine the result using the above table.

Step 3
If it is completely divisible by 4 (i.e. zero remainder), consider the exponent as 4, i.e. $(2)^4$ which will mean 6 is the unit digit.

Let's consider some examples.

Example 1:
Find the unit digit in $(2)^{53}$

1. Divide the exponent of 2 by 4, i.e. divide 53 by 4. The remainder is 1.
2. Since 1 is the remainder, we will consider it to be the exponent of 2, i.e. $(2)^1$.
3. As $(2)^1 = 2$, the unit digit of $(2)^{53}$ will be 2.

Example 2:
Find the unit digit in $(2)^{40}$

1. Divide 40 by 4, i.e. $40 \div 4$. The remainder is 0.
2. Since it is completely divisible by 4, take 4 as the exponent of 2, i.e. $(2)^4$.
3. From the above table, the unit digit of $(2)^4 = 6$. Hence, the unit digit of $(2)^{40}$ will be 6.

C. Finding the unit digit of any power with base 3

The following table shows the possible unit digits of 3^n.

Power	Unit digit
$(3)^1$	3
$(3)^2$	9
$(3)^3$	7
$(3)^4$	1

The above pattern of unit digits repeats itself after interval of 4. Hence, to find out the unit digit of 3^n, follow these steps:

Step 1
Divide the exponent of 3 by 4.

Step 2
If there is any remainder, take it as the exponent and determine the result using the above table.

Step 3
If it is completely divisible by 4 (i.e. zero remainder), take 4 as the exponent, i.e. $(3)^4$, which will always mean 1 is the unit digit.

Let's consider some examples:

Example 1:
Find the unit digit in $(3)^{74}$

1. Divide 74 (the exponent of 3) by 4, i.e. $74 \div 4$; the remainder is 2.
2. Since 2 is the remainder, we will take it as the exponent of 3, i.e. $(3)^2$.
3. As $(3)^2 = 9$, the unit digit of $(3)^{74}$ will be 9.

Example 2:
Find the unit digit in $(3)^{32}$

1. Divide 32 (exponent of 3) by 4, i.e. $32 \div 4$; the remainder is 0.
2. Since it is completely divisible by 4, take 4 as the exponent of 3, i.e. $(3)^4$.

3. From the above table, the unit digit of $(3)^4 = 1$. Hence, the unit digit of $(3)^{32}$ will be 1.

D. Finding the unit digit of any power with base 4

- If the exponent is even, the unit digit will be 6.
- If the exponent is odd, the unit digit will be 4.

Examples:

The unit digit of $(4)^{64} = 6$
The unit digit of $(4)^{63} = 4$

E. Finding the unit digit of any power with bases 5 and 6

The unit digit of 5^n and 6^n will always remain 5 and 6, respectively.

F. Finding the unit digit of any power with base 7

The following table shows the possible unit digits of 7^n.

Power	Unit digit
$(7)^1$	7
$(7)^2$	9
$(7)^3$	3
$(7)^4$	1

The above pattern of unit digits repeats itself after interval of 4. To determine the unit digit of 7^n, follow these steps:

Step 1
Divide the exponent of 7 by 4.

Step 2
In case of any remainder, take it as the exponent of 7 and determine the result using the above table.

Step 3
If it is completely divisible by 4 (i.e. zero remainder), take 4 as the exponent, i.e. $(7)^4$, which will mean 1 is the unit digit.

Let's consider some examples.

Example 1:
Find the unit digit in $(7)^{23}$

1. Divide 23 (exponent of 7) by 4, i.e. 23 ÷ 4; the remainder is 3.
2. Since 3 is the remainder, we will consider it to be the power of 7, i.e. $(7)^3$.
3. As the unit digit of $(7)^3 = 3$, the unit digit of $(7)^{23}$ will be 3.

Example 2:
Find the unit digit in $(7)^{48}$

1. Divide 48 (exponent of 7) by 4, i.e. 48 ÷ 3; the remainder is 0.
2. Since it is completely divisible by 4, take 4 as the exponent of 7, i.e. $(7)^4$.
3. From the above table, the unit digit of $(7)^4 = 1$. Hence, the unit digit of $(7)^{48}$ will be 1.

G. Finding the unit digit of any power with base 8

The following table shows the possible unit digits of 8^n.

Power	Unit digit
$(8)^1$	8
$(8)^2$	4
$(8)^3$	2
$(8)^4$	6

The above pattern of unit digits repeats itself after interval of 4. To find out the unit digit of 8^n, follow these steps:

Step 1
Divide the exponent of 8 by 4.

Step 2
In case there is any remainder, take it as the exponent of 8 and determine the result using the above table.

Step 3
If it is completely divisible by 4 (i.e. zero remainder), take 4 as the exponent, i.e. $(8)^4$, which will always give 6 as the unit digit.

Let's consider some examples.

Example 1:
Find the unit digit in $(8)^{23}$

1. Divide 23 (exponent of 8) by 4, i.e. $23 \div 4$; the remainder is 3.

2. Since 3 is the remainder, we will take it as the exponent of 8, i.e. $(8)^3$.
3. As the unit digit of $(8)^3 = 2$, the unit digit of $(8)^{23}$ will be 2.

Example 2:
Find the unit digit in $(8)^{48}$

1. Divide 48 (exponent of 8) by 4, i.e. $48 \div 4$; the remainder is 0.
2. Since it is completely divisible by 4, take 4 as the exponent of 8, i.e. $(8)^4$.
3. From the above table, the unit digit of $(8)^4 = 6$. Hence, the unit digit of $(8)^{48}$ will be 6.

H. Finding the unit digit of any power with base 9

-   If the exponent is even, the unit digit will be 1.
-   If the exponent is odd, the unit digit will be 9.

Examples:

The unit digit of $(9)^{64} = 1$
The unit digit of $(9)^{63} = 9$

Now, we can easily solve the questions based on finding the unit digit of large powers.

Example 1:
Find the Unit Digit in $(295)^{98} + (612)^{33} + (893)^{72}$

Unit digit of $(295)^{98}$ = unit digit of $5^{98} = 5$.
Unit digit of $(612)^{33}$ = unit digit of 2^{33} = unit digit of $2^{(4 \times 8) +1}$ = unit digit of $2^1 = 2$.

Unit digit of $(893)^{72}$ = unit digit of 3^{72} = unit digit of $3^4 = 1$.

$$5 + 2 + 1 = 8$$

Hence, the final answer will be 8.

Example 2:
Find the Unit Digit in $(743)^{85} - (625)^{37} + (986)^{98}$

Unit digit of $(743)^{85} = 3$
Unit digit of $(625)^{37} = 5$
Unit digit of $(986)^{98} = 6$

$$3 - 5 + 6 = 4$$

Hence, the final answer will be 4.

?   **Riddle Time**

Which of the following sentences is correct?
Nine and five are thirteen.
or
Nine and five is thirteen.

? Neither is correct: 9 + 5 = 14

13

SHORTCUT TO FIND THE SUM

In quizzes, interviews and competitive exams, some questions test your calculation skills. Solving them using traditional methods takes up a lot of time, which is crucial in such situations. In this chapter, we will use a formula to quickly calculate the sum of all possible numbers formed using a given set of numbers.

Question: What is the sum of all three-digit numbers that can be formed using the numbers 1, 2 and 3, without repeating any digit?

Answer: In this case, we can simply write all the possible combinations of three-digit numbers and add them up:

123
213
132
312
321
231

So, their sum will be:

123 + 213 + 132 + 312 + 321 + 231 = 1332

But, what if the number of digits increases?

Say, you have to find the sum of all four-digit numbers that can be formed using the numbers 1, 2, 3 and 4, without repeating a digit.

In such cases, writing all possible four-digit numbers and then adding them is very time consuming and difficult.

Let's learn a smart way to calculate it;

Let the four digits be A, B, C and D. Then, the number formed using them can be written in the following format:

$$1000A + 100B + 10C + D$$

Now, as we start placing numbers at the unit place, we have four options.

Then, for the tens place, three options will remain, as we cannot repeat a number.

For the hundreds place, two options will remain.

And for the thousands place, only one option will be left.

Hence, the total number of ways in which we can form four-digit numbers are:

$$4 \times 3 \times 2 \times 1 = 24$$

Or using the 'permutation and combination' formula, there are $^4P_4$ ways in which four-digit numbers can be formed from a given set of four numbers, with each number appearing only once:

$$^4P_4 = 4! = 4 \times 3 \times 2 \times 1 = 24$$

Also, all four of these digits (1, 2, 3, 4) will be placed at each digit place an equal number of times. As the total possible numbers are 24, so we can say each of these four numbers will appear six times at each place. That means at the unit place 1 will appear six times, 2 will appear six times, 3 will appear six times and 4 will also appear six times.

Therefore, the total of the unit digits in all 24 numbers will be:

$$6(1 + 2 + 3 + 4)$$

Similarly, the total of the tens digits will be:

$$6 \times 10(1 + 2 + 3 + 4)$$

In short, if we add all the digit places, we get:

$6 \times 1000(1 + 2 + 3 + 4) + 6 \times 100(1 + 2 + 3 + 4) + 6 \times 10(1 + 2 + 3 + 4) + 6(1 + 2 + 3 + 4)$

$= 6 \times [1000(1 + 2 + 3 + 4) + 100(1 + 2 + 3 + 4) + 10(1 + 2 + 3 + 4) + (1 + 2 + 3 + 4)]$

$= 6 \times (1 + 2 + 3 + 4) \times [1000 + 100 + 10 + 1]$

$= 6 \times 10 \times (1111)$

$= 66660$

As you have understood the concept now, we can see the direct formula for it as:

> The sum of all the numbers that can be formed by using
> n non-zero digits is
> *If repetition is not allowed:*
> (n-1)! × (sum of the digits) × (1 . . . n times)
> *If repetition is allowed:*
> $n^{(n-1)}$ × (sum of the digits) × (1 . . . n times)

Let's see some more examples to better understand the formula:

Example 1:
Find the sum of all four-digit numbers that can be formed using 1, 2, 3 and 4, if repetition of digits is allowed.

The formula when repetition of digits is allowed is:
$n^{(n-1)}$ × (sum of the digits) × (1 . . . n times)
= 4^3 × (1 + 2 + 3 + 4) × (1111)
= 64 × 10 × 1111
= 711040

Example 2:
Find the sum of all 4-digits numbers that can be formed using the digits 2, 3, 4, 5, if repetition of digits is not allowed.

The formula when repetition of digits is not allowed is:
(n-1)! × (sum of the digits) × (1 . . . n times)
= 3! × (2 + 3 + 4 + 5) × (1111)
= 6 × 14 × 1111
= 93324

?

Riddle Time

How many birthdays can an average person have?

? One. All the others are anniversaries of one's birthday.

14

MAGIC BY 11

Multiplication by the number 11 is very interesting and fast. In many cases the answer can be determined by just looking at the given numbers.

Let's take a look at a few examples.

Example 1:
34 × 11

The answer can be given at a glance, i.e. 374. Here's how:

To get the answer write 3 and 4 as it is and their sum (i.e. 7) in the middle.

So, 34 × 11 = **374**.

Similarly, $61 \times 11 = 671$ (the sum of 6 and 1, i.e. 7, in the middle).

Example 2:
53172 × 11

For a bigger number like this, we write the first and the last numbers, i.e. 5 and 2 as it is and then starting from either end, keep writing the sum of the two digits at a time as shown below:

So, the answer is **584892**.

This trick is easier to apply when the addition of numbers do not require a carry-over.

When a number needs to be carried over, we make a Dot Sandwich of the number, i.e. put a dot on both the sides of the number and carry on with the successive addition steps, as we will see in the next example.

Example 3:
6258 × 11

1. Put two dots, one on each side of the number, i.e. · 6 2 5 8 ·

2. Starting from the dot on the right-hand side, taking two digits at a time, keep on adding in pairs till you reach the dot on the left; consider the value of a dot as 0.

Note: If at any step, addition results in a two-digit number, we write down the unit digit and carry over the tens digit to be added in the next step.

$$·6258· \times 11$$

$$\downarrow\downarrow\downarrow\downarrow\downarrow$$

$$6\,87\,3\,8$$

$$1$$

So, the answer is **68838**.

Example 4:
5619 × 11

The answer can be directly given as

$$·5619· \times 11 = 5\ \underset{1}{1}\ 7\ \underset{1}{0}\ 9 = \textbf{61809}$$

For more such tricks of calculation using Vedic maths, visit our website, www.aditisinghal.com, or refer to our book *How to Become a Human Calculator?*

?

Riddle Time

How many times can you subtract 2 from the number 21?

? Only once. After that it becomes 19.

15

WONDER OF 9s

Multiplication by 9 often lends itself to many tips and tricks, which can be quite handy not just for examinations but also for performing quick mental maths.

If a number is to be multiplied by another number consisting of only 9 or a series of 9s, the answer can be arrived in an amazingly simple way.

Example 1:
84 × 99

The answer will be in two parts, LHS (left-hand side) and RHS (right-hand side).

For LHS, subtract 1 from 84, i.e. 84 − 1 = 83.

For RHS, subtract this LHS answer from 99, i.e. 99 − 83 = 16.

The answer can simply be written as:

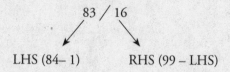

83 / 16

LHS (84– 1)   RHS (99 – LHS)

So, the answer is **8316**.

Example 2:
752 × 999

The answer can be written in two parts as:

751 / 248

LHS (752 – 1)   RHS (999 – LHS)

So, the answer is **751248**.

This trick can be applied to any number provided that the number of digits in the multiplicand and the multiplier (the number comprising only of 9s) are the same.

Example 3:
810256 × 999999

LHS = 810256 – 1 = 810255
RHS = 999999 – 810255= 189744
So, the answer is **810255189744**.

When there are more 9s in the multiplier than there are digits in the multiplicand, the same trick can be applied with a little modification, as shown below.

Example 4:
58 × 999

Since the multiplier here has three 9s, convert the multiplicand 58 into a three-digit number by adding a 0 in front. So, it becomes:

$$058 \times 999$$

The answer can be directly written in two parts as:

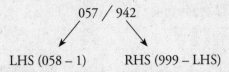

057 / 942

LHS (058 – 1)   RHS (999 – LHS)

So, the answer is **57942**.

The process can be simplified even more:

1. Reduce 1 from the multiplicand
2. Write the extra 9(s) in the centre
3. Subtract the answer of step 1, from rest of the 9s in the multiplier.

The next example should make this method clear.

Example 5:
542 × 9999

Here the multiplicand, 542, has three digits and the multiplier, 9999, has four digits. So in this case, there is one 9 extra in the multiplier.

The answer can be arrived directly as

$$541 \; / \; 9 \; / \; 458 = \textbf{5419458}$$

       ↓

   extra 9

Example 6:
453 × 9999999

$$453 \times 9999999 = 452 \; / \; 9999 \; / \; 547$$
$$= \textbf{4529999547}$$

For more such tricks of calculation using Vedic maths, visit our website, www.aditisinghal.com, or refer to our book *How to Become a Human Calculator?*

Riddle Time

Which is heavier, milk or cream?

 Cream is actually lighter than milk, which is why cream will rise to the top.

16

LEARNING THE TIMES TABLES

Times tables are the basic foundation concepts for doing calculations. Most students find it easy to memorize tables till 10 or 11, but not beyond that. Most children, as well as adults, tend to turn to calculators for calculations even as simple as 16 × 8.

In this chapter you will learn a magical technique of working out tables mentally, from 12 right up to 99. Using this technique, we set the Guinness World Record for teaching the largest maths class, in which 2312 students were taught tables till 99. We also share this technique in almost all our workshops, and thousands of teachers have given very positive feedback after teaching it to their students.

Times Tables from 12 to 19

Let's understand the table of 12 first. It is easy to work out the table of 12 from the table of 2. Observe the pattern outlined on the next page:

$$2 \times \mathbf{1} = \mathbf{2} \qquad\qquad 12 \times 1 = \mathbf{12}$$

$$2 \times \mathbf{2} = \mathbf{4} \qquad\qquad 12 \times 2 = \mathbf{24}$$

$$2 \times \mathbf{3} = \mathbf{6} \qquad\qquad 12 \times 3 = \mathbf{36}$$

$$2 \times \mathbf{4} = \mathbf{8} \qquad\qquad 12 \times 4 = \mathbf{48}$$

Till 2 times 4 and 12 times 4, we are just shifting the factor to the tens place beside the product, i.e. in '2 × 3 = 6', we are taking the factor 3 to the tens place beside the product 6 to get '12 × 3 = 36'.

For 12 × 5 too, we will follow the same process. But 2 × 5 = 10 has two digits in the product, so we will add the factor '5' to '1' at the tens place to get 6, and the ones place will remain as it is, as shown below, to get the product:

$$2 \times \mathbf{5} = \mathbf{10} \qquad\qquad 12 \times 5 = \mathbf{60}$$
add

Similarly,

$$2 \times \mathbf{6} = \mathbf{12} \qquad\qquad 12 \times 6 = \mathbf{72}$$

$$2 \times \mathbf{7} = \mathbf{14} \qquad\qquad 12 \times 7 = \mathbf{84}$$

$$2 \times \mathbf{8} = \mathbf{16} \qquad\qquad 12 \times 8 = \mathbf{96}$$

$$2 \times \mathbf{9} = \mathbf{18} \qquad\qquad 12 \times 9 = \mathbf{108}$$

- In the same way, using the table of 3, we can write the table of 13.
- From the table of 4, we can get the table of 14.
- From the table of 5, we can get the table of 15.
- From the table of 7, we can get the table of 17.
- From the table of 9, we can get the table of 19.

You do not need to write out the entire table to determine only one particular product. Let's make this clearer with an example.

Suppose you need to find the answer to **13 × 6**.

We know that the table of 13 can be worked out from the table of 3, so visualize the corresponding multiplication from the table of 3 in your mind, and do the remaining calculation mentally, as shown below:

$$3 \times \mathbf{6} = \mathbf{18} \qquad\qquad 13 \times 6 = \mathbf{78}$$
add

Practise this with any random product of tables 12 to 19 and check for yourself.

Some more examples are given below:

$$6 \times \mathbf{8} = \mathbf{48} \qquad\qquad 16 \times 8 = \mathbf{128}$$

$$7 \times 7 = \mathbf{49} \qquad\qquad 17 \times 7 = \mathbf{119}$$

$$9 \times \mathbf{6} = \mathbf{54} \qquad\qquad 19 \times 6 = \mathbf{114}$$

Rules to remember

- Before applying the above technique, the learner must know the tables till 9.
- The learner must be able to add two digits mentally.
- To arrive at the product, you need to add just the factor (of the corresponding table) in the ten's place. The one's digit remains as it is.

A Myth about Learning Tables

Tables are always thought of as something to be learnt by heart, by repetitively chanting or reciting them. Because we have been taught this way for generations, we assume that this is the best way to teach or learn tables. But if this is the best way, why is memorizing tables such a big problem for students, their parents and teachers?

Through our experience of working with thousands of students of different age groups, and experiences shared by other teachers, we observed that more than 80 per cent of students feel unequipped to tackle even the most basic arithmetic operations because they don't know their tables thoroughly.

Learning anything becomes easy if we understand the pattern in it. For example, if someone tells you their number is 9810199101, you don't have to put in effort to memorize it, as there is a pattern to it, i.e. 98-101-99-101, so it gets automatically stored in your brain. This is how our brain works, and mathematics is all about understanding patterns.

Learning tables will also become easy if we understand the patterns in them instead of just mugging them up.

Times Tables up to 99

Once you practise tables till 19 for a week, you may learn the following method to do tables mentally till 99.

For example, let's take the table of 87.
First write down the table of 8 and then the table of 7 beside it:

Table of 8	Table of 7	Process	Table of 87
16	14	(16 + 1)4	174
24	21	(24 + 2)1	261
32	28	(32 + 2)8	348
40	35	(40 + 3)5	435
48	42	(48 + 4)2	522
56	49	(56 + 4)9	609
64	56	(64 + 5)6	696
72	63	(72 + 6)3	783
80	70	(80 + 7)0	870

Or you can calculate any single product as follows:

$$\overset{(8 \times 6)}{} \quad \overset{(7 \times 6)}{}$$
$$8\,7 \times 6 = \mathbf{4\,8} \qquad \mathbf{4}\,2 = \mathbf{52}2$$

add

This way one can work out tables from 21 to 99 mentally.

To access the activity sheets for practising times tables, visit our website: www.aditisinghal.com

Riddle Time

I add five to nine, and get two. The answer is correct, but how?

 When it is 9 a.m., add 5 hours to it and get 2 p.m.

17

AMAZING SQUARES

In this chapter we will learn an interesting trick that lets us easily find the squares of numbers with 5 as the last digit.

We follow this procedure for the trick:

1. The answer comes in two parts—LHS and RHS.
2. LHS is computed by multiplying the digit before 5 by its next consecutive number.
3. RHS is always 25 as the number ends in 5, and we know that $5^2 = 25$.

Let's take an example to understand it better.

Example 1:
Find the square of 35.

35^2 LHS = The digit before 5, i.e. 3, is multiplied by its next consecutive number, 4.

$3 \times 4 / 5^2$ i.e. $3 \times 4 = 12$

35^2 RHS = as the number ends in 5,
$$\downarrow \quad \downarrow$$ $5^2 = 25$
12 / 25

So, $35^2 =$ **1225**.

Example 2:
Find 75^2.

LHS = $7 \times 8 = 56$
RHS = $5^2 = 25$

So, $75^2 =$ **5625**.

Example 3:
Find 115^2.

LHS = $11 \times 12 = 132$
RHS = $5^2 = 25$

So, $115^2 =$ **13225**.

Some More Solved Examples:

85^2 = $(8 \times 9)/25$ = 7225
25^2 = $(2 \times 3)/25$ = 625
15^2 = $(1 \times 2)/25$ = 225
125^2 = $(12 \times 13)/25$ = 15625
405^2 = $(40 \times 41)/25$ = 164025

For more such calculation tricks using Vedic maths, visit our
website, www.aditisinghal.com, or refer to our book *How to
Become a Human Calculator?*

? Riddle Time

A certain number when written in words has four letters.
Take two letters away and you have four left.
Take one more letter away and you have five left.
What is the word?

? The word is FIVE.
Take away F and E, and you get IV (the Roman numeral for 4).
Take away I and you get V (the Roman numeral for 5).

18

SIMPLIFYING MULTIPLICATION

The following tricks will help you perform calculations just by taking a look at the question.

Multiplying Any Number by 5

Since $5 = \dfrac{10}{2}$, first multiply the number by 10 and then divide it in half.

Example 1:
62 × 5

Just put one 0 at the right of 62 to multiply it by 10, and divide the number obtained in half:

$$62 \times 5 = \frac{620}{2} = 310$$

Multiplying Any Number by 50

Since $50 = \dfrac{100}{2}$, to multiply a number by 50 add two 0s to its right and divide it in half.

Example 2:
38 × 50

$$38 \times 50 = \frac{3800}{2} = 1900$$

Multiplying Any Number by 25

Since $25 = \dfrac{100}{4}$, to multiply a number by 25 add two 0s to its right and divide it in half twice.

Example 3:
84 × 25

$$84 \times 25 = \frac{8400}{2 \times 2} = 2100$$

Multiplication by	Step I	Step II	Example
$5 = \dfrac{10}{2}$	Add one 0 to the right	Divide the result in half	$42 \times 5 = \dfrac{420}{2} = 210$
$50 = \dfrac{100}{2}$	Add two 0s to the right	Divide the result in half	$42 \times 50 = \dfrac{4200}{2} = 2100$

Multiplication by	Step I	Step II	Example
$500 = \dfrac{1000}{2}$	Add three 0s to the right	Divide the result in half	$42 \times 500 = \dfrac{42000}{2} = 21000$
$25 = \dfrac{100}{4}$	Add two 0s to the right	Divide the result in half twice	$42 \times 25 = \dfrac{4200}{2 \times 2} = 1050$
$250 = \dfrac{1000}{4}$	Add three 0s to the right	Divide the result in half twice	$42 \times 250 = \dfrac{42000}{2 \times 2} = 10500$

Another Magical Multiplication

Now we will see a magical multiplication of two numbers, where:

- The digits in the units place add up to 10
- The digits in the tens place are the same

We will get the answer in two parts—LHS and RHS.

For LHS answer:
Multiply the tens place digit by its next consecutive number (i.e. $n+1$ if n is the digit).

For RHS answer:
Multiply the digits at the units place by one another.

Example 4:
24 × 26

$4 + 6 = 10$, so the digits in the units place add up to 10, and the digit at the tens place is 2 in both the numbers.

24
26
———
6/24

LHS = Multiply the digit at tens place, i.e. 2, by its next consecutive number.

$2 \times (2 + 1) = 2 \times 3 = 6$

RHS = Multiply the digits at the units place.

$4 \times 6 = 24$

So, $24 \times 26 = 624$.

Special Tip

The number of digits on RHS is always double the number of 0s in the base.

(By base, we mean 10^n, e.g. 10, 100, 1000, etc.)

Example 5:
59 × 51

At the units place, $9 + 1 = 10$. And the tens digit is 5 for both numbers.

LHS = $5 \times (5 + 1) = 5 \times 6 = 30$

5 9
5 1
———
30/09

RHS = $9 \times 1 = 9$, i.e. 09

(since the number of digits on RHS = double of the number of 0s in the base, and since $9 + 1 = 10$, the base is 10 and has one 0)

So, $59 \times 51 = 3009$.

Note: This trick also holds true for numbers with more than two digits as well, where the units digits add up to 10 and the remaining digits are the same in both numbers.

Example 6:
602 × 608

At the units place, $8 + 2 = 10$, and the remaining digits are 60 for both numbers.

$$
\begin{array}{l}
6\ 0\ 2 \\
\underline{6\ 0\ 8} \\
3660/16
\end{array}
$$

LHS $= 60 \times (60 + 1) = 60 \times 61 = 3660$

RHS $= 2 \times 8 = 16$

So, $602 \times 608 = 366016$.

Special Tip

This method can also be extended to cases where groups of digits on the right in both multiplicand and multiplier add up to other bases such as 1000, 10,000 and so on, and the remaining digits on the left are the same in both numbers.

Example 7:
293 × 207

In this case, 3 and 7 in the units place add up to 10, but 29 and 20 don't match.

So, we will just consider the common digits for the LHS and add the rest of the digits to check if they add up to a multiple of 10.

So, 93 + 7 =100 can be taken as base and the remaining digit, i.e. 2, in the hundreds place is the same for both numbers.

2 9 3   LHS = 2 × (2 + 1) = 2 × 3 = 6
2 0 7   RHS = 93 × 7 = 0651
―――   (RHS will have four digits as 100 is the base and
6/0651   has two 0s)

So, 293 × 207 = 60651.

For more such tricks using Vedic maths, visit our website, www.aditisinghal.com, or refer to our book: *How to Become a Human Calculator?*

?   **Riddle Time**

If 8 birds can eat 8 worms in 8 minutes, how long will it take 16 birds to eat 16 worms?

19

MAGICAL DIVISION

The following is an amazing trick that serves as the fastest method to divide when the denominator ends in 9, e.g. 19, 39, 69, 119, etc.

We simplify the division process by the use of auxiliary (supporting) fractions, where big denominators are converted into small, and thus more comfortable, denominators and the whole division is carried out by this new divisor through a very unique procedure.

Example 1:
Convert $\dfrac{4}{29}$ to its decimal form

Conventional method:

$$29)\overline{40}\ (0.13793103448$$
$$\underline{29}$$
$$110$$
$$\underline{87}$$
$$230$$
$$\underline{203}$$

270
<u>261</u>
 90
 <u>87</u>
 30
 <u>29</u>
 10
 <u>00</u>
100
 <u>87</u>
130
<u>116</u>
140
<u>116</u>
240
<u>232</u>
 80

Magical method:

$$\frac{4}{29} = 0.13793103448\ldots$$

Let's understand this magical method.

Step 1

Add 1 to the denominator 29 to make it 30, and remove 0 from it by introducing a decimal point in the numerator, as shown:

$$\frac{4}{29 + 1} = \frac{4}{30} = \frac{0.4}{3} = \text{Auxiliary Fraction (AF)}$$

This new fraction $\dfrac{0.4}{3}$ is called the auxiliary fraction of $\dfrac{4}{29}$, which will help to find the answer in a very easy and unique way. Now we will carry out step-by-step division by taking the divisor as 3 instead of 29.

Step 2
Divide 0.4 by 3. This will be a slightly different kind of division as $\dfrac{0.4}{3}$ is an auxiliary fraction, not the original one.

Put the decimal point first and divide numerator 4 by denominator 3.

$$4 \div 3 \Rightarrow Q = 1, R = 1.$$

Write Q = 1 after the decimal point in the answer and place R, i.e. 1, before the quotient as shown below. Reminder and quotient taken together gives our next dividend as **11**.

$$\frac{0.4}{3} = 0._11$$

Step 3
Now divide 11 by 3.

$$11 \div 3 \Rightarrow Q = 3, R = 2$$

Write 3 as the next number in the quotient and place 2 before 3 as shown to give **23** as next dividend.

$$\frac{0.4}{3} = 0._11_23$$

Step 4
Divide 23 by 3, i.e. $23 \div 3 \Rightarrow Q = 7, R = 2$

Write it as shown below:

$$\frac{0.4}{3} = 0._{.1}1_23_27$$

Step 5
Next dividend $27 \div 3 \Rightarrow Q = 9$, $R = 0$

$$\frac{0.4}{3} = 0._{.1}1_23_27_09$$

The process can be continued up to any number of decimal places.

$$\frac{4}{29} = \frac{0.4}{3}\,(AF) = 0._{.1}1_23_27_09_03_01_03_14_24_08...$$

Discarding all the remainders, we get the final answer as:

$$\frac{4}{29} = \mathbf{0.13793103448\ldots}$$

Example 2:

Convert $\dfrac{57}{149}$ to its decimal form.

$$\frac{57}{149} = \frac{57}{150} = \frac{5.7}{15}\,(AF)$$

$$\frac{5.7}{15} = 0._{.12}3_38_82_75_05_53_83...$$

$$\frac{57}{149} = \mathbf{0.38255033\ldots}$$

Example 3:

Convert $\dfrac{17}{69}$ *to its decimal form.*

$$\frac{17}{69} = \frac{17}{70} = \frac{1.7}{7}\,(AF)$$

$$\frac{1.7}{7} = 0._32_44_26_53_47_56_08_11\ldots$$

$$\frac{17}{69} = \mathbf{0.24637681\ldots}$$

Isn't it like tossing off one digit after another mentally as if you already know the answer? This process takes only as much time as that needed to write the answer. That is why we call it Magical Division.

Special Tip

If the denominator ends with 7 or 3, you can use this magical trick by multiplying both the numerator and the denominator by 7 or 3, respectively, so that the resulting denominator ends in 9.

You can use this trick to impress your friends, by asking them to give you a single-digit or two-digit number. Let's say your friend gives you 35. Write this number as the numerator of the fraction.

Now, you choose any number ending with 9 and greater than 35 and write it as the denominator of the fraction.

Let's say you choose 89, so the fraction becomes $\frac{35}{89}$.

As discussed above, find its auxiliary fraction as $\frac{3.5}{9}$ and find the answer up to the desired number of decimal places, using 9 as divisor.

For more such tricks using Vedic maths, visit our website, www.aditisinghal.com, or refer to our book *How to Become a Human Calculator?*

? Riddle Time

Divide 30 by a half and add 10. What is the answer?

20

QUICK CUBE ROOTS

Shakuntala Devi, popularly known as 'the human computer', was a great mathematician who often used to amaze her audience during her academic shows. One of these mathematical feats was finding the cube root of six-digit numbers at a glance.

What Is a Cube Root?

When a number is multiplied by itself twice, we get the cube of the number.

For example, cube of $4 = 4^3 = 4 \times 4 \times 4 = 64$

Finding a cube root is just the reverse procedure of calculating a cube. It is actually finding the number which has been multiplied twice by itself to obtain the cube.

For example, 64 is the cube of 4, and 4 is the cube root of 64.

Similarly, 8 is the cube of 2, and 2 is the cube root of 8.

Normally, a lengthy prime factorization method has to be followed to find the cube root of big numbers. For example, let us find the cube root of 592704.

Conventional method:

2	592704
2	296352
2	148176
2	74088
2	37044
2	18522
3	9261
3	3087
3	1029
7	343
7	49
7	7
	1

Cube root = 2 × 2 × 3 × 7 = 84

The magical method explained below is much simpler:

Magical Method of Cube Root

To know the magic, let's first take the cubes of numbers from 1 to 9.

Number	Cube	Last digit of the cube
1	1	1
2	8	8

Number	Cube	Last digit of the cube
3	27	7
4	64	4
5	125	5
6	216	6
7	343	3
8	512	2
9	729	9

We can see that each cube has a unique last digit. By observing the last digit of the cube, we can easily tell the last digit of its cube root.

Here is the chart of the last digits of cube roots:

If a cube ends in	Last digit of its cube root will be
1	1
2	8
3	7
4	4
5	5
6	6
7	3
8	2
9	9
0	0

Some observations from the above table:

- If a cube ends in 1, 4, 5, 6 or 9, its corresponding cube root also ends with the same digit.

- If a cube ends with 2, its cube root ends with 8 and vice versa.
- Similarly, the cube of 3 ends with 7, and the cube of 7 ends with 3.

Steps for Finding the Cube Root

Step 1
Starting from the right-hand side, divide the number into two groups by putting a slash after three digits.

Step 2
By observing the left-hand side group, the first digit of the cube root can be determined. Consider the perfect cube smaller than or equal to the number in this group and take its cube root as the first digit of the required cube root.

Step 3
By looking at the last digit of the given cube, we can find out the second digit of the cube root.

Example 1:
Find the cube root of 117649.

Step 1

117 | 649   Put a slash after three digits from the right side of the number.

Step 2

117 | 649   The perfect cube smaller than the first group
  ↓   number '117' is 64, and cube root of 64 is 4.
  4   So the first digit of the cube root is 4.

Step 3

117 | 649   The last digit of the given number is 9, so the last
              digit is 9.

4   9

So, the cube root of 117649 is 49.

Example 2:
Find the cube root of 19683.

19 | 683

27

So, $\sqrt[3]{19683} = 27$

Note: This method of finding cube roots is possible only for perfect cubes with a maximum of six digits.

For more such tricks using Vedic maths, visit our website, www.aditisinghal.com, or refer to our book *How to Become a Human Calculator?*

?

Riddle time

If you take 3 apples from a group of 5, how many do you have?

? 3! You just took them yourself.

21

QUICK CALCULATIONS OF COMPOUND INTEREST

We all want to get maximum return on our savings or investments, so we look for the options where we can get more interest, i.e. return on investment is more. Let's look at why compound interest is always more beneficial than simple interest.

What Is Compound Interest?

At the end of a fixed period, the interest that has become due is not paid to the lender, but is added to the sum lent (i.e. the principal amount), and the amount thus obtained becomes the principal amount for the next period. This process is repeated till the final amount is paid. The difference between the original principal and the final amount is called compound interest (CI). Thus, compound interest includes interest on interest.

General Formula for Calculating Compound Interest

Let, Principal = P, Rate = R% per annum, Time = n years, Amount = A.

When interest is compounded annually, the formula is:

$$A = P\left(1 + \frac{R}{100}\right)^n$$

$$CI = A - P$$

$$CI = P\left[\left(1 + \frac{R}{100}\right)^n - 1\right]$$

Let's take an example.

Example 1:
₹12,000 is borrowed at CI at the rate of 10% per annum. What will be the amount to be paid after 2 years?

P = ₹12000
R = 10% p.a.
T = 2 years

$$A = P\left(1 + \frac{R}{100}\right)^n$$

$$= 12000\left(1 + \frac{10}{100}\right)^2$$

$$= 12000 \times \frac{11}{10} \times \frac{11}{10}$$

$$= 120 \times 121$$

$$= 14520$$

So, CI = A – P
          = 14520 – 12000
          = ₹2520

But there is another easier way of finding compound interest which will take less time.

Easiest Method of Calculating Compound Interest

Case 1: When the rate of interest is the same in both the years

If the rate of interest is R% per year, for 2 years, compound interest would be:

$$\textbf{Compound Interest (CI)} = \left[2R + \frac{R^2}{100} \right] \% \textbf{ of P}$$

Let's take the previous example again. Here, R = 10 and P = 12000.

$$CI = \left(20 + \frac{100}{100} \right) \% \text{ of } 12000$$
$$= 21\% \text{ of } 12000$$
$$= \frac{21}{100} \times 12000$$
$$= 2520$$

So, using the above formula we calculated that CI is actually 21% and thus we directly found it for 2 years.

Case 2: When the rate of interest is different for each year

If the rate of interest is different in each of the two years, the formula will become:

$$\textbf{Compound Interest (CI)} = \left[a + b + \frac{a \times b}{100} \right] \% \textbf{ of P}$$

Where *a* and *b* are the two different rates of interest.

Case 3: When the time period is 3 years

The formula in Case1 is applicable only when the time period is 2 years. If the time period is 3 years, we use the formula twice, i.e. first we calculate the effective rate of interest for the first 2 years and then use that along with the second formula for the third year.

Example 2:
Find the compound interest on ₹14,000 at 20% per annum for 3 years.

P = ₹14000
R = 20 % p.a.
T = 3 years

Here, the rate of interest for the first, second and third year is the same, i.e. 20%.

So, for the first 2 years, $CI = \left[2R + \dfrac{R^2}{100} \right]\%$ of P

$$= \left[2(20) + \dfrac{20^2}{100} \right]\% \text{ of P}$$

$$= \left[40 + \dfrac{400}{100} \right]\% \text{ of P}$$

$$= 44\% \text{ of P}$$

We then take this interest rate as *a*, for the first two years, and the original interest rate, i.e. 20%, as *b* and put them in the formula presented in Case 2.

So, for 3 years, $CI = \left[44 + 20 + \dfrac{44 \times 20}{100} \right]\%$ of P

$$= \left(64 + \frac{88}{10} \right) \% \text{ of P}$$

$$= 72.8\% \text{ of P}$$

Thus, at the end of three years,

$$CI = \frac{72.8}{100} \times 14000$$

$$= 728 \times 14$$

$$= ₹10,192$$

Thus, we have directly calculated 72.8% of the principal amount to get the compound interest for 3 years.

Example 3:
If the compound interest (CI) on a certain sum for 2 years at 5% is ₹115.50, what would be the simple interest (SI)?

Traditional method:

$$CI \text{ on } ₹1 = \left(1 + \frac{5}{100} \right)^2 - 1 = \left(\frac{105}{100} \right)^2 - 1 = \frac{441}{400} - 1 = ₹\frac{41}{400}$$

$$SI \text{ on } ₹1 = \frac{2 \times 5}{100} = \frac{1}{10}$$

$$\therefore \quad \frac{SI}{CI} = \frac{1}{10} \times \frac{400}{41} = \frac{40}{41}$$

$$\therefore \quad SI = \frac{40}{41} \text{ of } CI = \frac{40}{41} \times 115.5 = ₹112.68$$

Shortcut method:

SI $= 2 \times 5 = 10\%$ of principal amount.

CI $= 10 + \dfrac{5^2}{100} = 10.25\%$ of principal amount.

Here, 10.25% of principal is ₹115.5.

$\therefore$ 10% of principal $= \dfrac{115.5}{10.25} \times 10 = \dfrac{4620}{41} = ₹112.68$

So, now you have learnt a way of calculating compound interest that is very simple and easier to calculate than the traditional method.

Riddle Time

I am an odd number; take away a letter and I become even. What number am I?

22

THE PRIME CHECK

A prime number is a whole number that is greater than 1 and has only two factors, namely 1 and the number itself. For example, 2, 3, 5, 7, etc. are prime numbers.

In this chapter we will see how to check whether a given number is a prime number or not. Let's take the number 39.

One way is to check its divisibility by all the numbers from 2 to 38. This method is very time-consuming and becomes increasingly difficult with larger numbers. For example, if we need to check whether 9837 is a prime or not, it is very difficult to use this method.

Shortcut Method

1. If the number is even, surely it is not a prime number as it will at least have the number 2 as one of its factors.
2. If the given number is odd and we do not know the factors of that number—as in the case of 239 or 541 or 9476571—take the square root of the number and check the divisibility of the number with the prime numbers less

than its square root only; no need to check with the prime numbers beyond that.

How does it work?

If a and b are two factors of the given number, say N, and if a is smaller than the square root of N, the other factor b must be larger than its square root. So, checking the divisibility with prime numbers up to its square root will surely cover one of the factors and then there is no need to check it with the rest of the numbers.

Let's consider a few examples.

Example 1:
Check if 37 is a prime number or not.

Since, 37 is an odd number, let's find its square root first.

$$\sqrt{37} \sim 6.08$$

(In this case we can directly take it approximately 6 as we know $\sqrt{36} = 6$ and the square of 7 is 49.)

Now, we need to check the divisibility of 37 only with the prime numbers less than 6, i.e. 2, 3, 5.

Divisibility by 2

37 is not even, so it is not divisible by 2.

Divisibility by 3

The sum of the digits is 3 + 7 = 10, which is not divisible by 3, so 3 is not a factor.

Divisibility by 5

37 does not end in 0 or 5, so 5 is not a factor.

So, 37 has no factors, other than 1 and 37 itself. Hence, 37 is a prime number.

Example 2:
Check if 239 is a prime number or not.

Since, 239 is an odd number, let's find its square root first.

$$\sqrt{239} \sim 15.459$$

(If you remember that $15^2 = 225$ and $16^2 = 256$, you can simply take 15 as the approximate square root.)

Now, we need to check the divisibility of 239 only with the prime numbers less than 15, i.e. 2, 3, 5, 7, 9 and 11.

Divisibility by 2

As 239 is not even, it is not divisible by 2.

Divisibility by 3

The sum of the digits of 239 is 2 + 3 + 9 =14, which is not divisible by 3, so 3 is not a factor.

Divisibility by 5

239 does not end in 0 or 5, so 5 is not a factor.

Divisibility by 7

Double the last digit and subtract it from the rest of the digits and check the divisibility with the resulting number, i.e. for 239, double of 9 is 18 and $23 - 18 = 5$, which is not divisible by 7, so 7 is not a factor.

Divisibility with 9

The sum of the digits of 239 is 14, which is not divisible by 9, so 9 is not a factor.

Divisibility with 11

Check if the difference of the sum of even-place digits and the sum of odd-place digits is 0 or a multiple of 11. In the above number it is $(2 + 9) - (3) = 11 - 3 = 8$, which is not a multiple of 11, so 11 is not a factor.

So, 239 has no factors, other than 1 and 239 itself. Hence, 239 is a prime number.

Special Tip

To check the divisibility of all the numbers less than 100, we just need to check the divisibility of the given number with 2, 3, 5, 7 and 9, since $\sqrt{100} = 10$.

Prime numbers between 1 and 1000									
2	3	5	7	11	13	17	19	23	29
31	37	41	43	47	53	59	61	67	71
73	79	83	89	97	101	103	107	109	113
127	131	137	139	149	151	157	163	167	173
179	181	191	193	197	199	211	223	227	229
233	239	241	251	257	263	269	271	277	281
283	293	307	311	313	317	331	337	347	349
353	359	367	373	379	383	389	397	401	409
419	421	431	433	439	443	449	457	461	463
467	479	487	491	499	503	509	521	523	541
547	557	563	569	571	577	587	593	599	601
607	613	617	619	631	641	643	647	653	659
661	673	677	683	691	701	709	719	727	733
739	743	751	757	761	769	773	787	797	809
811	821	823	827	829	839	853	857	859	863
877	881	883	887	907	911	919	929	937	941
947	953	967	971	977	983	991	997		

You can also do the primality test online using the following website: http://www.onlineconversion.com/prime.htm

Riddle Time

There are twelve ₹1 coins in a dozen, how many ₹2 coins are there in a dozen?

12

23

COMPARING SURDS

In competitive exams, some questions require you to arrange the given numbers in ascending or descending order. Most of the time, these are numbers with large exponents or surds, like $\sqrt[2]{4}$, $\sqrt[3]{3}$, etc.

So, in this chapter we are sharing a trick to solve such questions especially with surds.

What Is a Surd?

Surds are numbers left in root form ($\sqrt{}$) to express their exact value, as it has an infinite number of non-recurring decimals. Therefore, surds are irrational numbers. For example, $\sqrt{2}, \sqrt[4]{3}$ or $5^{\frac{1}{3}}$, etc.

In general, a surd is of the form: $\sqrt[n]{a}$ or $a^{\frac{1}{n}}$, where a is the radicand and n is the order of the surd, i.e. the nth root of a.

Comparison of Surds

Step 1
Check if the order of surds is same. Two surds of the same order can be easily compared by just comparing their radicands, e.g. $\sqrt{3} > \sqrt{2}$.
Hence, $\sqrt[n]{a} > \sqrt[n]{b}$, if $a > b$.

Step 2
If the orders of two surds are different, e.g. $\sqrt[n]{a}$, $\sqrt[m]{b}$, then first we reduce them to the surds of same order, by taking the LCM of the orders of the given surds and applying the following method:

$$\sqrt[n]{a} = \sqrt[mn]{a^m} \text{ and } \sqrt[m]{b} = \sqrt[mn]{b^n}$$

Step 3
After making the order of surds the same, compare the radicand as in Step 1. The greater the radicand, the greater the surd would be.

Let's take a few examples.

Example 1:
Which is greater $\sqrt{3}$ or $\sqrt[3]{5}$?

First of all, we will take the LCM of the orders of the given surds. LCM of 2 and 3 is 6.

$$\sqrt{3} = \sqrt[2 \times 3]{3^3} = \sqrt[6]{27}$$
$$\sqrt[3]{5} = \sqrt[3 \times 2]{5^2} = \sqrt[6]{25}$$

Clearly, $\sqrt[6]{27} > \sqrt[6]{25}$ $\therefore \sqrt{3} > \sqrt[3]{5}$

Example 2:
Which is greater, $\sqrt[3]{3}$ or $\sqrt[4]{5}$?

LCM of 3 and 4 is 12.

$\sqrt[3]{3} = \sqrt[3 \times 4]{3^4} = \sqrt[12]{81}$

$\sqrt[4]{5} = \sqrt[4 \times 3]{5^3} = \sqrt[12]{125}$

Clearly, $\sqrt[12]{125} > \sqrt[12]{81}$

$\therefore \sqrt[4]{5} > \sqrt[3]{3}$

Example 3:
Which is greater, $\left(\dfrac{1}{2}\right)^{\frac{1}{2}}$ or $\left(\dfrac{2}{3}\right)^{\frac{1}{3}}$?

LCM of 2 and 3 is 6.

$\left(\dfrac{1}{2}\right)^{\frac{1}{2}} = \sqrt[2]{\dfrac{1}{2}} = \sqrt[2 \times 3]{\left(\dfrac{1}{2}\right)^3} = \sqrt[6]{\dfrac{1}{8}}$

$\left(\dfrac{2}{3}\right)^{\frac{1}{3}} = \sqrt[3]{\dfrac{2}{3}} = \sqrt[3 \times 2]{\left(\dfrac{2}{3}\right)^2} = \sqrt[6]{\dfrac{4}{9}}$

Clearly, $\dfrac{4}{9} > \dfrac{1}{8}$

$\therefore \sqrt[3]{\dfrac{2}{3}} > \sqrt[2]{\dfrac{1}{2}}$

Example 4:
Arrange the following surds in descending order:

$$\sqrt[3]{2}, \sqrt[6]{3}, \sqrt[9]{4}$$

LCM of 3, 6 and 9 is 18.

$$\sqrt[3]{2} = \sqrt[3\times 6]{2^6} = \sqrt[18]{64}$$
$$\sqrt[6]{3} = \sqrt[6\times 3]{3^3} = \sqrt[18]{27}$$
$$\sqrt[9]{4} = \sqrt[9\times 2]{4^2} = \sqrt[18]{16}$$
$$\sqrt[18]{64} > \sqrt[18]{27} > \sqrt[18]{16}$$
$$\therefore \sqrt[3]{2} > \sqrt[6]{3} > \sqrt[9]{4}$$

Similarly, you may also compare powers of numbers by converting their exponents to the same number.

Example 5:
Which is greater, $(2)^{40}$ or $(3)^{30}$?

$$(2)^{40} = (2)^{4\times 10} = (2^4)^{10} = (16)^{10}$$
$$(3)^{30} = (3)^{3\times 10} = (3^3)^{10} = (27)^{10}$$

Clearly, $27 > 16$
$\therefore (3)^{30} > (2)^{40}$

Example 6:
Which is greater, $(2)^{125}$ or $[32 \times (10)^{36}]$?

$$
\begin{aligned}
(2)^{125} &= (2)^{5+120} \\
&= 2^5 \times 2^{120} \\
&= 32 \times 2^{10\times 12} \\
&= 32 \times (2^{10})^{12}
\end{aligned}
$$

$$
\begin{aligned}
32 \times (10)^{36} &= 32 \times (10)^{3\times 12} \\
&= 32 \times (10^3)^{12}
\end{aligned}
$$

Clearly, $2^{10} > 10^3$ (As $2^{10} = 1024$ and $10^3 = 1000$)
$\therefore (2)^{125} > [32 \times (10)^{36}]$

Riddle Time

How many eggs can you put in an empty basket that is one foot in diameter?

Only one egg, because after that the basket doesn't remain empty any more!

PART C

INTERESTING MATHS FACTS

24

RACES ON TRACKS

Why Athletes Start from Different Positions

In track races that are run in multiples of 200 m, competitors in each lane begin at different points around the track. At first glance, it appears as though everybody is running a different length. However, on the contrary, this is done to make sure that all athletes run the same distance. Confused? Read on for the explanation.

Running tracks are oval in shape and are made this way on purpose. If the participants are running a short race, say, 100 m, it is convenient to run in a straight line. Longer races of 200 or 400 metres could also be run in a straight line, but in that case, the required track would be very long and it would be a poor spectator sport. The reason making fields oval is that it is easier to build spectator arenas around them.

An official oval running track has two straights of length 84.39 m and two semi-circular ends with an inside radius of 36.50 m so that the track is 400 m around (using the inside lane). The runner is assumed to be running 0.30 m (approximately

1 foot) away from the inside edge. This gives a running radius of
36.80 m for the innermost track.

You can see now how the maths works out. A 400 m oval has
two straights of 84.39 m and two curved sections of 36.80 m × π
in length.

Total track length = (2 × 84.39 m) + (2 × 36.80 m × π)
= 168.78 m + 231.22 m = 400 m

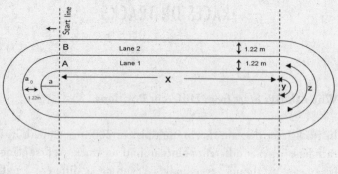

400 m Track

If the starting point is the same for athletes A and B, as shown in
above figure, the total length covered by athlete A in lane1 is equal
to (2x + 2y) = 400 m.
The total length covered by athlete B in lane 2 is equal to
(2x + 2z) > 400 m.

So, to compensate for this error, athlete B is asked to start in a
different position.

To find this position, we use the formula circumference = $2\pi r$

The distance covered along the straight path $(2x)$ is the same for all the lanes. The variation occurs only along the curved path. The two arcs, which are semicircles, together constitute a circle.

The first lane has a radius of a.

So, $2y = 2\pi a$

The second lane has a radius of $a + a_0$.

So, $2z = 2\pi(a + a_0)$

$2z = 2\pi a + 2\pi a_0$

Thus, the difference in the curved length of lane 2 and lane 1 is:

$2z - 2y = 2\pi a + 2\pi a_0 - 2\pi a = 2\pi a_0$

In accordance with the requirements of the International Association of Athletics Federations, each lane is 1.22 m wide.

So, $a_0 = 1.22$ m.

Therefore, $2\pi a_0 = 2 \times 3.14 \times 1.22 = 7.66$ m

So, to compensate this defect of excessive length covered in lane 2, the athlete B is made to start from a location B_1, 7.66 m ahead of the starting line.

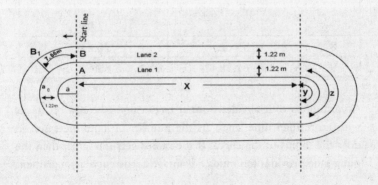

This same concept is applied to all the nine lanes.

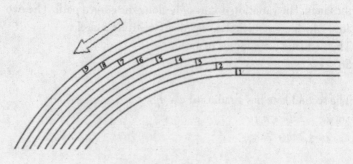

Lanes	Length Advanced	
	Adjustment (approx. in m) for 400 m (2 arcs)	Adjustment (approx. in m) for 200 m (1 arc)
1	0.00	0.00
2	7.66	3.83
3	15.32	7.66
4	22.98	11.49
5	30.64	15.32
6	38.30	19.15
7	45.96	22.98
8	53.62	26.81
9	61.28	30.64

According to official rules, formal races cannot be run on tracks with more than nine lanes. As the number of lanes increases, so does the radius of the curve. If the radius gets too large, then the outer lane provides too much advantage as the curve is so gentle it seems to be a straight section of track; runners find it easier to run on a straight track instead of a curve.

Cautioning the witness to remember that she was under oath,
the lawyer asked, 'How old are you?'
'Twenty-nine years and some months,' she replied.
'How many months?'
'A hundred and ten.'

25

MATHS BEHIND CREDIT/DEBIT CARD NUMBERING

All credit and debit cards have numbers printed on them (generally 16 digits). This signifies a unique account number for a particular card and reveals some information about the card issuer and its associated account. The card numbers are not randomly generated numbers, but rather have interesting maths behind them.

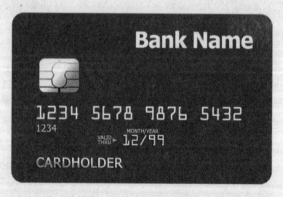

Let's break it down cluster by cluster.

1. Card Number

Credit/debit card numbers are all numeric and between 12 and 19 digits. For example, MasterCard has 16 digits and American Express has 15 digits.

2. Major Industry Identifier

The first digit of the credit/debit card is the Major Industry Identifier (MII). It indicates the category of the entity which issued the card.

- 1 and 2: Airlines
- 3: Travel and entertainment
- 4 and 5: Banking and financial services
- 6: Merchandising and banking
- 7: Petroleum
- 8: Health care, telecommunications
- 9: National assignment

3. Issuer Identification Number

The first six digits are the Issuer Identification Number (IIN). These denote the institution that issued the card. For example, Visa cards begin with a 4, while MasterCard ones start with numbers between 51 and 55.

Here is a list of some of the common card issuers and their IINs:

Issuing network	IIN ranges	Number of digits
American Express	34, 37	15
China Union Pay	62	16–19
Diners Club International	300–305, 309, 36, 38, 39	14
Discover	6011, 622126–622925, 644–649, 65	16, 19
JCB	3528–3589	16
Maestro	50, 56–69	12–19
MasterCard	51–55 2221–2720	16 16
RuPay	607	16
Visa	4	13, 16, 19

The Maths behind the Card Numbering

In a typical sixteen-digit credit card number, the first fifteen digits are determined by the issuing bank, but the last digit, called the *check digit*, is mathematically determined based on all the other digits.

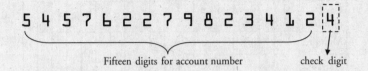

Fifteen digits for account number   check digit

It is very common to make a mistake while typing out a sixteen-digit number. Hence, the last digit is used to check if there are any errors.

Although, not all errors can be detected with a single check digit, one can still find out if one digit is wrong. Whenever an e-commerce application, for example, has to validate a card number, it checks this last digit before sending the rest of the information to the bank.

The exact mathematical formula for the check digit was invented by Hans Peter Luhn in 1954. The Luhn algorithm works in the following way.

Let's suppose the number for which we need a check digit is 545762279823412 and the check digit is x. Then our final sixteen-digit card number is

$$545762279823412x$$

To calculate the check digit, follow these steps:

Step 1
Starting from the rightmost digit (i.e. the check digit), multiply every second digit (i.e. digits at even positions) by 2, e.g. $4 \times 2 = 8$. If you get a two-digit number after the multiplication, add these digits to get a single digit, e.g. $6 \times 2 = 12$, then $1 + 2 = 3$.

Card number	5	4	5	7	6	2	2	7	9	8	2	3	4	1	2	x
Multiply even position digits by 2 (starting from the right)	10		10		12		4		18		4		8		4	
Add double digits	1+0		1+0		1+2		4		1+8		4		8		4	
New result	1		1		3		4		9		4		8		4	

Step 2

Add the resulting digits to the digits at the odd positions.

Card number	5	4	5	7	6	2	2	7	9	8	2	3	4	1	2	x
New result	1		1		3		4		9		4		8		4	
Odd position digits		4		7		2		7		8		3		1		x
Total	$1 + 4 + 1 + 7 + 3 + 2 + 4 + 7 + 9 + 8 + 4 + 3 + 8 + 1 + 4 + x = 66 + x$															

Step 3

The total obtained in Step 2 (i.e. $66 + x$), should be divisible by 10, only then this number is a valid card number, according to the Luhn algorithm.

Thus the check digit (x) should be calculated accordingly, so that the final total is divisible by 10. In the above example, x must be 4, so that the total will be $66 + 4 = 70$. (Remember, x can only be a single digit.)

Hence, the final valid card number is 5457622798234124.

Let's see a few more examples.

Example 1:
Check whether the following would be a valid credit card number or not.

$$4162\ 0012\ 3456\ 7893$$

Step 1
Starting from the right, multiply the digits at even positions by 2. In case the result is a two-digit number, add the digits to make it a single digit.

Step 2
Add the digits resulting from the previous step to the digits at the odd positions.

Card number	4	1	6	2	0	0	1	2	3	4	5	6	7	8	9	3
Multiply even position digits by 2 (starting from the right)	8		12		0		2		6		10		14		18	
Adding double digits	8		1+2		0		2		6		1+0		1+4		1+8	
New result	8		3		0		2		6		1		5		9	
Odd position digits		1		2		0		2		4		6		8		3
Total	8 + 1 + 3 + 2 + 0 + 0 + 2 + 2 + 6 + 4 + 1 + 6 + 5 + 8 + 9 + 3 = 60															

Since, the total (60) is a multiple of 10, 4162 0012 3456 7893 may be a valid credit card number.

Example 2:
Check whether the following would be a valid credit card number or not.

$$6070 \quad 6432 \quad 1023 \quad 2453$$

Step 1
Starting from the right, multiply the digits at even positions by 2. In case the result is a two-digit number, add the digits together to get a single digit.

Step 2
Add the digits resulting from the previous step to the digits at the odd positions.

Card number	6	0	7	0	6	4	3	2	1	0	2	3	2	4	5	3
Multiply even position digits by 2(starting from the right)	12		14		12		6		2		4		4		10	
Adding double digits	1+2		1+4		1+2		6		2		4		4		1+0	
New result	3		5		3		6		2		4		4		1	
Odd position digits		0		0		4		2		0		3		4		3
Total	3 + 0 + 5 + 0 + 3 + 4 + 6 + 2 + 2 + 0 + 4 + 3 + 4 + 4 + 1 + 3 = 44															

Since, the total (44) is a not a multiple of 10, ᏏᏆᏆᏋᏍᏣᏅᏝᏆᏆᏤᏅᏅᏦᏯᏍᏫ ᏍᏝᏍ is not a valid credit card number.

A mathematician organizes a lottery in which the prize is an infinite amount of money. When the winning ticket is drawn, and the jubilant winner comes to claim his prize, the mathematician explains the mode of payment: '1 dollar now, 1/2 dollar next week, 1/3 dollar the week after that . . .'

26

WHY IS 1 ONE, WHY IS 2 TWO?

Arabic numerals or Hindu–Arabic numerals are made up of ten digits: 0, 1, 2, 3, 4, 5, 6, 7, 8, 9. These are the most common symbolic representations of numbers in the world today.

The decimal Hindu–Arabic numeral system was developed in India by AD 700. The development was gradual, spanning several centuries, but the decisive step was probably provided by Brahmagupta's formulation of zero as a number in AD 628.

The Arabs picked up these numerals and popularized them, and they stood in contrast to the Roman numerals (I, II, III, IV, V, etc.).

Have You Ever Thought about Why 1 Is One, 2 Is Two, 3 Is Three?

It's simple—check the number of angles in each figure!

Look at these numbers written in their primitive form, as shown in the following images:

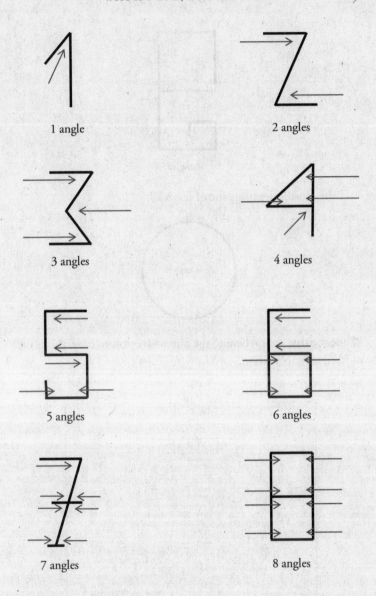

1 angle

2 angles

3 angles

4 angles

5 angles

6 angles

7 angles

8 angles

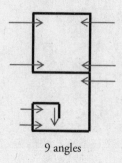

9 angles

And the most interesting one of them all,

Zero angles!

While the true reason behind the numerals is lost to time, this is the most likely explanation.

27

IS ZERO EVEN OR ODD?

What do you think?
Is zero an odd number or an even number?
Can you explain why?

This is a common question we ask in many of our workshops, be it with teachers, students or working people.

Almost everyone has an answer to this one. Some say it's even and some think it cannot be classified as even or odd. But when it comes to justifying this with a reason, they are dumbfounded.

So let us examine this matter.

For a number to be even, the following must be true:

1. The number must be divisible by 2

Divisible by 2 means when a number is divided by 2, it should leave 0 as remainder.

For example:

$26 \div 2$ gives quotient 13 and remainder 0.

Hence, 26 is even.

2. If you can write the number as 2 times something

For example:

$26 = 2 \times 13$

Hence, 26 is even.

3. If it can be represented as a number plus itself

For example:

$26 = 13 + 13$

Hence, 26 is even.

Let us check the above conditions with 0,

1. $0 \div 2 = 0$

2. $2 \times 0 = 0$

3. $0 + 0 = 0$

All the above three conditions are true with 0. Therefore, zero is an even number.

28

WHY IS DIVISION BY 0 NOT DEFINED?

The mathematician Bhaskara II (AD 1114–85) was the first to give the correct explanation of what division by zero means in his book *Lilavati*. Before him, Brahmagupta was the one who started working with 0 as a separate number, and tried to define operations using 0.

When someone needs to answer a question where they need to divide a number by zero, it sometimes leads to confusion and most of the times it is done wrong.

For example, they write: $\dfrac{3}{0} = 0$ or $\dfrac{3}{0} = 3$

Although some people are aware of the fact that division by zero is not defined, they usually do not know the reason behind it.

Let's understand why this is so.

Reason 1: Division is a process of repeated subtraction, till the remainder is 0

For example:

$$16 \div 2 = ?$$

$16 - 2 = 14$	First stage
$14 - 2 = 12$	Second stage
$12 - 2 = 10$	Third stage
$10 - 2 = 8$	Fourth stage
$8 - 2 = 6$	Fifth stage
$6 - 2 = 4$	Sixth stage
$4 - 2 = 2$	Seventh stage
$2 - 2 = 0$	Eighth stage

The final remainder 0 is reached at the eighth stage. Hence, $16 \div 2 = 8$.

Now, let's divide a number, say 1, with 0 and try to solve it, using the process of repeated subtraction:

$$1 \div 0 = ?$$

$1 - 0 = 1$	First stage
$1 - 0 = 1$	Second stage
$1 - 0 = 1$	Third stage
$1 - 0 = 1$	Fourth stage

You can't achieve the final remainder of 0, no matter how many attempts you make.

Reason 2: Division is the inverse process of multiplication

For example:

$$6 \div 2 = 3$$
$$2 \times 3 = 6$$
Or
If $a \div b = c$, then $b \times c = a$

Suppose $1 \div 0 = x$.
Then $x \times 0 = 1$.
But the product of any number with zero can never be 1.

So, it becomes clear why division by 0 is undefined.

PART D

MATHEMAGICIAN TECHNIQUES FOR COMPETITIVE EXAMS AND INTERVIEWS

29

AN INTERVIEW QUESTION

Interviews are an integral part of not just the hiring process in companies, but also of the admission process of reputed educational institutions. Let's take a look at an interesting interview question.

A company was looking to hire a person for one of its senior posts. They made the final round of selection a tricky one to ensure that the most suitable candidate was picked. There were six candidates who reached the final round. They all were given this situation to solve:

There are five men. Two of them have red pens and three of them have blue pens. The men having 'red pens' always give the right answer whereas the ones having 'blue pens' always give the incorrect answers. Without looking at their pens you have to identify which of these men have red pens and which ones have blue pens. For this you are allowed to ask only one question to any of these men.

All the five men were made to stand in a row with their pens hidden in their pockets.

All the candidates were confused. They racked their brains trying to come up with a suitable question. The task seemed impossible.

After a few minutes, one candidate stepped forward.

Can you guess what question he asked?

He asked the first man in the row, 'Who has which pen?'

The man pointed to each of the pen holders, starting with himself, and said, 'Red, blue, red, red, blue.'

The other candidates started smiling. They had also thought of asking this question but, for them, this was not enough to solve the puzzle. This fellow is a simpleton, they thought.

The candidate smiled and said, 'I have the solution. The second and the fifth man in the row have red pens and the rest have blue pens.'

The interviewers asked all the men to reveal their pens. The candidate's answer was correct, and he was selected for the post. The rest were baffled as how he got the solution with just one question.

Can you figure it out?

SOLUTION

The chosen candidate was really smart—he had already judged that there are only two possible replies to the question he was going to ask.

If the first man has a blue pen, he will give an incorrect answer and in his reply there will be three men carrying red pens and two carrying blue, in this case 'red, blue, red, red, blue'.

In case the first man has a red pen, his reply will be correct and he will only point out two men as carrying red pens, with the other three men having blue pens. Thus, his answer will be the actual solution.

In this case, the man replied, 'Red, blue, red, red, blue.' Since the candidate already knew that there are only two red pens, this is clearly the wrong answer, and all he had to do to get the right one is switch all the colours, i.e. 'blue, red, blue, blue, red'.

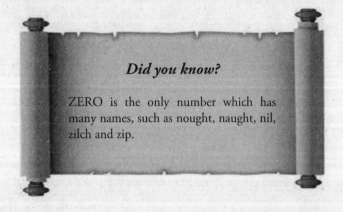

Did you know?

ZERO is the only number which has many names, such as nought, naught, nil, zilch and zip.

30

HANDSHAKES

Handshakes are a favourite topic of question setters, whether for puzzles, competitive exams or interviews, probably because they lend themselves so easily to problems of permutations and combinations.

For instance, how many handshakes occur when a group of 26 people shake hands exactly once with every other person at a party?

SOLUTION

The first person A can shake hands with 25 other people.
The second person B can shake hands with only 24 other people, as he/she has already shaken hands with person A.

In the same way, the third person C can shake hands with 23 people.

(Remember, A and B have already been greeted and no person shakes hands with themselves.)

So the total number of handshakes will be 25 + 24 + 23 + 22 + . . . + 3 + 2 + 1 = 325.

What if the number of people is higher, say 166, or n? Is there any formula to calculate it?

Considering that each person shakes hands $(n-1)$ times, and there are n people, there would be $(n-1)(n)$ handshakes, but this includes each handshake twice (A with B, B with A) so dividing it by 2 gives the correct answer.

Thus we can calculate it using the formula $\frac{(n-1)n}{2}$, where n is the number of people.

Another way of finding the formula:

We have seen above that if there are n people, then the total number of handshakes is:

$$(n-1) + (n-2) + . . . + 3 + 2 + 1$$

So we can use the formula of finding sum of first n natural numbers, which is $\frac{n(n+1)}{2}$. Here, we just need to find the sum of first $n-1$ natural numbers. So substituting n with $n-1$ we get the final formula for total number of handshakes as $\frac{(n-1)n}{2}$.

Another way of looking at this puzzle is:

At a party, everyone shook hands with everybody else. There were 66 handshakes. How many people were there at the party?

As we have discussed above that we can get the total number of handshakes using

$$\frac{(n-1)n}{2}$$

where, n is the number of people.

So, $66 = \frac{(n-1)n}{2}$

Therefore, $n = 12$.

Let's look at another example.

There are 10 cricket teams in a tournament. How many games must be played so that each team plays with every other team exactly once?

This is similar to the handshake puzzle. Each team playing every other team is similar to each person shaking hands with every other person.

Therefore the number of games that need to be played is

$$= \frac{(10)(9)}{2} = 45$$

The concept can also be used to solve some traditional maths problems. Let's see how we can relate the handshake problem to finding the number of diagonals in a polygon. The following are some shapes with their diagonals:

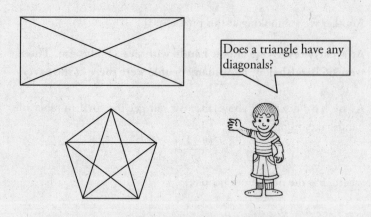

Number of sides	Number of diagonals
4	2
5	5
6	9
7	14
8	20
9	27

Let's represent the handshake problem in pictorial form. Draw a rectangle and label it ABCD.

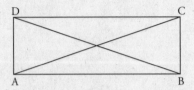

Think of the four points as persons A, B, C and D. A diagonal is a handshake with everyone except yourself and the two people adjacent to you.

Thus, in this case, person A cannot shake hands with themselves, or persons B and D. This would imply here that if the total number of people is n, A will shake hands with $n - 3$ people.

Person B can only shake hands with D, since A and C are adjacent, and B won't shake hands with themselves. Again we have $n - 3$ handshakes rather than $n - 1$.

So, just as the total number of handshakes was $\frac{(n)(n-1)}{2}$, the total number of diagonals = $\frac{(n)(n-3)}{2}$, where n is the number of sides of the polygon.

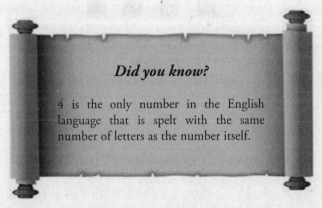

Did you know?

4 is the only number in the English language that is spelt with the same number of letters as the number itself.

31

INVESTIGATING SQUARES

How many squares are there on a chessboard?

Observe a chess board having 8 rows and 8 columns.

It has 8 squares in each row and 8 squares in each columns, so most people initially would say the answer is quite simple as:

$$8 \times 8 = 64 \text{ squares}$$

But this is *incorrect*.

It requires a methodical approach to count squares in such investigations. The detailed solution follows on the next page.

SOLUTION

As you can see that apart from 64 '1 × 1' squares, there is one '8 × 8' square, and similarly more such squares as shown below:

1. Counting '8 × 8' squares:

'8 × 8' square – ONE

2. Counting '7 × 7' squares:

'7 × 7' squares – FOUR

3. Counting '6 × 6' squares:

'6 × 6' squares – NINE

4. Counting '5 × 5' squares:

'5 × 5' squares – SIXTEEN

5. Counting '4 × 4' squares:

'4 × 4' squares – TWENTY-FIVE

6. Counting '3 × 3' squares:

'3 × 3' squares – THIRTY-SIX

7. Counting '2 × 2' squares:

'2 × 2' squares – FORTY-NINE

8. Counting '1 × 1' squares:

'1 × 1' squares – SIXTY-FOUR

We can summarize the square's pattern in the table as shown below.

Square size	Number of appearances on the board
8 × 8	64
7 × 7	49
6 × 6	36
5 × 5	25
4 × 4	16
3 × 3	9
2 × 2	4
1 × 1	1

Total number of squares on a chess board are = 1 + 4 + 9 + 16 + 25 + 36 + 49 + 64

$= 1^2 + 2^2 + 3^2 + 4^2 + 5^2 + 6^2 + 7^2 + 8^2$ = **204**

Formula for '$n \times n$' Square Board

It's clear from the above analysis that the solution in the case of '$n \times n$' is the sum of the squares from n^2 to 1^2, that is to say $n^2 + (n-1)^2 + (n-2)^2 + \ldots + 2^2 + 1^2$

The formula to calculate the sum of the squares of the first n natural numbers is:

$$\frac{n(n+1)(2n+1)}{6}$$

Now, find the total number of squares in a '10 × 10' square board using the above formula.

Did you know?

From numbers 0 to 1000, the letter 'a' appears only once, and that is in 1000 (one thousand).

32

INVESTIGATING TRIANGLES

Counting the number of triangles in a given image is a common question in most types of exams. While it is always possible to individually count out the triangles, it's often time-consuming and you're likely to make a mistake. Hence, we are going to show you the traditional method and then a simple one to quickly determine the answer.

How Many Triangles Can You Count in This Figure?

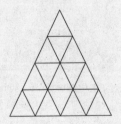

In the above figure, an equilateral triangle is filled with some smaller triangles, dividing the sides of the biggest triangle into four equal parts. Investigate and find how many triangles, large or small, you can see in the above figure.

Traditional Solution:

A methodical approach is needed to count the total number of triangles in such investigations.

Let's count the triangles by first counting the bigger triangles and then the smaller ones. Add the two figures, as we did in the last chapter, 'Investigating Squares'.

Let us consider the length of the side of the smallest triangle as 'one unit'. Then the length of the side of the biggest outermost triangle would become 'four units'. Now we count the triangles.

Step 1
First count the bigger triangle with length 'four units'.

There is only one triangle with length 'four', i.e. the outermost triangle, as shown in the Figure 32.1 below.

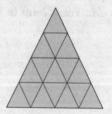

Figure 32.1

Step 2

Count the number of triangles with length 'three units'.

Figure 32.2

There are three such triangles with length 'three', as shown above in Figure 32.2.

Step 3

Count the number of triangles with length 'two units'.

Figure 32.3

Figure 32.4

There are six such triangles with length 'two', as shown above in Figures 32.3 and 32.4.

Do you notice that all these triangles are with the vertex facing upwards? Is there any triangle of length 'two' or more that is facing downwards?

Just see the image below (Figure 32.5) to identify one such possible triangle:

Figure 32.5

Step 4

Count the number of triangles with length 'one unit'.

Figure 32.6

In Figure 32.6, you can see that there are ten such triangles with length 'one', facing upwards.

1 triangle in the first row, 2 in the second row, 3 in the third and 4 in the fourth.

Some triangles of length 'one unit' that are facing downwards as well are shown below in Figure 32.7.

Figure 32.7

In Figure 32.7, there are six triangles of length 'one unit' facing downwards.

So, the total number of triangles in the given equilateral triangle are = 1 + 3 + 7 + 16 = 27.

But this process is cumbersome and there are chances that you will miss out some triangles while counting. So let's learn how you can get the answer directly without counting each triangle.

Formula for an Equilateral Triangle

The formula to calculate the maximum number of triangles formed by dividing a side of an equilateral triangle, having each side of length n units, in equal parts is:

$$\frac{n(n+2)(2n+1)}{8}$$

Using the above formula, find the total number of triangles possible in the given image (Figure 32.8) and then verify it by counting them using a pattern method as discussed above.

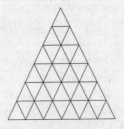

Figure 32.8

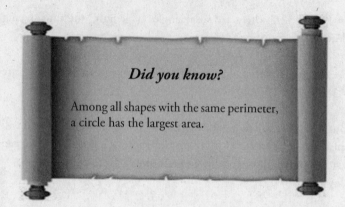

Did you know?

Among all shapes with the same perimeter, a circle has the largest area.

33

CRACK THE CODE

In these puzzles, you have to crack the code using the given clues.

Cracking the Code—1

Clues

6	8	2	One number is correct and correctly placed

6	1	4	One number is correct but at the wrong place

2	0	6	Two numbers are correct but at the wrong place

7	3	8	Nothing is correct

8	7	0	One number is correct but at the wrong place

CODE

Cracking the Code—2

Study the seven clues given below and place the numbers 1 to 9 into the nine positions. Each number should appear exactly once.

x   x   x
x   x   x
x   x   x

Clues

1. 1 is next to and directly to the left of 9
2. 9 is next to and directly above 6
3. 6 is further right than 4
4. 4 is next to and directly to the right of 8
5. 8 is next to and directly above 2
6. 2 is next to and directly to the left of 5
7. 5 is not next to 7

Cracking the Code—3

If ROSE is coded as 6821,

CHAIR is coded as 73456 and

PREACH is coded as 961473,

What will be the code for
SEARCH?

Read more different interesting methods of cracking the code in our other book, *How to Crack Mysteries*.

SOLUTIONS

Cracking the Code—1

- All the possible numbers are 6, 8, 2, 1, 4, 0, 7 and 3.
- In the fourth clue, it is given that 7, 3, and 8 are all incorrect.
- The remaining numbers are 6, 2, 1, 4 and 0.
- In the fifth clue, 0 is the correct digit, as we have already ruled out 7 and 8.
- In the first clue, out of 6, 8 and 2, 8 is already incorrect. Assuming 6 is the correct number and in the right place, it will not satisfy the second clue (i.e. only one number is correct but wrongly placed). This means it is not 6 but 2 is the correct digit.
- In the third clue, two numbers are correct but placed wrong. Obviously, it is 2 and 0. So, 2 must be placed in the last place of the code and 0 in the first.
- In the second clue, out of 6, 1 and 4, 6 is not correct, so we are choosing between 1 and 4.
- As we already have 0 in the first place and 2 in the last place, the missing number is placed in the middle.
- Assuming 1 to be the correct number it should be placed correctly, but the second clue states that 'one number is correct but in the wrong place'. That means it is not 1 but 4.
- So, the final code is 042.

Cracking the Code—2

Top Row	7 1 9
Middle Row	8 4 6
Bottom Row	2 5 3

Cracking the Code—3

- If you observe closely, you will notice that each letter corresponds to one number;
- For example, R in ROSE and R in CHAIR both correspond to 6.
- Similarly, you have to find codes for all the letters in the word SEARCH.
- The last two letters in ROSE, i.e. SE = 21
- The next two letters can be found out from PREACH and CHAIR, i.e. A = 4 and R = 6.
- The last two letters can be found from PREACH, i.e. CH = 73,
- So the solution is: SEARCH = 214673.

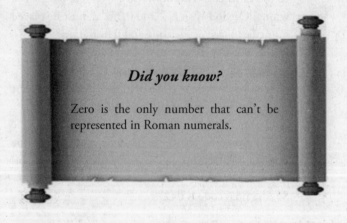

Did you know?

Zero is the only number that can't be represented in Roman numerals.

34

OUT-OF-THE-BOX THINKING

While solving mathematical problems, we tend to follow specific steps using the standard formulas, etc. to reach the final answer. But in some situations, it is better not to follow the routine and think out of the box, maybe starting from the final answer and working backwards.

Let us illustrate this point with an example:

The sum of two numbers is 3 and their product is 5. Find the sum of the reciprocal of the two numbers.

If we follow the common method of solving this problem, we will initially create two equations and then solve them as given below.

Let the two numbers be x and y.

$$x + y = 3$$
$$xy = 5$$

Solving first equation for y, we get $y = 3 - x$

Substituting this value of y in the second equation, we get:

$$x(3 - x) = 5$$
$$3x - x^2 - 5 = 0$$
$$x^2 - 3x + 5 = 0$$

Using the quadratic formula, we get:

$$x = \frac{3 \pm \sqrt{9 - 20}}{2}$$
$$= \frac{3 \pm \sqrt{-11}}{2} = \frac{3 \pm \sqrt{(-1)(11)}}{2}$$
$$= \frac{3 \pm i\sqrt{11}}{2}, \text{ where } i \text{ stands for } \sqrt{-1}$$
$$= \frac{3 + i\sqrt{11}}{2} \text{ or } \frac{3 - i\sqrt{11}}{2}$$

So, $x = \dfrac{3 + i\sqrt{11}}{2}$ and $y = \dfrac{3 - i\sqrt{11}}{2}$ or $x = \dfrac{3 - i\sqrt{11}}{2}$ and $y = \dfrac{3 + i\sqrt{11}}{2}$

Sum of the reciprocals of x and y is:

$$\frac{1}{x} + \frac{1}{y} = \frac{1}{\frac{3 + i\sqrt{11}}{2}} + \frac{1}{\frac{3 - i\sqrt{11}}{2}} = \frac{2}{3 + i\sqrt{11}} + \frac{2}{3 - i\sqrt{11}}$$
$$= \frac{2(3 - i\sqrt{11}) + 2(3 + i\sqrt{11})}{(3 + i\sqrt{11})(3 - i\sqrt{11})} = \frac{12}{3^2 - (i\sqrt{11})^2}$$
$$= \frac{12}{9 - (11)(i^2)} = \frac{12}{9 + 11} = \frac{12}{20} = \frac{3}{5}$$

Now let us try the other approach, viz., working backwards from the solution.

We have to find:

$$\frac{1}{x} + \frac{1}{y}$$

It's already given in the questions that

$$x + y = 3$$
$$xy = 5$$

Thus the required solution of our problem is:

$$\frac{1}{x} + \frac{1}{y} = \frac{x + y}{xy} = \frac{3}{5}$$

This example clearly shows how much time and effort can be saved by taking an out-of-the-box approach in some cases.

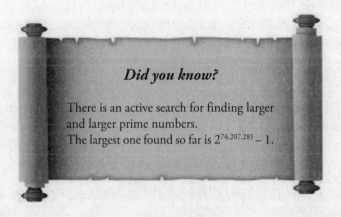

Did you know?

There is an active search for finding larger and larger prime numbers.
The largest one found so far is $2^{74,207,281} - 1$.

35

PRESENTATION OF DATA

In this chapter we will learn how presentation of data is important and can make even a complex problem simple to work out.

Question:

Find the numerical value of the following expression:

$$\left(1-\frac{1}{4}\right)\left(1-\frac{1}{9}\right)\left(1-\frac{1}{16}\right)\left(1-\frac{1}{25}\right)...\left(1-\frac{1}{225}\right)$$

The normal method to solve this problem is to simplify the terms in the bracket:

$$\left(\frac{3}{4}\right)\left(\frac{8}{9}\right)\left(\frac{15}{16}\right)\left(\frac{24}{25}\right)...\left(\frac{224}{225}\right)$$

After this, you will convert them into decimals or cancel out the common factors of some, and then multiply it. But this method is very lengthy and cumbersome.

Now, let us try to convert the problem in a simpler way by changing the way it is presented and then solve it, as shown below:

$$\left(1-\frac{1}{4}\right)\left(1-\frac{1}{9}\right)\left(1-\frac{1}{16}\right)\left(1-\frac{1}{25}\right)...\left(1-\frac{1}{225}\right)$$

$$=\left(1^2-\frac{1}{2^2}\right)\left(1^2-\frac{1}{3^2}\right)\left(1^2-\frac{1}{4^2}\right)\left(1^2-\frac{1}{5^2}\right)...\left(1^2-\frac{1}{15^2}\right)$$

Using the formula $(a^2 - b^2) = (a - b)(a + b)$, we get:

$$\left(1-\frac{1}{2}\right)\left(1+\frac{1}{2}\right)\left(1-\frac{1}{3}\right)\left(1+\frac{1}{3}\right)\left(1-\frac{1}{4}\right)\left(1+\frac{1}{4}\right)\left(1-\frac{1}{5}\right)\left(1+\frac{1}{5}\right)$$

$$...\left(1-\frac{1}{15}\right)\left(1+\frac{1}{15}\right)$$

$$=\left(\frac{1}{2}\right)\left(\frac{3}{2}\right)\left(\frac{2}{3}\right)\left(\frac{4}{3}\right)\left(\frac{3}{4}\right)\left(\frac{5}{4}\right)\left(\frac{4}{5}\right)\left(\frac{6}{5}\right)...\left(\frac{14}{15}\right)\left(\frac{16}{15}\right)$$

$$=\left(\frac{1}{2}\right)\left(\frac{16}{15}\right)$$

$$=\left(\frac{8}{15}\right)$$

You can see how a problem which seemed so complex in the beginning is solved in a simple way just by changing the way it is presented.

Did you know?

10! means '10 factorial'. 10! = $10 \times 9 \times 8 \times 7 \times 6 \times 5 \times 4 \times 3 \times 2 \times 1$ = 3628800.
3628800 seconds exactly equals 42 days, or 6 weeks.

36

ARE YOU MATHS SMART?

Using your calculator, how would you work out the following?

1. Two consecutive numbers whose product is 5402.
2. Three consecutive numbers whose product is 32736.
3. Two two-digit numbers whose quotient is 0.578125.
4. Two two-digit numbers whose product is 1357.
5. Two consecutive numbers whose squares add up to 3613.
6. Two numbers with a sum of 100 and a product of 1539.
7. Three numbers with a sum of 100 and a product of 31248.
8. The sum of two numbers is 14 and their difference is 10. Find the product of the two numbers.
9. The difference between a two-digit number and the number obtained by interchanging the digits is 27. What is the difference between the two digits of the number?
10. A number on being divided by 5 and 7 successively leaves the remainders 2 and 4 respectively. Find the remainder when the same number is divided by 5 × 7 = 35.

Before looking at the solutions on the next page, first try to solve the questions yourself.

SOLUTIONS

1. Two consecutive numbers whose product is 5402

By trial and error we could find that $60 \times 61 = 3660$ and $80 \times 81 = 6480$.

So we then try some pair in between. And to reduce the search we look for pairs which will give 2 as the units (or ones) digit.

A better strategy is to find the square root, which lies between the two consecutive numbers.

$\sqrt{5402} \simeq 73.498$

So, $73 \times 74 = 5402$

Hence the consecutive numbers whose product is 5402 are 73 and 74.

2. Three consecutive numbers whose product is 32736

Let's find the cube root of 32736, which should be close to any of the three numbers:

$$\sqrt[3]{32736} \simeq 31.989$$

So, $31 \times 32 \times 33 = 32736$

Hence the three consecutive numbers whose product is 32736 are 31, 32 and 33.

3. Two two-digit numbers whose quotient is 0.578125

$$0.578125 = \frac{578125}{1000000}$$
$$= \frac{578125 \div 125}{1000000 \div 125}$$

$$= \frac{4625}{8000}$$

$$= \frac{4625 \div 125}{8000 \div 125}$$

$$= \frac{37}{64}$$

Hence the two two-digit numbers are 37 and 64.

4. Two two-digit numbers whose product is 1357

Expressing 1357 as a product of prime factors, we have $1357 = 23 \times 59$.

Hence, the two two-digit numbers whose product is 1357 are 23 and 59.

5. Two consecutive squares whose sum is 3613

Let's find half of 3613.

$$\frac{1}{2} \times 3613 = 1806.5$$

Now, look for the squares immediately above and below

$$\sqrt{1806.5} \simeq 42.502$$

Therefore, $42^2 + 43^2 = 1764 + 1849 = 3613$

6. Two numbers with a sum of 100 and a product of 1539

By prime factorization:

$$1539 = \underbrace{3 \times 3 \times 3 \times 3}_{81} \times 19$$

$$= 81 \times 19$$

Also, $81 + 19 = 100$.

So, the numbers are 81 and 19.

7. Three numbers with a sum of 100 and a product of 31248

$$31248 = \underbrace{2 \times 2 \times 2 \times 2 \times 3}_{48} \times \underbrace{3 \times 7}_{21} \times 31$$
$$= 48 \times 21 \times 31$$

Also, $48 + 21 + 31 = 100$.

So, the three numbers are 48, 21 and 31.

8. The sum of two numbers is 14 and their difference is 10. Find the product of the two numbers.

The product can be directly found using the formula:

$$\text{Product} = \frac{(\text{Sum} + \text{Difference})(\text{Sum} - \text{Difference})}{4}$$
$$= \frac{(14 + 10)(14 - 10)}{4} = 24$$

The two numbers, x and y, can also be easily found as:

$$x = \frac{\text{Sum} + \text{Difference}}{2} = \frac{14 + 10}{2} = 12$$

$$y = \frac{\text{Sum} - \text{Difference}}{2} = \frac{14 - 10}{2} = 2$$

Hence, the product of the two numbers is 24 and the numbers are 12 and 2.

9. **The difference between a two-digit number and the number obtained by interchanging the digits is 27. What is the difference between the two digits of the number?**

Difference between the two digits =

$$\frac{\text{Difference between the original and the interchanged number}}{9}$$

$$= \frac{27}{9} = 3$$

10. **A number on being divided by 5 and 7 successively leaves the remainders 2 and 4 respectively. Find the remainder when the same number is divided by $5 \times 7 = 35$.**

The required remainder = $d_1 \times r_2 + r_1$

Where, d_1 = the first divisor $\quad = 5$

$\quad r_1$ = the first remainder $\quad = 2$

$\quad r_2$ = the second remainder $\quad = 4$

The required remainder = $5 \times 4 + 2 = 22$.

Did you know?

40 when spelt out ('forty') is the only number with letters in the alphabetical order, while 'one' is the only one with letters in the reverse order.

37

CALENDAR AT YOUR FINGERTIPS

This chapter will cover an amazing technique that will let you master 500 years of the calendar. Using this trick, you can instantly tell the day on which any particular date of a given year falls.

You can tell your friends and relatives the day they were born just by asking their date of birth. And of course, the technique is very useful in competitive exams that ask tricky questions related to dates and ages.

Memorizing 500 Years of the Calendar

If we observe any date, there are four main things:

- Date
- Month
- Century
- Year

We give each of these some particular codes. The sum of all these codes helps determine the day of the week on which any given date falls.

Let's understand the process and memorize the codes:

Code for Date

Divide the date by 7. Then write the remainder as the code of the date.

Let's say the date is 23, then 23 ÷ 7 will result in 2 as the remainder. So, the code for the date (23) is 2.

If the date is 6, then 6 ÷ 7 will result in 6 as the remainder So, the code for the date (6) is 6.

Codes for Months

Month	Code
January	1
February	4
March	4
April	0
May	2
June	5
July	0
August	3
September	6
October	1
November	4
December	6

Table 37.1

The month codes seem difficult to memorize as they don't follow any immediately discernible logic. Here are some easy ways to memorize these codes with the help of some associations:

Month	Code	Association
January	1	January is the 1st month of the year.
February	4	A leap year comes about every 4th year.
March	4	March is immediately after February, and so it shares the same code of February.
April	0	On April Fool's day we become 0s (fools) from heroes.
May	2	May reminds us of 2 options—may be or may not be.
June	5	June ends in 'e', the 5th letter of the alphabet.
July	0	July can be pronounced as jOOly, where the Os look like 0s.
August	3	15th August (Independence Day) reminds us of India's tricolour flag, so the code is 3.
September	6	September begins with the letter 'S' and so does 'six'. Hence, the code is 6.
October	1	The 't' of October is reminiscent of 1.
November	4	The 'N' of November looks like the Roman numeral for 4 (IV).
December	6	Think of December as Dicember. A dice has 6 sides, so the code is 6.

Codes for Years

Year	Code	Year	Code	Year	Code	Year	Code
01	1	26	4	51	0	76	4
02	2	27	5	52	2	77	5
03	3	28	0	53	3	78	6
04	5	29	1	54	4	79	0
05	6	30	2	55	5	80	2
06	0	31	3	56	0	81	3
07	1	32	5	57	1	82	4
08	3	33	6	58	2	83	5
09	4	34	0	59	3	84	0
10	5	35	1	60	5	85	1
11	6	36	3	61	6	86	2
12	1	37	4	62	0	87	3
13	2	38	5	63	1	88	5
14	3	39	6	64	3	89	6
15	4	40	1	65	4	90	0
16	6	41	2	66	5	91	1
17	0	42	3	67	6	92	3
18	1	43	4	68	1	93	4
19	2	44	6	69	2	94	5
20	4	45	0	70	3	95	6
21	5	46	1	71	4	96	1
22	6	47	2	72	6	97	2
23	0	48	4	73	0	98	3
24	2	49	5	74	1	99	4
25	3	50	6	75	2		

Table 37.2

To learn techniques to memorize the codes of years, refer to our book
How to Memorize Anything.

Codes for Centuries

Century	Code
1600s	6
1700s	4
1800s	2
1900s	0
2000s	6
2100s	4

Table 37.3

Observe that the pattern 6, 4, 2, 0 repeats.
The code for the current century 2000 is 6 or –1.
(Instead of adding 6 you can subtract 1 to simplify the calculation,
it will give the same result.)

Example 1
Now, let's consider the date 23 May 1992.

Date: 23 ÷ 7 gives remainder 2.
Month: May = 2 (refer to Table 37.1).
Year and century: 1992 = 0 + 3 = 3 (refer to Tables 37.2 and 37.3).

Date	Month	Year	Century
2	2	3	0

Adding all the codes together, we get:

$$2 + 2 + 0 + 3 = 7$$

This final sum 7 will indicate the day of the week. Each day has its own code, as shown in the table below.

Codes for Days

Day	Code
Sunday	1
Monday	2
Tuesday	3
Wednesday	4
Thursday	5
Friday	6
Saturday	7 or 0

Table 37.4

Clearly, 23 May 1992 was a Saturday.

Let's consider a few more examples.

Example 2
28 March 1980

Date: $28 \div 7$ gives remainder = 0.
Month: March = 4 *(refer to Table 37.1).*
Year and century: 1980 = 0 + 2 = 2 (refer to Tables 37.2 and 37.3).
Adding all, we get $0 + 4 + 2 = 6$.
6 is the code corresponding to Friday (refer to Table 37.4).

Hence, 28 March 1980 was a Friday.

Example 3
5 April 2010

Date: 5 ÷ 7 gives remainder = 5.
Month: April = 0 (refer to Table 37.1).
Year and century: 2010 = 6 + 5 = 11 (refer to Tables 37.2 and 37.3).
Total: 5 + 0 + 11 = 16.
Again, 16 ÷ 7 gives remainder = 2.

2 stands for Monday.

Note: When the final total is more than 7, divide it again by 7. The remainder thus obtained corresponds to the code of the day.

In Case of a Leap Year

If the given year is a leap year, and the months are January or February, the day will be the one previous to what you have calculated. For example, if by your calculation it is a Thursday, the actual day will be Wednesday.

Example 4
23 February 1976

Date: 23 ÷ 7 gives remainder = 2.
Month: February = 4 (refer to Table 37.1).
Year and century: 1976 = 0 + 4 = 4 (refer to Tables 37.2 and 37.3).
$$2 + 4 + 4 = 10$$
10 ÷ 7 gives remainder as 3, so the answer is Tuesday.

Ideally the day should be Tuesday, but 1976 is a leap year, so we subtract a day to arrive at the correct answer: Monday.

Note: As soon as you hear the months of January and February, immediately check if it is a leap year (if the given year is divisible by 4, it means it is a leap year).

If the year is a leap year, but the date for which the day needs to be calculated is between March and December, there is no need for any adjustment.

With practice you can tell the day of any date within a few seconds.

How to Calculate Year Codes

Instead of referring to the table, there is a method to calculate the code for the year.

Let's find the code for the year 98.

Step 1
Divide the year by 4.
98 ÷ 4 gives quotient = 24, remainder = 2.

Step 2
Ignore the remainder and add the quotient obtained to the year, i.e. 24 + 98 = 122.

Step 3
Divide 122 by 7 and consider the remainder obtained as the code, i.e. 122 ÷ 7 gives quotient = 17, remainder = 3.
This remainder (3) is the code for the year 98.

Another Method for Calculating the Year Code

You will find that calendar codes repeat themselves after every 28 years. So, we can subtract maximum multiples of 28 (84, 56 or 28) from the given year and then add the quarter of that number to itself, i.e. if the year is 98, subtracting 84 (multiple of 28) from it, we get:

$$98 - 84 = 14$$

Now, add the approximate quarter of 14, i.e. 3, to itself to get 17.

Divide it by 7 and find its remainder, i.e. 3.
So, 3 is the code for 98.

This method of first subtracting the multiple of 28 allows us to work with smaller numbers, thus speeding up our calculations.

Let's consider a few more examples.

Example 5
Rohit was born on the first Monday of March 1952. On which date was he born?

First, let's find the day of 1 March 1952.

1 March 1952
$$1 + 4 + 0 + 2 = 7$$

7 means the day was Saturday.
If 1 March 1952 was a Saturday, the date on the first Monday was 3 March.
So, Rohit was born on 3 March 1952.

Example 6
Which day of the week did 8 September 1783 fall on?

8 September 1783
1 + 6 + 4 + 5 = 16
16 ÷ 7 gives 2 as the remainder.
2 indicates Monday.

Hence, 8 September 1783 was a Monday.

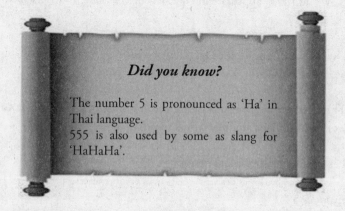

Did you know?

The number 5 is pronounced as 'Ha' in Thai language.
555 is also used by some as slang for 'HaHaHa'.

38

COOL MATHS

While solving maths problems, you have to utilize time in the best possible manner. In this chapter, you will learn some revolutionary techniques we call Cool Maths. These techniques will enable you to determine answers in almost a quarter of the time the traditional approach requires. Let's understand it using some maths problems:

1. Consider the nine-digit numbers formed by using each of the digits 1 to 9 once and only once, e.g. 145673928 or 938267145. How many of these are prime numbers?

2. The ratio of the ages of A and B is 7:4. After five years, the ratio of their ages becomes 11:7. Find the age of A.
   (a) 14 years   (b) 21 years   (c) 28 years   (d) 16 years

3. If $x^2 + 79^2 = 172^2 - 88^2 - 8203$. Find the value of x.
   (a) 86   (b) 89   (c) 83   (d) 93

SOLUTIONS

1. Traditional Method:

First we try finding the possible nine-digit numbers formed using each digit from 1 to 9.
Total such possible numbers are 9! = 362880
It is very difficult to find all the numbers and then check for primality.

Cool Maths:
The nine-digit numbers are formed using each digit once and the sum of digits from 1 to 9 is:

$$1 + 2 + 3 + 4 + 5 + 6 + 7 + 8 + 9 = 45$$

That means if you add up the digits of each of the numbers so formed, you will always get a total of 45, which is divisible by 9.

Any number the sum of whose digits is divisible by 9 is itself divisible by 9.
This means that each of the possible 9! (362880) nine-digit numbers is divisible by 9.

So, we can easily say that none of these numbers are prime.

2. Traditional Method:

Given the ratio of the ages of A and B = 7:4
Let the common ratio be x.

Then, the age of A = $7x$ years
And the age of B = $4x$ years

After 5 years, age of A = $(7x + 5)$ years and age of B = $(4x + 5)$ years.
As after 5 years ratio of their ages = 11:7
Therefore,

$$\frac{7x + 5}{4x + 5} = \frac{11}{7}$$

$(7x + 5) \times 7 = 11 \times (4x + 5)$
$\quad 49x + 35 = 44x + 55$
$\qquad\qquad 5x = 20$
$\qquad\qquad\ x = 4$

So, present age of A = $7 \times 4 = 28$ years.

Using this method we spend about a minute or so (time may vary from person to person) to solve it. But with Cool Maths, we can solve it in just 10 seconds.

Cool Maths:
We use substitution method (also known as reverse engineering) to solve such questions.

The ratio of the present ages of A and B = 7:4
This shows that the present age of A is a multiple of 7.
After 5 years, the ratio of their ages becomes 11:7.
So, after 5 years, the age of A is a multiple of 11.

Now we use the above understanding and start eliminating the options given.
Let's start by checking multiples of 7.

Option (a): 14 years, 14 is a multiple of 7, but after 5 years it becomes 19, which is not a multiple of 11. So reject this option.

Option (b): 21 years, 21 is a multiple of 7, but after 5 years it becomes 26, which is not a multiple of 11. So reject this option as well.

Option (c): 28 years, multiple of 7. After 5 years it becomes 33, which is a multiple of 11.

Hence, option (c), i.e. 28 years is the right answer.

So instead of solving for the correct answer, we just eliminate the wrong answers to get the correct answer easily.

3. Traditional Method:

Given that:

$$x^2 + 79^2 = 172^2 - 88^2 - 8203$$
$$x^2 + 6241 = 29584 - 7744 - 8203$$
$$x^2 + 6241 = 13637$$
$$x^2 = 7396$$
$$x = \sqrt{7396}$$
$$x = 86$$

This method will take a few minutes to solve, but using the Cool Maths method, you can solve it in less than a minute.

Cool Maths:

We use the units digit method (refer to Chapter 12, 'Determining the Unit Digit at a Glance' for more details).

$$x^2 + 79^2 = 172^2 - 88^2 - 8203$$

Let's find out the units digit of RHS first:

172^2 : as the number ends in 2, so its square ends in 4.
88^2 : as the number ends in 8, so its square ends in 4.
8203 : ends in 3.

So, using the above units digits we can easily get the units digit of '$172^2 - 88^2 - 8203$', which is same as:

$$4 - 4 - 3 = 0 - 3 = 7$$

It will not be –3, as we are finding the units digit.
So to subtract '3' after getting '0' at the units place, we take one 10 from the tens place and it becomes $10 - 3$ (using the concept of place value).
Thus the RHS units digit will be 7.

Now let's take the LHS:

79^2: as the number ends in 9, its square ends in 1.
So, to make the units digit of LHS = RHS, x^2 must end in 6, so that $6 + 1$ (units digit of x^2 + units digit of 79^2) will become 7.

Given options for x are:
(a) 86   (b) 89   (c) 83   (d) 93

You can see that out of the given options, the square of only 86 ends in 6.

So the correct answer is option (a), i.e. 86.

Did you know?

1729 is known as the Ramanujan's number. When the great Indian mathematician was lying ill in the hospital, Dr Hardy came to visit him. He said the number of the taxi in which he had come, 1729, was a boring number. Suddenly Ramanujan's face lit up and he said that it is not a boring number. It is the only number that is the sum of two cubes in two different ways.

$10^3 + 9^3 = 1729$ and $12^3 + 1^3 = 1729$

ACKNOWLEDGEMENTS

We would first like to thank the God Almighty for empowering us with the intellect and belief to write this book.

We thank our parents, for their belief in our capabilities and for their unconditional love and support.

A big thanks to our teachers from school and college, especially respected R.L. Singhal and Rajendra Kalra, whose encouragement and guidance laid the foundation for all our work in mathematics.

Thanks to M. Saquib, for transforming our imagination into illustrations that enlivened the pages of this book.

We extend our special thanks to Milee Ashwarya, editor-in-chief (commercial and business), Penguin Random House. It is because of her persistent efforts that we could bring out with our third book.

We greatly appreciate the help of Roshini and Cibani, our editors, in the presentation of the content—they gave the book its present shape and enabled us to make it better.

A warm thanks to our friend Jaya Kalwani, for her constant feedback and support throughout the making of this book. Her keen interest and valuable inputs helped us refine and fine-tune the text.

Thanks to our kids, Devansh and Ishaan, who are the first ones with whom we played all these maths tricks. Their excitement encouraged us to share it with others.

We'd like to thank all the students and teachers who participated in our numerous maths workshops over the years. It was their valuable feedback and constant encouragement that motivated us to spread our knowledge, both magical and mathematical.

Finally, thanks to everyone whose names we have missed out but who have lent their support, in any way, to the book.